Kintyre Instructions

The 5th Duke of Argyll's Instructions to
his Kintyre Chamberlain, 1785-1805

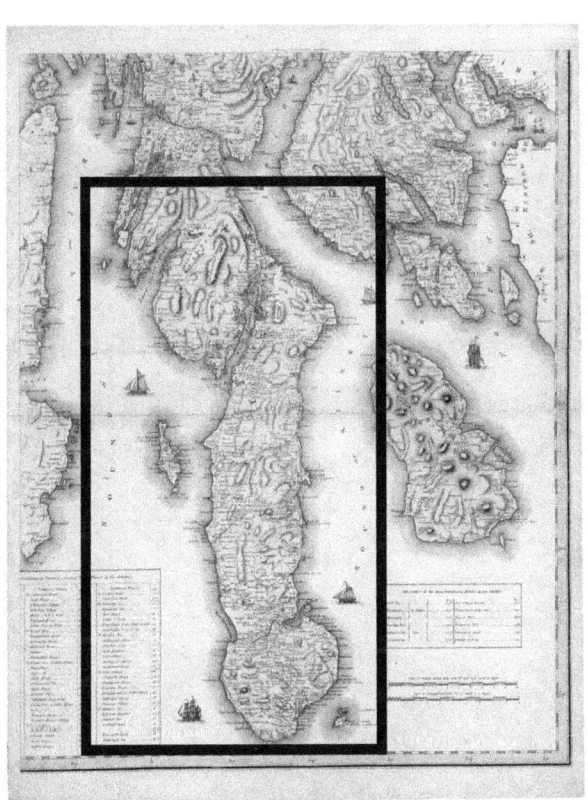

Kintyre, outlined by the box, in George Langlands'
1801 map of Argyll (above) is reproduced in sections
on the following four pages. Map reproduced
courtesy of National Library of Scotland.

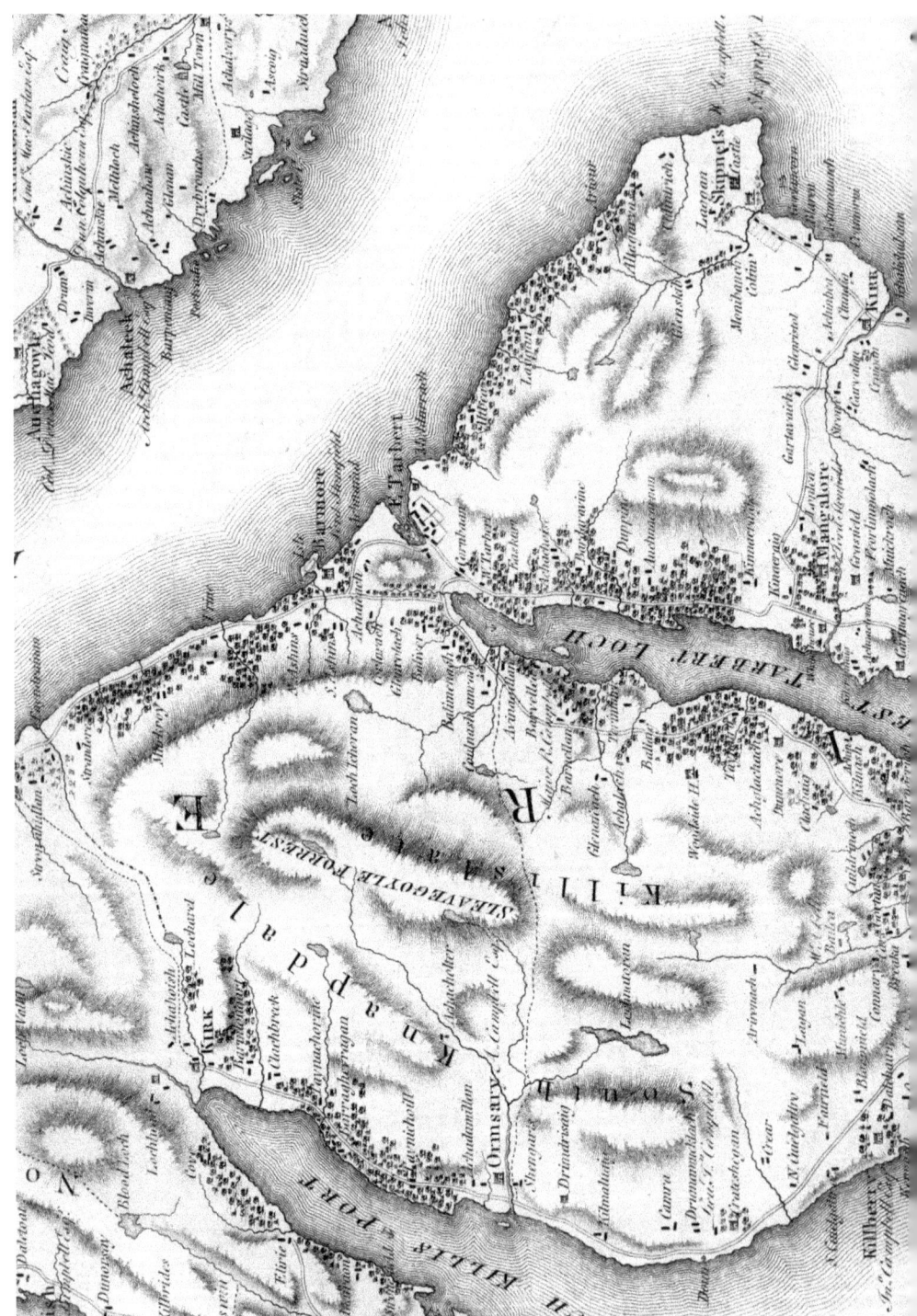

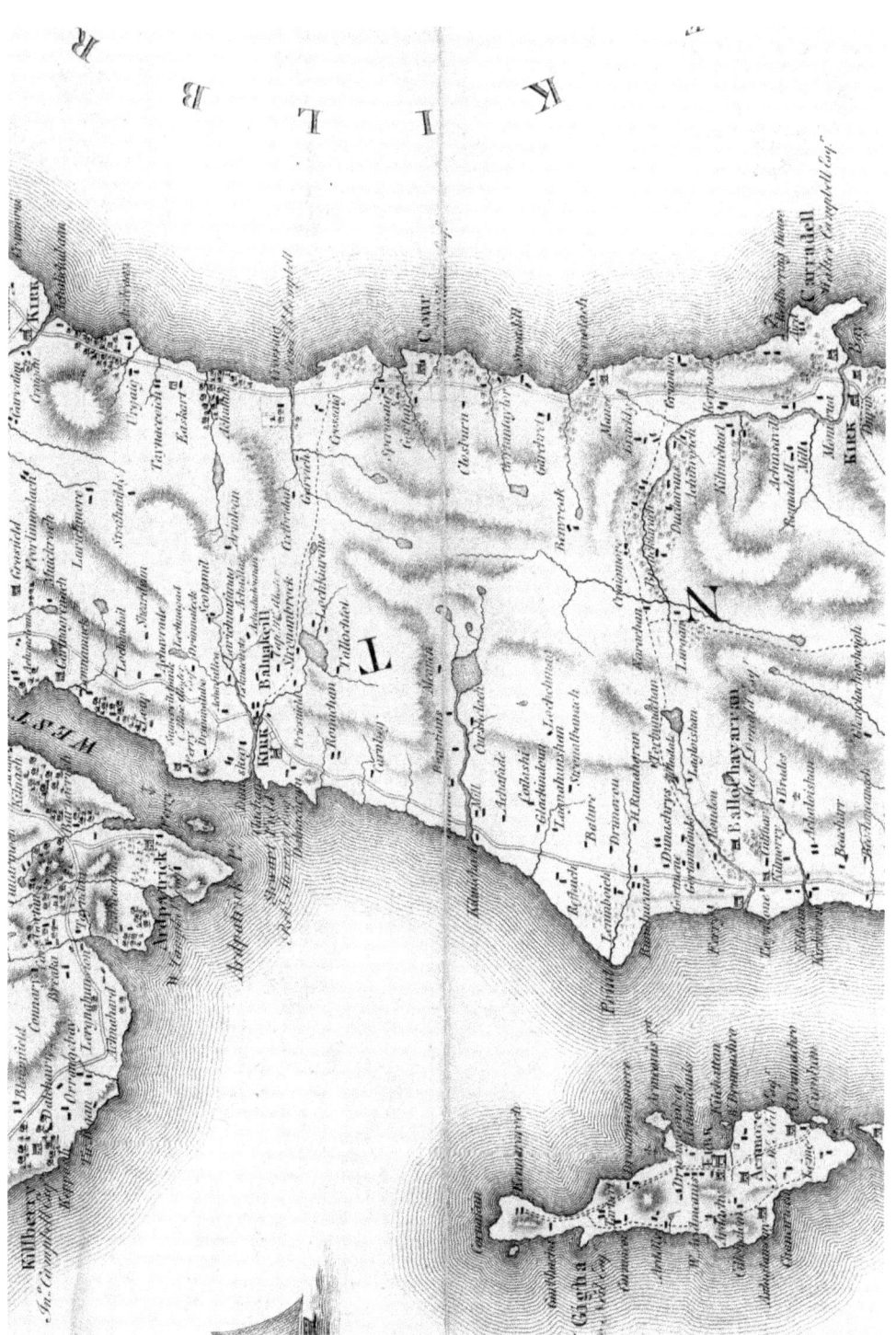

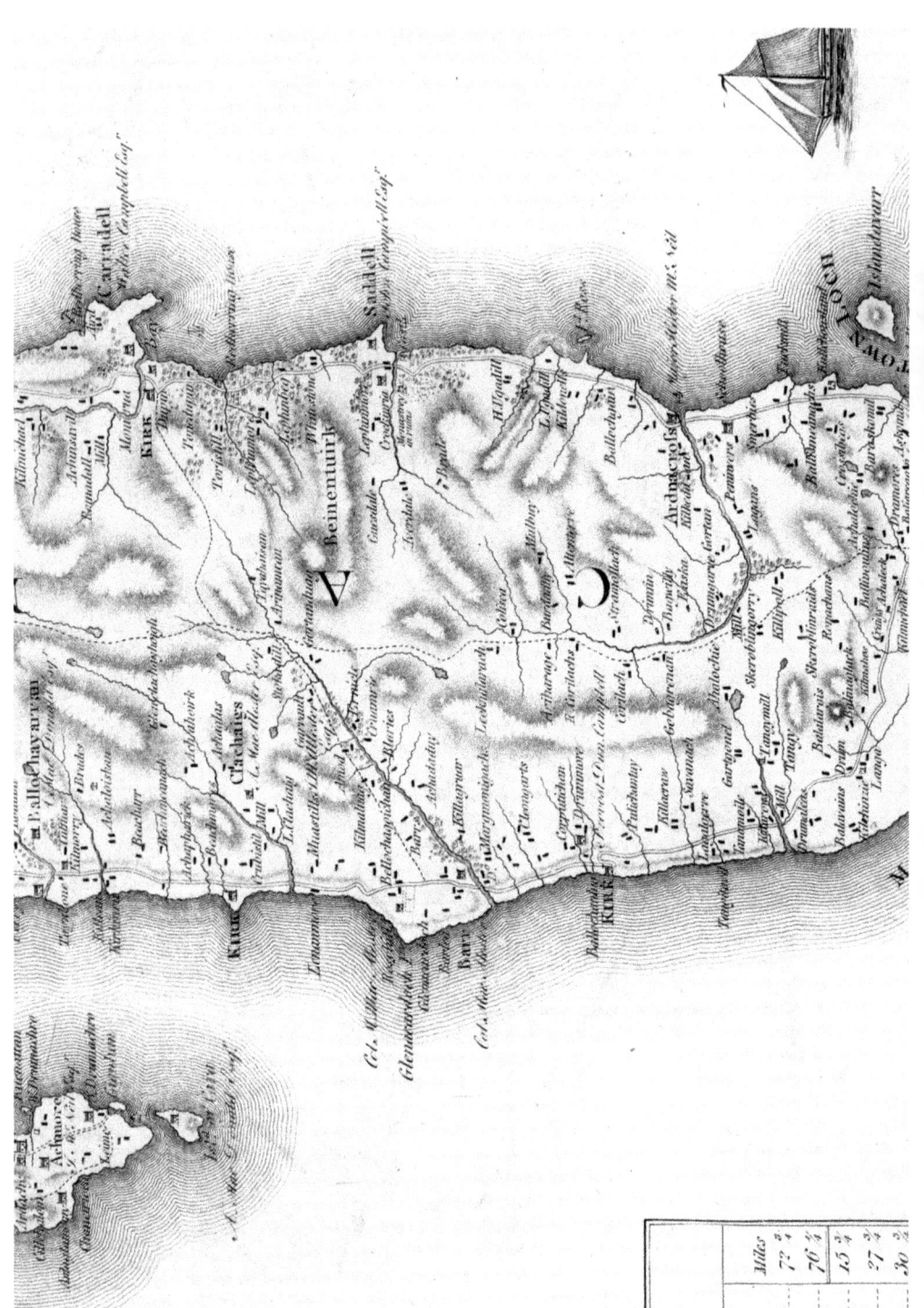

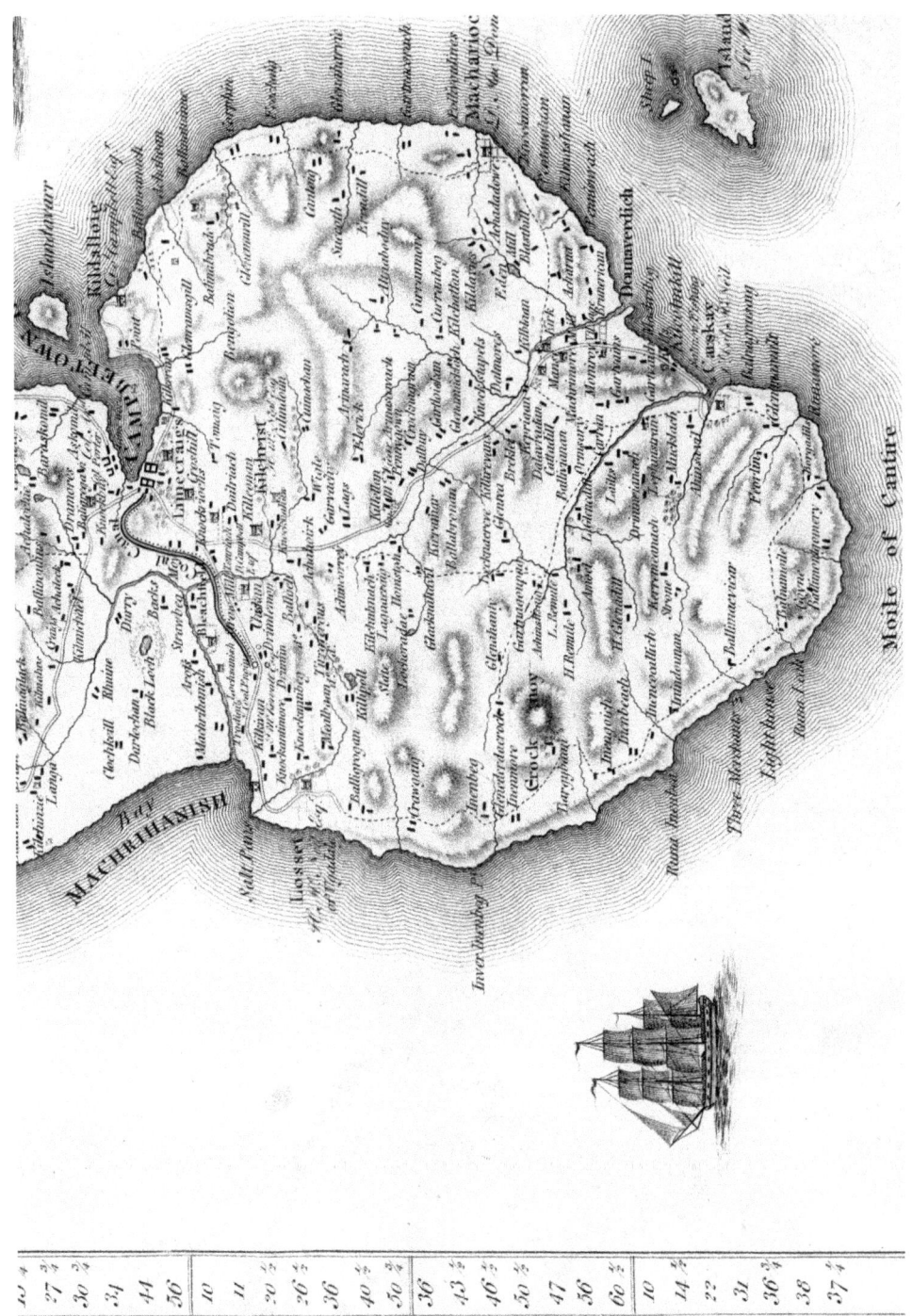

Previous books by Angus Martin

History

The Ring-Net Fishermen
Kintyre: The Hidden Past
Kintyre Country Life
Fishing and Whaling
Sixteen Walks in South Kintyre
The North Herring Fishing
Herring Fishermen of Kintyre and Ayrshire
Fish and Fisherfolk
Memories of the Inans, Largybaan and Craigaig, 1980-85
An Historical and Genealogical Tour of Kilkerran Graveyard
Kintyre Birds
The Place-Names of the Parish of Campbeltown (with Duncan Colville)
The Place-Names of the Parish of Southend (with Duncan Colville)
Kilkerran Graveyard Revisited
Kintyre Families

Poetry

The Larch Plantation
The Song of the Quern
The Silent Hollow
Rosemary Clooney Crossing the Minch
Laggan Days: In Memory of George Campbell Hay
Always Boats and Men (with Mark I'Anson)
One Time in a Tale of Herring (with Will Maclean)

Kintyre Instructions

The 5th Duke of Argyll's Instructions to
his Kintyre Chamberlain, 1785-1805

Transcription by
Eric R. Cregeen M. A.

Commentaries by
Angus Martin

The Grimsay Press

Published by:

The Grimsay Press
An imprint of Zeticula
57, St Vincent Crescent,
Glasgow,
G3 8NQ,
Scotland
http://www. thegrimsaypress. co. uk

Copyright © Angus Martin 2011

Cover illustration: 'Saddell House and Castle, Cantire', by Rev. Edward Bradley ('Cuthbert Bede'), from Volume I of his *Glencreggan* (1861).

Angus Martin has asserted his right to be identified as author of this work in accordance with the Copyright, Designs and Patents Act, 1988.

ISBN 978-1-84530-109-5

All rights reserved. No reproduction, copy or transmission of this publication may be made without prior written permission.

'No Highlander sets great store by the possession of "estates". He knows that the land can never really belong to him: it is he belongs to the land. But in these days of universal change, the links of affection and of memory become more sacred than ever, and these can be preserved as well by the "landmark" of a cottage and field as by a large house and many acres.'

J. A. Campbell, Achanduin and Barbreck, in letter to *Campbeltown Courier*, 6/3/1924.

Our Ruined Townships

Seanlagan and Allt Beithe,
they are awaiting old days;
they are more lasting and more eternal
than stately realms.

From George Campbell Hay's *Ar Laraichean*, translated from Gaelic by Michel Byrne.

'The landscape was the paper on which everything was written, and afterwards it gets torn and nobody looks at the paper.'

S. Yizhar, quoted in *London Review of Books*, 26/2/2009, p. 31.

Contents

George Langlands' Map of Argyll	*i-v*
Acknowledgements	*xiii*
List of Illustrations	*xv*
Preface	*xvii*
Introduction 1	1
Introduction 2	9
Instructions to the Chamberlain of Kintyre	37
Commentaries on Instructions	81
Appendix: A Kintyre Boundaries Dispute	198
Sources and Notes: Introductions	199
Sources and Notes: Commentaries	203
Index	211

Acknowledgements

For assistance with this work, I am indebted to Robert W. Smith, Linlithgow, who read the penultimate draft; to Dr Donald William Stewart, University of Edinburgh, who read my Introduction; to my wife Judy, for scanning illustrations, for her photographs and for sharing the proof-reading; to Mary Davidson, Edinburgh, for various acts of assistance; to Mrs Maureen Bell, Drumlemble, for allowing me to raid her splendid collection of local postcards; to Mike Smylie, Bristol, for sourcing fishing illustrations; to all others who contributed illustrations and are acknowledged individually in the captions; to the National Library of Scotland for permission to reproduce the Kintyre section of the Langlands map of Argyll; to the Scottish History Society for permission to reproduce parts of Eric R. Cregeen's Introduction to *Argyll Estate Instructions*; to the staff of Campbeltown Public Library and to Murdo MacDonald, Lochgilphead; and, finally, to Lily Cregeen for entrusting this work to me, taxing though it proved to be!

Angus Martin

List of Illustrations

1. John, 5th Duke of Argyll. — xx
2. Craigaig from south. — 10
3. Craigaig ruins, with corn-kiln. — 12
4. The Gaelic-speaking Armour family of Rosehill, c. 1871. — 14
5. Ben Gullion, lair of the mythical serpent. — 17
6. Gleneadardacrock. — 19
7. Ruins of Allt Beithe. — 21
8. 'Sheggan' or 'shellister' at Knockbay. — 25
9. A stretch of the original Learside road. — 29
10. Old coastal track south of Inneans Bay. — 32
11. Backs Water from Parkfergus bridge. — 83
12. Campbeltown meal mill, c. 1905. — 83
13. The Mill Dam, c. 1935. — 84
14. Carved MacNeill stone at Low Tifergus farmhouse. — 84
15. Knocknaha Mill c. 1900. — 87
16. The Ugadale Brooch. — 87
17. Frontal view of Lossit House. — 88
18. The Island of Sanda from Polliwilline Hill. — 91
19. Largie Castle, 1861. — 91
20. Carskey House, c. 1925. — 93
21. Miss Campbell of Kildalloig. — 95
22. The foreshore at Dalintober, c. 1900. — 97
23. Saddell Castle, c. 1920. — 97
24. John Campbell, last laird of Saddell, c. 1920. — 98
25. Salt Pans, c. 1835. — 101
26. Surviving hedgerow on High Tirfergus road. — 103
27. Hawthorn forming part of hedge at Tomaig. — 103
28. Mull of Kintyre and Lighthouse, c. 1910. — 105
29. Presumed knockin stane in rock outcrop at Auchenhoan. — 105
30. Knockin stane at Innean Dunain ruin. — 107
31. Shipwreck on the Kintyre coast, c. 1900. — 109
32. Smack aground near Battle Isle. — 111
33. Limecraigs House. — 115
34. Kilchousland Church, c. 1865 — 117
35. Kilchousland, looking north-east. — 117
36. Memorial tablet to Rev. Dr John Smith with Smith's portrait. — 118
37. Remains of the Lintmill village. — 123

38. A Travellers' camp in Kintyre, c. 1935.	125
39. 'Mainland coast, Argyll' thatched cottage, 1946.	128
40. Glenmurril ruin.	128
41. Balnabraid ruin.	129
42. 'Interior of a cottage, Kintyre', c. 1859	129
43. Nineteenth century Kintyre farmhouse and steading.	131
44. Main Street of Campbeltown, c. 1835.	133
45. Kelp-kiln on Island of Gigha, 1987.	135
46. Kelp-making near Glencreggan.	137
47. Campbeltown canal, c. 1795.	139
48. 'Bubly Jock'.	143
49. Campbeltown Grammar School, c. 1910.	145
50. Walled-in wood, behind Limecraigs House.	149
51. A trading wherry.	158
52. Highland Parish Church, Campbeltown.	160
53A. Portrait believed to be of Gilles Campbell.	162
53B. Portrait believed to be of Scipio Duroure Campbell.	163
54A. Portrait of Christian Hamilton Campbell.	164
54B. Portrait of Daniel Mactaggart.	165
55. Nineteenth century 'twinning-pen'.	167
56. The ruins of Innean Mor.	169
57. Sheep at the ruins of Erradil.	171
58. Parish Church Southend, c. 1900.	175
59. The former United Free Church, Southend, c. 1935.	175
60. Looking north across Balinatunie ruins.	177
61. Late eighteenth century herring busses.	179
62. Drift-net fishing in Loch Fyne, c. 1835.	180
63. Neil Kelly, Lochside, with cartload of Moss peats, c. 1925.	180
64. Robert McInnes digging peats.	182
65. John Harvey with his father's Moss peat-spade.	183
66. Kilwhipnach lime-kiln and quarry.	189
67. Strath steading, with foal, c. 1960.	191
68. Archibald Ronald, with Daisy (left) and Jean 1939.	194
69. Illicit whisky-distillers at work.	196
70/71. The sheep-fank at Innean Mor.	202

Preface

Angus Martin

In 1964 the Scottish History Society published *Argyll Estate Instructions: Mull, Morvern, Tiree, 1771-1805*, which were the instructions of John, 5th Duke of Argyll, to his Chamberlain of Mull and Morvern and his Chamberlain of Tiree. The volume was edited by Eric R. Cregeen, who, in a footnote to his introduction, remarked that it was hoped to publish the 5th Duke's instructions to his Chamberlain of Argyll and his Chamberlain of Kintyre in a future volume. This volume contains only the Kintyre instructions and the chamberlains' replies, transcribed by Eric from the originals in Inveraray Castle.

Of the other set of instructions to which he referred in 1964, I have no knowledge. The Kintyre instructions alone seemed challenging enough considering that all that existed in the way of editorial preparation was several pages of notes which Eric compiled: useful to me as indicators of what Eric, in his initial reading of the instructions, considered the points most worthy of expansion, but, in the final analysis, just notes.

It was clear to me from the outset that this was never going to be the book which Eric envisaged, and those readers who are familiar with the Mull, Morvern and Tiree volume will soon realise that his approach and mine are different. The Duke's instructions and the chamberlains' responses in that volume are altogether more detailed, more varied in content and more interesting than the Kintyre material. The main reasons for these differences seem to me to be that the Duke's Kintyre estate was in a more advanced state of improvement, the tenantry less disaffected and the crofting system still-born. These factors, taken together, meant that the Kintyre estate required rather less management.

Whereas Eric's method was to furnish the basic text with a comprehensive introduction and to confine editorial interventions to footnotes, mine has been to furnish the text with lengthy commentaries. In effect, the text became a vehicle for my extended interpretations, and I believe it had to, because the original typescript ran to just short of 13,000 words, more a booklet than a book.

In these commentaries, I have tried to illuminate the background to some of the instructions, which are, in themselves, little more than bare, businesslike jottings. Therefore, where an individual is referred to, I have, if possible, supplied biographical notes, and if he (women are almost entirely absent) belonged to a notable family – whether of recent origin in Kintyre or of old stock – I have given some of the history of that family. Likewise, I have explained agricultural and other industrial practices, and sketched in some of the social, ecclesiastical and political features of the period.

The original text has been preserved as Eric transcribed it, except in cases where place-names, for example, appear to have been either clearly mis-spelt or mistranscribed, or where I felt that the clarity of the text would be improved by the addition of punctuation marks.

Eric appears not have written an introduction to these Kintyre instructions, which is understandable in the absence of a plan to publish them in his lifetime. Since his understanding of the Duke's life and times was deeper than mine, it seemed to me important that his overview should be represented. I therefore approached the Scottish History Society, which holds the copyright of *Argyll Estate Instructions*, and asked if I could reproduce the relevant parts of his introduction to that volume, in other words parts non-specific to Mull, Morvern and Tiree. I was granted permission and acknowledge here my gratitude. Introduction I is therefore an adaptation of Eric's introduction to *Argyll Estate Instructions*.

This work was undertaken at the request of Mrs Lily Cregeen, Eric's widow, in whose custody his unpublished papers are kept. She and Eric met in Kintyre, after Eric's appointment in 1954 as extra-mural tutor in Argyll, a post which he held until 1966, when he joined the School of Scottish Studies at the University of Edinburgh. Before his untimely death in 1983, Eric edited two books, *Inhabitants of the Argyll Estate 1779* (1963) and *Argyll Estate Instructions: Mull, Morvern, Tiree, 1771-1805* (1964), which were published by the Scottish History Society, and in 2004 a selection of his papers, edited by Margaret Bennett, was published under the title *'Recollections of an Argyllshire Drover' and other West Highland Chronicles*.

Eric's work as an historian was by no means confined to documentary research. His interests were wide-ranging and included anthropology, archaeology and oral history. When he was appointed Assistant Director of the Manx Museum in 1948 – his forebears were Manx – one of his functions was to collect the oral traditions of the island, and when he came to Argyll he continued his tape-recording activities here. Indeed, it was through oral history that I came to meet Eric. I was researching and writing my first book, *The Ring-Net Fishermen*, with which project he gave me valuable encouragement and assistance. He also brought me into the community of oral history researchers, and when the Scottish Oral History Group was formed in 1978, Eric became its Chairman and I was given its newsletter, *By Word of Mouth*, to edit.

I seldom had the pleasure of meeting Eric, so my memories of him are sparse, but he was both – if I may resort to a cliche – a gentleman and a scholar. I remember staying a night with him and Lily at their house in Perthshire, and two remarks of his lodge in my mind from that visit. The first was his observation that Kintyre had been well served by local historians of a high calibre, such as Duncan Colville, Andrew McKerral and Colonel Charles Mactaggart. The second was a rather more mundane piece of domestic advice: an egg which had been kept in a refrigerator should be allowed an extra minute's boiling!

I also remember a timely intervention of Eric's on the occasion of my first public lecture – probably at that 1978 conference – for which I had chosen the topic of the specialised vocabulary of Kintyre ring-net fishermen in herring-detection. Since I knew the subject well at that time, in my inexperience I didn't bother to prepare notes, assuming that the knowledge would pour forth when required; but when I rose to speak, I managed only 'Ladies and gentlemen . . . ' before my mind went completely blank. Eric at once rose from his seat, stood beside me, and by judicious prompting was able to elicit a series of responses which, if they didn't quite amount to a lecture, at least saved me from total humiliation.

There will no doubt be errors in this book, and I would appreciate being informed of them so that they may be corrected if the book is reissued. If any readers can add information to the text, I would appreciate that too. My address is 13 Saddell Street, Campbeltown, Argyll, Scotland PA28 6DN; e-mail is judymartin733@btinternet. com.

Angus Martin,
16 April 2011,
Campbeltown.

1. John, 5th Duke of Argyll, by Gainsborough, part-reproduced from *Argyll Estate Instructions*, in which Eric R. Cregeen acknowledges the kind permission of the 11th Duke, Ian Douglas Campbell, and the generous co-operation of the Scottish National Portrait Gallery. The original is in Inveraray Castle.

Introduction 1

Eric R. Cregeen

The present volume contains the instructions which John, 5th Duke of Argyll, gave to his Chamberlain of Kintyre. They reflect the interests and work of an exceptional man. He was born in 1723, the second son of General John Campbell of Mamore and Mary Bellenden, his wife. He had a distinguished military career, but saw no action after early service abroad and in the 'Forty-five when he served under General Hawley at Falkirk and under the Duke of Cumberland at Culloden.[1] He represented the Glasgow burghs in Parliament from 1744 until his father succeeded to the dukedom of Argyll in 1761. He was briefly in Parliament again, sitting for Dover in 1765, but in 1766 he was created a peer of Great Britain with the title of Baron Sundridge of Coombank and in 1770 he succeeded his father as 5th Duke of Argyll.[2]

The Instructions [– including those of Mull, Morvern and Tiree –] show us one of the most able and energetic landlords of his day going about his business, changing the face of the land, moving populations, setting down towns and villages, founding industries, meticulously controlling the life of the inhabitants of his estate. Yet it was partly a trick of circumstance that turned the Duke's energies into these channels and away from the political career which he would certainly have followed if it had been open to him. The tradition of the family dictated it. Its members had, one after another, played a leading role in the history of Scotland and had helped to shape the destinies of the country.

They had espoused the Reformation, and for more than a decade in the religious struggles of the mid-seventeenth century the kingdom had been dominated by the massive figure of the Marquess of Argyll. Among the Duke's immediate predecessors, the 2nd Duke and his brother, the 3rd Duke, had frequently enjoyed vast power and patronage in the northern kingdom. They were the principal pillar in Scotland of the Whig and Protestant cause, with whose fortunes those of the house of Argyll rose and fell. The dukedom conferred on the 10th Earl in 1701 was a reward for a family which had twice in a century suffered forfeiture and execution for this cause. The accession of George III, the rise of Lord Bute, and the jockeying for position inevitable at the beginning of a new reign, meant for the house of Argyll the loss of the ascendancy in Scotland which they had come to regard as a birthright.

The 5th Duke did not cease to be active in politics, but exclusion from high office gave him time and leisure for other things. One can think of few major enterprises in the Highlands in which he did not play a leading part. He was one of the pioneers of the Crinan Canal, Governor of the British Society, founded in 1786 to develop the resources of the Highlands and in particular the fishing industry, and first President of the newly formed Highland Society. But it was his estates in Argyll that enabled him to express his passion for improvement. Once again, as under the 3rd Duke, the domanial lands at Inveraray were the focus of vast and expensive schemes of building and improving, and from here his apparently inexhaustible energy flowed out in orders that penetrated to the remotest corners of his estate.

It is surprising to realise that, until he grew old, he passed most of his time in London, and rarely spent more than several months in the year at Inveraray and Rosneath. Technically he was an absentee landlord, but in actuality he controlled his estate with tighter reins than any of his predecessors and most of his contemporaries and had a far more intimate and detailed knowledge of his lands and tenants than did the 3rd Duke. Absence brought no real interruption to the Duke's interest and activity. He had a regular correspondence with James Ferrier, his Edinburgh agent, and with his chamberlains. He required a weekly budget of news from his Rosneath chamberlain, and his own letters burst with advice on crops, prices, the treatment of animal ailments and whatever else seemed relevant to the better management of his lands. Meanwhile, his Instructions, given in person at the time of the October meeting at Inveraray for the clearing of accounts, were in the hands of each chamberlain to reprove his past errors, encourage his zeal and control his future activities.

The Duke's interest in improvement was to a great extent controlled by the need for revenue. The management of a Highland estate was then, as now, a matter of business. This was an age of fast-rising rents, but it was also an age of insolvent landlords. In the county of Argyll, the 200 proprietors of the middle of the century had dwindled to 156 by the end of it. [3] There is scarcely an estate that comes to one's attention but is encumbered by debts, a large part of them due to a more lavish style of living.

The old chief, as Dr Johnson observed, had lost his prestige as the leader of his followers, and must compensate by a larger income and grandeur of living. [4] The Highland chiefs followed in the wake of such pioneer-lairds as Archibald Campbell of Knockbuy (1693-1790), who, from about 1728, devoted much of his estate on Lochfyneside to the grazing of cattle for the market, went in for extensive cattle-dealing, and raised the rental to fourfold its earlier level in the sixty following years. Even so, this practical and long-headed laird was often financially embarrassed, and by 1786 was in debt to the tune of £8,000. [5]

It was clear that careful financial management would be indispensable if the Argyll estate was not to fall into similar but much greater embarrassment. The 5th Duke had the experience of his predecessors to guide, and, at times, to warn him. They had long led the field both in the magnificence of their expenditure and in the development of the resources of their estate. The beginnings of commercial management can be seen at least as early as the 9th Earl of Argyll's time in the third quarter of the seventeenth century, [6] but it was the 2nd Duke, who succeeded in 1703 and died in 1743, who finally broke with tradition, removed the great tacksmen and so established the principle which might lead to the expansion of the commercial opportunities open to him and his successors.

The apogee of the improving movement was reached under the 3rd Duke of Argyll, who succeeded his brother in 1743 and died in 1761. Inveraray became the focus of improvements of unprecedented splendour and expense. The new town of Inveraray was begun, the new castle built, and the surrounding policies developed as gardens, farms and woodlands. These works in some years absorbed almost the whole of the property rents of the Argyll lands. Such immense outlays were made possible by the Duke's considerable revenues from his lands, offices and prerogatives. These he augmented by expanding the domain lands in the neighbourhood of Inveraray and Rosneath, and exploiting them fully by grazing cattle for the market, by selling farm produce and by growing timber for sale to the new iron foundry on Lochfyneside. Domanial rights were extended to include minerals, fishings and timber wherever they were on the estate.

Rents, too, could be increased, now that the tacksmen were removed, though the increase was governed by the resources of the tenantry. The gross revenue from the lands in Argyll (including the small neighbouring estate of Rosneath) rose from about £5,000 in 1703, when the 2nd Duke succeeded, to £6, 687 in 1743, when his brother inherited, and to nearly £10,000 in 1761 at the 4th Duke's succession. Since feu-duties and teinds were relatively static, most of the increase is attributable to rents and domanial products. In the eighteen years of the 3rd Duke's administration, the increase in rents was of the order of 40 per cent, and over the whole period from 1703 to 1770, rents on the average roughly tripled.

The 5th Duke inherited a princely estate in Argyll. It had reached the limits of its long career of expansion and now extended from Kintyre in the south to the confines of Inverness-shire in the north, and from Cowal and the tamed magnificence of Inveraray in the east to Coll and Tiree in the west. The rent-paying property lands were probably not less than 500 square miles, but, as superior, the Duke was ultimate owner of the greater part of a county of three thousand square miles, and beyond Argyll of all or part of the estates of chieftains like Clanranald and Glengarry.

He had besides a number of properties elsewhere: Rosneath in Dunbartonshire, the lands of Castle Campbell in Clackmannanshire, the Kinneil estate in West Lothian and others of less importance. This collection of Scottish estates formed a principality perhaps greater in extent than any other in these islands. Combined, they yielded a gross revenue, in 1770, of nearly £13,000, the bulk of it derived from his lands in Argyll. His revenue from Argyll was made up of rents, feu-duties and teinds, as follows:

Rents (including the domanial lands in his own hands)	£7, 539
Feu-duties	1, 551
Teinds (most of which were paid out again in stipends)	£1, 194
	£10, 284[7]

After paying the expenses of management, land-tax and other public burdens, the Duke received about £9,000 nett. The amounts collected in 1700-1 by the chamberlains of the various districts in which the estate was organised were:

The lands in the Argyll Collection[8]	£2,965
Kintyre	£4,811
Mull and Morvern	£1,656
Tiree and the two ends of Coll	£852

It is clear that the lands in the 'Argyll Collection' – the ancient core of the estate in central Argyll, under the management of the Chamberlain of Argyll – yielded considerably less than the lands that had been gained from the Macdonalds and the Duart Macleans. The fall of the Macdonalds had brought the Knapdale lands to the House of Argyll in 1476, and the valuable Kintyre estate in 1607. The annexation of the Duart lands had brought them truly vast territories in Mull, Morvern and the islands of Tiree and Coll (1674).

* * *

In the world of commerce and industry to which the Argyll estate had become an adjunct in the eighteenth century, the old social order of the Highlands was rapidly dissolving away. Tacksmen and tenants, mailers and cottars were now subject to forces originating far beyond the Highlands and outside their control; outside the control, for that matter, of the Duke of Argyll and landlords in general. They managed their estates in accordance with the dictates of changing prices, and the more fortunate survived and even made fortunes. Those, like the 5th Duke, who felt a sense of responsibility for the inhabitants of their estates, were restrained from heartless behaviour towards their tenants, but could not turn a blind eye to their own needs and the swelling rentals of their neighbours. At no time were the Duke's finances easy. Frequently they were in a state of acute embarrassment. 'Is it fair,' he writes peevishly to Ferrier in January 1806, 'in these eventful days that I should have no more than £1,600 at my command?'

There were many calls upon his purse. His great programme of building and improving at Inveraray (which included nothing less than the construction of a new town) rarely ran at less than £4,000 to £5,000 a year in the seventies and eighties. It demanded not less than £10,000 a year by the beginning of the century. The building of a new house at Rosneath in his last few years, to take the place of the castle destroyed by fire in 1802, was a crippling expense, especially as his eldest son had a hand in the plans. 'Two houses of expense and taste are sufficient to ruin any family,' the Duke wrote warningly to the Marquess in early 1803. By 1805 Rosneath was costing the Duke £4,000 a year.

Throughout his life, the Duke was generous to a fault to his children and dependants. When to his already straitened finances were added the Marquess's heavy debts, a series of crises was produced which required all Ferrier's financial skill to surmount. In 1802-3, farms to the value of £20,000 were sold off. Later the Duke was persuaded, much against his will, to part with several superiorities. These exigencies partly explain the Duke's growing involvement, against his own better judgement, in kelp manufacture as the source of much of his revenue. They lie behind the urgent demands for the punctual collection of rent in his Instructions and his anxiety to expand the domanial revenues and bring the kelp shores within the domain.

What is remarkable is not that he asked more but that his demands remained so moderate. Increases in rent were related to the tenants' capacity to pay and were accompanied by real improvements in the farms. Frequently he waived rent increases in favour of solid improvements which the tenants undertook to carry out. His administration opened with substantial increases, but from c. 1778 rents remained fairly static until the early nineties.

The 5th Duke was already something of a legend in his lifetime. Under his successor, George, 6th Duke, when the estate was in low water and enormous sales of land were once more necessary, with bad blood and legal proceedings between the Duke and his brother, it was natural for those who remembered the old Duke's pride of family and careful management, to hark back to better days. 'What would the late Duke of Argyll say to such measures?' asked a devoted friend of the family. [9]

The Instructions reveal the Duke as a benevolent despot transmitting his commands to his servants, and undoubtedly he was an exacting and autocratic master. But it is necessary to consider the Instructions together with the Reports which the chamberlains submitted in the following year. It is clear that the chamberlains exercised considerable influence on the Duke's policies. Their detailed reports, their carefully compiled census lists and their correspondence (though little of the latter seems to have survived) contributed not only to the Duke's encyclopaedic knowledge of his lands and tenants but to the progress of his ideas and the development of his policy.

The most important appointment made by the Duke was that of James Ferrier, W. S., to be his Receiver-General in succession to the loyal Archibald Campbell of Succoth in 1778. Thenceforward he was indispensable. Not only did he introduce stricter standards of accounting and efficiency into the management of the estate – and thereby made himself the terror of muddled or neglectful chamberlains – but his superb handling of the Duke's financial affairs and his well-informed advice contributed essentially to the whole administration. In spite of his brusque and overbearing personality, his intervention appears to have produced greater lenity and tolerance in the Duke's management of the more intransigent districts.

A change of some importance occurred in the administration in the 5th Duke's time for which Ferrier's influence is perhaps largely responsible. The dominance of the Campbells in the administration virtually ceases after c. 1790. Hitherto the Campbell gentry had enjoyed a monopoly of the offices of chamberlains, treasurer and the like. Such families as Stonefield, Airds, Sonochan and Asknish were closely identified with the administration of the estate. By the end of the Duke's life, only old Baillie Campbell at Rosneath survived of the old chamberlains. The rest were new men of less exalted rank, with higher salaries but reduced privileges, more burdensome duties but more restricted powers, greater expertise in accountancy and business, but less independence. This development of a salaried bureaucracy had been gradually on its way since the abolition of the tacksmen and the commercial management of the estate threw greater burdens on the chamberlains.

With all their virtues, the old, dignified chamberlains lacked the capacities which so recommended Maxwell, the Campbeltown lawyer, to James Ferrier and the Duke. They too, then, changed with the times, and only Baillie Rosneath soldiered on, a respected but somewhat tolerated old gentleman, immersed as deeply as the Duke in breeding and selling cattle, experimenting with composts and noting the yields of potatoes. He sent in his rents punctually, but accountancy was something he had never mastered, and his own private affairs were in an appropriate state of embarrassment. On receiving the news of the Duke's paralytic stroke, this devoted servant, who was at dinner, 'read the letter, laid it down on the table, said no other word than these, "Then it is time for me to go too", rose and went to bed, which he never left'. [10]

Duke John did not live to see the events that followed the end of the Napoleonic War – the decline of agricultural prices, the collapse of the kelp market, the eventual disappearance of nearly all the old Highland landlords, the crop failures and famine conditions which set in motion those immense tides of emigration that since have washed over the Highlands and scattered the population to distant lands. Pilot of innumerable enterprises, the Duke belonged, like Baillie Rosneath, to a more sanguine, bustling age, when it seemed still possible to divert the trend of industry from its Lowland concentrations, to irrigate the Highlands with channels of new wealth and keep the Highlanders at home. Under his aegis, as both landlord and chief, he had hoped and striven to find a sure place for his people in the industrial world.

The Instructions [– these and the others already published –] tell of achievements that would bring any man a measure of admiration and fame. But perhaps the significance of the 5th Duke's career lies less in what he accomplished than in what he attempted to do. His administration marks the last, and perhaps the best-conceived attempt, before the deluge of the nineteenth century, to preserve the Scottish Highlands from depopulation and decay. The future lay with other forces. Within a generation, much of his work had been undone. His memory has been neglected in favour of the statesmen and soldiers of the family of Argyll. It is hoped that the publication of these papers will help to restore the 5th Duke to that place in the history of his country that his vision, his humanity and his strength of character deserve.

* * *

My special thanks are due to His Grace the Duke of Argyll for permission to publish the documents which follow and for his kindness, over a number of years, in according me access to the papers at Inveraray Castle and generous hospitality. I have benefited much from his wide knowledge of the Argyll family papers.

(From E. R. Cregeen's Preface to *Argyll Estate Instructions: Mull, Morvern, Tiree, 1771-1805.*)

Introduction 2

Angus Martin

On 28 June 2009, I was in a party which set off from Ballygroggan and crossed the moors to the Inneans Bay. The others were Murdo MacDonald, Jimmy MacDonald, my wife Judy, Dr Gary Robinson, Genevieve Tellier and Chris Kerns, the latter three members of an archaeological team which at the time was excavating the chambered cairn at Blasthill, Southend. The main object of the walk was to examine a group of ruins at Earadale, on the coast between the Inneans and Machrihanish, to determine whether they were prehistoric in origin.

After cooking lunch on a driftwood fire, we parted from Jimmy and set off along the steep, rugged coast, following the well-trodden but erratic goat-tracks. Having looked at Earadale, we continued north, and, as I noted in a brief account published in the *Kintyre Magazine*, 'Our final stop was at the ever-evocative ruins of Craigaig'. [11]

Behind these words lay an experience which at the time of writing seemed more elusive than it does now. Craigaig – from Gaelic, 'Rocky Place' – is better preserved than any of the other townships on that coast. The buildings, while ruinous, retain a certain integrity, and on the edge of the settlement a corn-kiln still stands, so well preserved one might imagine that a day's work would have it operational again. An atmosphere of history clings to Craigaig, and a little knowledge of that history – the families which lived there and some of the events which shaped their lives – helps define the atmosphere, but it might also exist for those who know nothing of the place, perhaps not even its name.

Location is part of the appeal. The township stands on a green terrace overlooking a deeply indented bay which still bears the marks of cultivation. To the south, the land rises as it sweeps in cliffs and headlands towards the Mull. West is the Atlantic, continuous ocean all the way to the coast of Canada, with Rathlin Island and the north coast of Ireland to the south and Islay and Jura to the north.

When we stopped at Craigaig the sun was sinking. After the newcomers had explored the township and its environs, we all assembled to finish our flasks of tea and coffee. Inspired, I suppose,

2. Craigaig from south. The township ruins stand on the headland above the level bay, with the further headland, Dun Bhan, in distance. Photograph by A. Martin, 1984.

by the atmosphere of the place, I began relating tales of the Civil War in Argyll and the ravages committed by Alasdair MacColla (p. 89) in the Royalist cause. While I was describing the inexplicable rout of the Covenanting army, with its backbone of Campbells, at Inverlochy in 1645, Murdo broke in with a Gaelic song on the battle, composed by the MacDonald bard *Iain Lom* ('Bald John'). It was as though, close to the end of a day which had brought us scenic grandeur, the peace of remoteness, and the pleasures of companionship, the final pieces of an extraordinary mosaic of experiences had unexpectedly fallen into place. Somehow, Murdo's spontaneous song, in the language of its first and last inhabitants, had stirred from Craigaig's ruins the sleeping spirit of the place.

I relate all this by way of explaining what follows in this introduction, which strays far beyond the bounds of the 5th Duke's concerns. While recognising the historical value of the texts, I have felt compelled to look beyond the flat, logical view they present to a background of some cultural complexity. A good deal of this is old ground, well trodden in the past, but I trust that, here and there, as at Craigaig on that June evening two years ago, some new insight may emerge.

Mr Cregeen, in his introduction, refers to 'the Duke's encyclopaedic knowledge of his lands and tenants', but this evaluation may be unintentionally misleading. His knowledge, as Mr Cregeen acknowledges in the same sentence, derived substantially from the reports and correspondence of his chamberlains, who were, in effect, intermediaries in his dealings with his tenants and with the owners of adjoining estates. There is no evidence that the Duke had any direct contact with his Kintyre tenantry or was familiar with the nature of their lives. He was a 'semi-absentee', as Mr Cregeen has described him, 'confining his sojourns in Argyll to the summer or early autumn'. [12]

How different, then, from clan chiefs of a few centuries earlier, who lived and died among their people and shared their language and culture. Indeed, among the 5th Duke's common tenants in Kintyre were descendants of those families of hereditary poets and musicians – MacMurchy, MacMarquis and MacShannon – who had served Clan Donald before its fall from power and been rewarded with large tacks of rent-free land. [13]

The concerns of the instructions are largely administrative, which is right and proper; but in these pages the Duke's tenants appear as

3. Craigaig ruins, with corn-kiln in bottom left corner.
Photograph by A. Martin, 1986.

cloud-shadows on a landscape: fleeting and indistinct. Given the nature of the material, it would be unreasonable to expect more. But, of course, there was much more to their lives than labour on the land and contractual obligations. The commentaries I have added to the text attempt to broaden the view of their lives, but more is required if a fuller and clearer background is to emerge.

During the Duke's lifetime, and beyond it, there were two cultural groups in South Kintyre, Gaelic speakers and Scots (or English) speakers. The Lowland Plantation of Kintyre has been definitively documented in Andrew McKerral's *Kintyre in the Seventeenth Century* (1948), and its cultural impact in the present writer's *Kintyre: The Hidden Past* (1984). Since the Plantation was initiated by the Campbells of Argyll, that cultural divide was as much the 5th Duke's inheritance as the lands he owned in Kintyre. Yet, reading the instructions one would hardly guess that it existed. Tenants were tenants, and – rightly – subject to the same conditions of lease, whether they bore a native Gaelic surname or an Ayrshire settler surname; and, regardless of origins or racial stamp, they were subject to the same environmental, social and economic conditions – crop failures, market slumps, rent arrears, eviction, the tragedies of infant mortality and widowhood. All these trials, and more, were shared in common. Yet intermarriage between the two groups was rare in South Kintyre until the nineteenth century, and the barrier was primarily linguistic.

In North Kintyre – the present parishes of Killean and Kilchenzie, Kilcalmonell, and Saddell and Skipness – an altogether different pattern prevailed. Since the seventeenth century settlement of Lowlanders on Campbell lands was concentrated in South Kintyre – the present parishes of Campbeltown and Southend – it was in the south of the peninsula that the displacement of Gaelic by Scots first took hold. In the north, Gaelic retained its strength into the nineteenth century, and even, in a slow death by bi-lingualism, into the early twentieth century. Such Lowland families as settled in the north became Gaelic speaking in order to integrate, and, by the nineteenth century, Gaelic speakers with such names as Armour, Watson, and Greenlees appear in censuses and in legal records which attest to their need of translators.

During the period in which the Duke was firing off directions and rebukes to his chamberlains in the English language, hundreds

4. The Gaelic-speaking Armour family of Rosehill, c. 1871.
Back row: Margaret, b. 1857, later Mrs McLean, Kilmaho, d. 1934;
Janet, b. 1853, later Mrs Revie, d. 1919;
Isabelle, b. 1846, later Mrs McCorkindale, Eden, d. 1921;
Jean, b. 1855, d. 1884;
Donald, b. 1859, d. 1935, Dunfermline.
Front row: Mary, b. 1848, later Mrs Taylor, Crubasdale, d. 1932;
Catherine, b. 1868, later Mrs McDonald, Knocknaha, d. 1940;
Archibald, b. 1814, d. 1887;
James, b. 1865, d. 1895;
Jean McNiven, b. 1823, d. 1885;
John, b. 1861, later in Kilkeddan, d. 1942;
Archibald, Killarow, b. 1850, d. 1918.
All Armour farming families in Kintyre stem from the marriage of
Archibald Armour and Jean McNiven, above.
Photograph from Mrs Ina Semple, Kilkeddan.

of his tenants in Kintyre could not speak English. The point is worth emphasising, because here was a population for which the English language and the cultural values embodied in it were alien intrusions. But it remains possible to look back and glimpse the outlines of that embattled culture, in traditions which were recorded in the nineteenth and twentieth centuries, before the Gaelic language in Kintyre perished.

Peter MacIntosh's *History of Kintyre*, first published in 1857 and reissued thrice, is largely unreliable as history, but contains many tales from Gaelic oral tradition. A teacher and then a catechist, he was a Kintyre man, born at Ardnacross, and also wrote verse in Gaelic and English. He died in Campbeltown in 1876 in his ninetieth year. [14]

Another Kintyre man who collected Gaelic oral tradition was the Rev. Daniel or Donald Kelly (1791-1843), the son of a Campbeltown merchant. He was minister in Southend and afterwards in the Lowland Church, Campbeltown, and wrote the *Second Statistical Account* for both parishes. He was decidedly eccentric and obstructive, however, and in 1836, by order of the General Assembly, he was suspended as minister of the Lowland Church for 'irregularities'. Described as an 'ardent collector of ancient memoirs and legendary tales', his collection was not published in his lifetime and only partially thereafter. It passed on to his equally eccentric son Neil (1823-1906), who styled himself Neil Munro Kelly Robertson. Neil, a 'first rate raconteur of old legends, stories and events', clearly shared his father's interests, and, when he retired to Campbeltown after a career at sea, published items from his father's papers and allowed other writers access to them; but he never married and had no family, and the collection has evidently not been heard of since his death. [15]

The manuscript collection of Edinburgh doctor Robert Craig Maclagan (1839-1919) contains in excess of a hundred items of folklore from Kintyre and is lodged in the Department of Celtic and Scottish Studies, University of Edinburgh. [16] That collection was made between 1893 and 1902, during which period the Rev. D. J. Macdonald (1855-1930), a native of Benbecula and minister of Killean and Kilchenzie Parish for fifty years, was active in the Largieside collecting place-names and folklore, part of which collection was published posthumously in 1932 as *Antiquities of Killean and Kilchenzie*. [17]

With the appearance of tape-recording equipment in the twentieth century, a more scientific approach became possible, particularly in the field of linguistics, and Kintyre was visited by, among other scholars, Nils M. Holmer of the Norwegian Linguistic Survey, whose *The Gaelic of Kintyre* was published some twenty years later, in 1962, and included a section of 'texts', which are largely traditional tales. [18] Even when the present writer was hitch-hiking and cycling around Kintyre in 1977, visiting and tape-recording elderly farmers and shepherds, there remained a small harvest of tales to be gathered in.

By that time, no trace remained of the ancient, complex Gaelic tales; but D. J. Macdonald, eighty years earlier, recorded a few, including one about the great *Fionn Mac Cumhaill*'s henchman *Gille Cochull nan Craiceann* – 'Lad of the Skin Hoods' – who slew a terrifying supernatural bull-like creature at Muasdale. [19] Among the Maclagan tales from Kintyre are several which describe a white pig-shaped thing known as the *Sac Ban*, which would follow people who were out at night, and grip and bite their heels. [20]

Gigantic serpents lurked in the hills. One such, 'of most enormous power, size, and ferocity', had its lair on Ben Gullion and was 'the terror alike of man and of beast'. It remained invincible until a hero named MacMurchy appeared and lured it to a trap, in which, with agonized writhings and hissings, it was roasted to ashes. [21] A more docile, but none the less dangerous serpent frequented Barr Glen at Cnocan nam Ban (below). It could be seen coiled around that roadside knoll, from which it could extend itself across the road to drink from the river, and still keep its tail around the knoll. [22]

Certain remote lochs were inhabited by water horses. Loch an Eich, 'The Horse Loch', in the hills west of Tayinloan, was said to contain no trout because the water horse had eaten them all; and a proposal to restock it was 'turned down on the plea that the horse would certainly eat them all'. A local shepherd claimed to have seen its hoof-prints in snow. [23]

The humble mole has been associated with the Campbells in Kintyre folklore. 'The moles were to drive the Campbells before them and take possession of their estates; and when the moles had reached the Mull, not a Campbell would remain throughout the length and breadth of Cantire.' [24] It is remarkable that the mole appears to have come into Kintyre only in the early part of the

5. Ben Gullion, lair of the mythical serpent, from Limecraigs Cottage, 2006. Photograph by A. Martin.

nineteenth century. When the Rev. Donald MacDonald, minister of Killean and Kilchenzie Parish, completed his *Statistical Account* in 1843, he was able to declare that 'the mole has not yet made its appearance in this parish'; but, before publication, he inserted the footnote: 'Since writing the above, the mole has advanced into the parish. ' The present writer noticed the first molehills on the coast between Machrihanish and the Mull around 1980, by which time, certainly, not a Campbell estate remained in Kintyre, though there were – and are – plenty of Campbells. [25]

Many supernatural beings live on inside those time-capsules which are place-names. One of the most mysterious in Kintyre must be Allt Leannan Sithe, 'The Stream of the Fairy Lover', which runs off Cnoc Moy and into the high end of Gleneadardacrock. The 'fairy lover' was one who enjoyed the sexual favours of mortal women, and the male child of such a union was *dubh-sith*, 'black fairy'. One such was *Sitheach*, a dwarf of whose exploits the present writer recorded stories in the 1970s. One story, from Willie McGougan in Largie, had the dwarf offering martial service to Sir Lachlan MacLean of Duart on the eve of the Battle of Traigh Ghruineart (1598) in Islay. MacLean, on the evidence of his eyes, rudely rejected the offer, so the dwarf approached MacLean's adversary, Sir James MacDonald, who looked him over and asked if he was 'any good'. The dwarf professed to be 'a first class hand wi the bow and arrow'. An apple was duly set up as a target, and the little man at once split it with a shot. He also subsequently – and fittingly – split Sir Lachlan, and the MacLeans fled the battlefield. The dwarf remained with the MacDonalds and became the 'Cara Broonie', famed in Largieside tradition. [26]

The name MacFarlane in Tarbert had a lingering association with sorcery even into the twentieth century. A man of that name appeared one hot summer's day at the township of Allt Beithe – 'Birch Burn' – on the coast south of Tarbert. Only women were there and he asked them for a drink of milk to appease his thirst and hunger, but was refused and advised to drink from the burn. He stepped inside the house and produced a hazel twig from a concealed pouch. He began stabbing it into the thatch, and all the time he was doing that, the women couldn't stop dancing. When they had all fallen to the floor exhausted, he said to them: 'The next time a man comes to this house for a drink of milk, you'll give it to him'. [27] Allt Beithe was deserted after an outbreak of plague in

6. Gleneadardacrock. Beyond the ruined shepherd's house lies Allt Leannan Sithe. John Brodie (left) and Jamie Girvan are standing amid a cluster of mounds, probably shieling huts.
Photograph by A. Martin, 7/5/2007.

1845. When visitors to the ruins in 1985 cleared a section of the floor in one of the houses, a flagstone near the hearth was lifted and underneath it was discovered 'a few locks of reddish hair'. [28]

Supernatural lore abounded: witches, wizards, fairies, ghosts, brownies, goblins, water-horses, evil eye, second sight, premonitions, and a host of other mysterious and alarming phenomena (some of which, of course, still haunt the human psyche). But there was a powerful natural force prevailing then, which has since been effectively banished from modern society – darkness.

Until the twentieth century, illumination was feeble, indoors and especially out. Candles and cruisies, and even the later lanterns, produced little light. In the ceilidh-houses where folk gathered in winter to hear songs sung and tales told, there was the security of the company, but when the time came to step outside and set off homeward, the prospect was often one of utter darkness. It was the custom to lift, with tongs, a burning peat from the fire and use it as a torch, but it was a poor light and little help in the banishment of fear.

For many folk, into the nineteenth century, malign forces were all around in the dark, and certain places were to be avoided, even should that involve a time-consuming detour. Cnoc Sithe, 'Fairy Knoll', near the crest of the Glenahanty-Largiebaan road, was one such spot, where fairies had supposedly been seen. [29] Cnocan nam Ban, 'The Women's Knoll', was another, in Barr Glen, where 'ould weemen' – witches no doubt – had been seen 'dancin oot in the field'. [30] Hares might not be hares at all, but witches transformed, and if a cow's milk-yield suddenly dropped or butter wouldn't form in the churn, witchcraft would immediately be suspected.

By the time the present writer was recording such traditions, they were regarded as ridiculous, and had been so regarded for a generation or two back, but at one time their influence was real enough. An emigrant, recalling the Campbeltown of his boyhood in the early years of the nineteenth century, remembered listening spell-bound on many a night as his grandfather related with 'solemn gravity . . . the most appalling stories about brounies, coinchachs, wizards and warlocks', which left the boy 'ready to start at [his] own shadow and trembling with fear'. [31]

But the spiritual illumination which religion ought to have brought to those who were disposed to receive it, might itself illumine only morbid terrors of another species. In his *History of Kintyre*, Peter

7. Ruins of Allt Beithe, looking east across Loch Fyne to Cowal, 27/3/2011.
Photograph by Judy Martin.

MacIntosh preserves several tales which afford a glimpse into the mentality of those times. As an instance of 'the fearful effects of Sabbath desecration', he relates an occurrence in the mid-eighteenth century 'which raised a great sensation throughout the district'. Some boys were amusing themselves one Sunday on Smerby shore, when one of them decided he would imitate a preacher and stood at the side of a rock to deliver a sermon. A part of the rock split off, fell on him and broke his back, 'which rendered him a miserable object for the rest of his life – living for many years as a warning to others'. [32]

Another of MacIntosh's stories, also ascribed to the mid-eighteenth century, concerned a man by the name of Beith who lived near Clachaig Glen, above Muasdale. Though 'very pious and intelligent', he was 'troubled by the arch-fiend, who appeared before him in frightful shapes'. Going home one night, he came to the gully of the stream he was to cross and 'perceived an elegant bridge over the steep place'. Considering it to be 'an invention of the enemy to entice him to go over', he spoke a short prayer, whereupon the bridge 'disappeared with a tremendous noise, as if ten thousand iron chains rattled down the glen'. MacIntosh adds cautiously: 'No doubt these things were not real, but sprung from a strong imagination; but they were formerly believed by the people of the place'. [33]

The surname Beith came into Kintyre with the Lowland settlement; indeed, it derives from the place-name in north Ayrshire, [34] which itself probably derives from Gaelic *beith*, 'birch', [35] identically spelled, but far apart in pronunciation. Although Beith families flourished in South Kintyre – John Jnr. , merchant and whisky distiller, for instance, was five times provost of Campbeltown in the mid-nineteenth century[36] – there were others who settled early in the North and were no doubt Gaelicised (though notice the Lowland forenames below). John Beith was recorded as a fencible man in Gartgunnell and Tangie in 1692, [37] and, further north, on the 'five merk land of Muisdale', Duncan Beith was a joint-tenant by 1729 and was followed by Duncan, Adam and Mathew in 1757, Hugh in 1770 and David and Robert in 1776. [38]

The Gaelicisation of elements of the Lowland settler stock is demonstrable from the records, but, setting that aside and returning to oral tradition, a question arises. What became of the cultural inheritance of the Lowlanders after their settlement in Kintyre? Certainly, their language prevailed – the extinction of Kintyre Gaelic in the mid-twentieth century testifies to that – although its vocabulary is fast wearing out and giving way to English. (The nineteenth century dialect poem, 'Flory Loynachan', illustrates the past richness of the Scots lexis in Kintyre.) But what of the stories they surely brought with them from Ayrshire and Renfrewshire?

That the Scottish Lowlands possessed such riches of oral tradition needs no explaining here – the legacies of Burns, Hogg and Scott alone amply testify to that – but that little or nothing survived in Kintyre is curious, especially as the nineteenth century brought another wave of Lowlanders: Millars, Hunters, Ronalds and Youngs among them. One explanation may be that no one bothered to collect their traditions, not even one of their own community, which prospered phenomenally in the nineteenth century, producing a host of whisky-distillers, merchants and industrialists. [39] Perhaps the root of the dearth was archetypal materialism or perhaps a stronger dose of Calvinism purged them quicker than it did the Highlanders!

An interesting – if tenuous – link with Burns appeared in Kintyre in the mid-nineteenth century in the person of Annie Sillars Paterson, who took the lease of Cattadalemore in Southend. When Jean Breakenridge married Robert Burns's brother Gilbert in 1791, her half-sister Annie Sillars was bridesmaid and was complimented at the wedding by the poet himself, who told her: 'Annie, somebody will break his heart over you yet. ' She married Archibald Paterson, farmer in Ashyard, Galston, and after his death moved to Southend, where she and her family remained for the duration of the 19-year lease, afterwards returning to Ayrshire. [40] When James Bickett, farmer in Cloanbeith, Kilwinning, secured the lease of Cattadalemore in 1863, the sitting tenant was named as David Paterson, [41] so presumably the family left in that year.

Kintyre's most enduring connection with the poet is, of course, 'Highland Mary' Campbell. She was born in Cowal in 1766, four years before John Campbell succeeded to the dukedom of Argyll upon his father's death. As a child, she moved to Dalintober, where her father, Archibald Campbell, had earlier been a seaman in the Revenue Service, whose fast, armed cutters were based at Campbeltown to suppress smuggling. Mary Campbell was brought up at Broombrae, where a maternal aunt, Elizabeth MacNeill, already lived, and she attended school nearby. Her relationship with the poet has been the subject of intensive research, yet remains controversial, but that she and Burns entered into a marriage contract is now indisputable. Whether Burns would have honoured that engagement is conjectural, because Mary died in Greenock, aged twenty, on 17 October, 1786, and Jean Armour became his wife. From such poems as 'To Mary in Heaven', 'Highland Mary' and 'The Highland Lassie O' was Mary Campbell's cult status formed, and she remains, by her brief, but intense, association with Scotland's most celebrated poet, Dalintober's most illustrious historical figure. [42]

While, by the nineteenth century, a small section of the Lowland community had come to identify itself with Gaelic, a large section of the Gaelic community was not only losing the language, but was losing, or discarding, its outward identity. Throughout Kintyre, scores of surnames were changed to make them appear less Gaelic or, in some cases, not Gaelic at all, but Scots or English. At a time when a Gaelic background was widely perceived to be a handicap, this transformative trend was in part motivated by social, economic and cultural aspirations; but it was also in part a consequence of officials' having to spell, as best they could, Gaelic names for which there was no available standard spelling; so the most awkward of the names were simplified or translated.

MacSporran, therefore, might become by part-translation 'Pursell', and MacEachran 'Cochrane' from a similarity in the sound; but neither of these alternatives lasted. Many did, however. O'Brolachan became 'Brodie' and O'Loynachan 'Lang', to give just two well-known examples. Of course, these spellings of Gaelic names are themselves modified: 'MacEachran', for example, is *Mac Eachtighearna*, which looks quite different, but is pronounced much the same. Most of the names which underwent radical transformation belonged to minor, localised families. The big surnames in Kintyre, which were also big elsewhere, such as Campbell, MacCallum, MacDougall, MacKay, MacIntyre, MacLachlan, and MacMillan, remain recognisably Gaelic, though anglicised to a degree. [43]

Although native Gaelic has disappeared from Kintyre, after an existence of 1500 or more years, hundreds of words survive in place-names and in dialect, though few folk give them much thought – like features in a landscape, they are simply there until noticed. But they have been collected and studied and published. The split between Gaelic and Scots can be represented by a flower, the beautiful

8. 'Sheggan' or 'shellister' at Knockbay.
Photograph by George McSporran, June 2010.

and botanically fascinating wild iris (*Iris pseudacorus*). In Scots, its name is 'sheggan' – a variant of Scots 'segg', which has a wide range of plant applications, and is a form of English 'sedge' – and in Gaelic 'shellister' (*seilisdeir*). The later Scots word prevailed in South Kintyre and the Gaelic word in North, and perhaps even fifty years ago, with a stint of research, a dividing line could have been drawn across Kintyre, with 'sheggan' below and 'shellister' above. [44]

Returning to Peter MacIntosh's Beith anecdote, he remarks of Clachaig Glen that, 'At present it is thinly inhabited . . . '; and he describes Ballochroy Glen as 'almost depopulated, in order to leave space enough for the sheep and heather fowl'. [45] This was in the mid-nineteenth century, yet the hinterlands of Kintyre were still populated to an extent which might appear incomprehensible now. Many settlements which were farms in the eighteenth century became herds' houses in the nineteenth and ruins in the twentieth.

George Langlands, the Northumbrian who was the 5th Duke's improver and surveyor (p. 120), produced an invaluable map of Argyll which was published in its final version in 1801. A look at the Kintyre section of that map will reveal the wide distribution of the population. The map is not accurate in scale, but it records settlements roughly where they were. Immediately noticeable is the number of habitations which lie far inland, dotted along the flanks of the big glens and amid the hills. Add to these the myriad shieling huts – clustered on traditional summer grazings – and the scale of occupation, both permanent and seasonal, becomes astonishing compared with the settlement evidence on a modern map, with its blocks of smothering coniferous plantations.

The Duke had many tenants in Campbeltown – 302 families in 1779 – but the greater part of his tenantry – 587 families – lived on farms throughout Kintyre (excepting Kilcalmonell Parish); however, as the present writer has elsewhere suggested, the term 'farm' should be treated with caution. Until the concept of the farm as an independent agricultural unit, worked by a single tenant, was forced into the frame of Gaelic society, the *baile* (anglicised in place-names as 'bally', 'balli', etc.) was a communal tenancy township in which farming was more or less taken for granted. The farm, as now understood, was a nineteenth century creation, the full-grown child of the Improvements. [46] By then, as now, farmers did little else but farm – it was their settled occupation, not least when dairying, with its heavy commitments in time and labour, was adopted in mid-century – whereas their grandfathers and great-grandfathers might turn their hands to almost anything: labouring, house-building, boatbuilding, cobbling, herring-fishing, whisky-distilling, cattle-raiding, and, a bit further back, by choice or by coercion, the dark arts of battle.

Principles of commercial estate management had been applied by the Earls of Argyll to their Kintyre lands well before the end of the seventeenth century, with the introduction of nineteen-year leases, the plantation of Campbells and their followers, along with the Lowlanders, and the 'profitable device' of auctioning leases. The tacksmen, or superior tenants, who, within the old clan system, had been the chief's kinsmen and enjoyed their lands at nominal rents by virtue of that kinship and in return for martial services, were the first to feel the impact of these changes. Under the 2nd Duke (1680-1743), they lost their privileges by the increase in their rents and the prohibition of sub-letting, on which they depended for their incomes. In Kintyre, the tacksmen, as a class, effectively ceased to exist in 1710 when the Duke accepted higher offers of rent from their sub-tenants. [47]

In an analysis of the 'List of People upon the Argyll Estate, 1779' – 'probably the earliest known Scottish census' – Eric R. Cregeen remarks of Kintyre:

> 'In the place of the privileged tacksmen and their numerous sub-tenants one finds that there has emerged a new tenant body, some 250 strong and ranging from fairly small runrig tenants to prosperous men holding one or two farms. They are of mixed origins, drawn from both the tacksman class and their former sub-tenants. They pay higher rents, on the average, than the tenants of other parts of the estate, and between the lowest and the highest ranks is a solid body of middling tenant-farmers, typical of the new age and rarely found north of the estate. Undoubtedly, in the emergence of this new tenant class, the trade and industry of Campbeltown played a significant part, by injecting new blood into the tenantry, by providing a demand for agricultural products, and by absorbing into its expanding life the less successful of the sub-tenants. In no other district were the dukes so successful in creating a viable agrarian organisation to take place of the old.' [48]

For Kintyre, unfortunately, that census did not ennumerate entire families, only males above the age of twelve; nor, contrary to the case in the other parts of Argyll Estate, were family names documented. The census reveals that several farms on the Mull were already under sheep. 'Borgadilmore' was uninhabited, while its neighbour 'Borgadilbeg' held one family, no doubt that of the shepherd. 'Innendownan' and 'Ballinamoile' and 'Ballimaacviccar' were also uninhabited, while others in the area, though occupied, were clearly not occupied by the lessees, but by sub-tenants, most likely shepherds (p. 168).

Some of the farms were populous. In Killean Parish, Beallachgoichan – which no longer exists – had 11 families on it. Six of the 17 men recorded there were 'tacksmen' – a term, by then, having no other significance in Kintyre than 'lease-holders', most of whom, as Eric R. Cregeen observed, were of 'humble origin'[49] – while 3 were 'tacksmen's sons', 3 'servants' and 5 'cottars'. Pollwuline (Polliwilline, in Kilblaan Parish) also supported 11 families, while Smerby (Kilchousland Parish) had 15 families, Killocraw (Kilchenzie) 11 and Torristill (Carradale) 10. Numbers ranged from these double figures to single families in the smallest of the farms, generally remote hill places, now ruinous – and some of them 'lost' – such as, in Kilchousland Parish, Altantarve and Mulbuy, and, in Kilkerran Parish, Laggs, Bailinatuine, Arinaschavach, Aultnaboduy and Arinarach.[50]

The following list of farms and crofts which are now uninhabited is merely a sample, fifteen from each Kintyre parish and seventy-five in all. Many, it should be stated, were on estates other than Argyll's. There are few people left alive who have heard a quarter part of these names spoken, let alone know where the places are.

> **Kilcalmonell**: Achachoish, Ariloan, Auchnaglaick, Brantian, Clackadunan, Cregan, Duppen, Lagnascavach, Lergnahuinsan, Monyliadh, Muckroy, Shirdrim, Sidrigill, Sron Albannach, Stronambrock.
> **Killean and Kilchenzie**: Achachoirk, Achaglass, Achapharick, Achnaha, Arichoraig, Balanacoille, Cruamrie, Gortanduag, Lecknalarach, Lorgie, Mucklach, Rudugh, Stelag, Stockadil, Teanchoisin.
> **Saddell and Skipness**: Ardnadamh, Auchameanach, Auchnastrone, Bailean-Cleirich, Breaclarach, Croit Bhridean, Garbhachaidh, Gortan a' Bhealaich, Granamhoine, Kirnashie, Lagan Geoidh, Stronovean, Tigh a' Chnoic, Toit Dubh, Uladil.

9. A stretch of the original Learside road, which ran overland between Glenramskill and Ballimenach brae, looking south-east towards the Ayrshire coast and Ailsa Craig.
Photograph by A. Martin, summer 1988.

Campbeltown: Arichlarie, Auchinbreck, Ballochnahuilly, Balure, Barn Croft, Bogwilly, Clachfin, Crocharie, Dalachlachan, Drumathrottan, Drumfin, Easca, Mealbaan, Mulbuy, Strathduie.
Southend: Achinsavil, Achnaclary, Altnaboduy, Balimacmurchie, Ballanacusag, Blarphern, Cantaig, Clachavulline, Corrylach, Gortein Labach, Knocknagrein, Lonachan, Mulbuy, Socach, Tigh Mhuilich.

Most of these settlements were indeed remote, but only by present standards. Until the mid-twentieth century, the generality of countryfolk – and many townsfolk too – thought nothing of walking ten or twenty miles or more to visit friends or family or to transact a piece of business. Many children, within living memory, walked several miles to school and back daily. A network of tracks linked settlements with one another, and, over longer distances, with shielings, peat-banks, mills, smiddies, harbours and the principal villages where provisions could be purchased when occasionally required. Tracks joined the east coast of Kintyre with the west, and social and economic contacts between the opposite communities flourished to a degree scarcely imaginable now, when the principal roads mainly follow the coasts.

In the Langlands map of 1801, already mentioned, most of the major geographical features are missing, but these faults are not surprising in a map of that period. Total surveying methods would come with the Ordnance Survey seventy years later, when Langlands' many blank or sketchy areas would be filled in. The Langlands map, on the contrary, captures mainly a basic landscape of settlements, roads and tracks, in other words a human geography. The settlements, which are all named, are only approximately located, but the lines of the roads and tracks are probably the most accurate features, since he would have traversed all of them, on foot or on horseback, in the making of the map.

The roads, which are indicated by parallel lines, are much as they are now, but the map also shows the main overland tracks or paths, indicated by a single broken line, and these have since fallen out of use. One long track begins at Drumore, Campbeltown, and runs north up the middle of Kintyre until it joins with an east-west track from north of Carradale to Tayinloan. Another track, further north, crosses the peninsula from Crossaig to Clachan. Others, in the southern part of the peninsula, may be located on the reproduction of the map in this book.

In the mid-nineteenth century, Carradale's postal links were with Tayinloan. A 'runner' went there twice a week in winter and thrice in summer, but a complaint was made in 1852 that the service was unsatisfactory and that Campbeltown would be preferred, the distance being shorter and the route 'incomparably better'. [51]

As recently as 1903, Archibald McArthur, farmer in Auchinreich, Carradale Glen, died of exposure on Deuchran Hill returning home in darkness from a ploughing match at Rosehill, Glenbarr. [52] A McCallum shepherding family in the nineteenth century would walk from Largiebaan, Southend, to Campbeltown, to attend Lorne Street Church, renting a room in town for the day so that they could attend morning and evening services before returning home. Their route was across the hills by Killypole, on a path marked with white stones. [53]

Parts of these old tracks can still be seen on the landscape, but afforestation in particular has obliterated much archaeological and historical evidence on the ground; how much will never be known. Sections of the coastal track from Machrihanish to Carskey are still visible, for example on the southern approach to the Inneans Bay, as illustrated on the following page. Its antiquity has not been established, but it certainly, as the Langlands map shows, connected the string of townships which escaped the agricultural improvements of the late eighteenth and early nineteenth centuries and were instead turned over to sheep.

In the Argyllshire Road Act of 1800, it was proposed to create a 'Path about Ten Feet Broad, from Glemanuilt to the Lighthouse on the Moyle of Cantyre, and from thence round about till it joins the High Road at Trodigal or Kilkivan', but the proposal was evidently never proceeded with, and the existing track – suited only, in its time, to pedestrians and pack-ponies – remained unimproved. [54] Two of these thirteen coastal townships, Innean Mor and Innean Beag, are examined on p. 166. All of them belonged to the Argyll Estate and all of them were farmed, from the commencement of records until the coming of sheep, by Gaelic families.

Until the mid-nineteenth century, housing conditions of tenant-farmers were uniformly primitive, and decidedly worse for the cottars, or 'day labourers', who congregated on the farms and were sub-tenants. These conditions are briefly examined on p. 127, but the following peculiar anecdote from the seventeenth century will give a flavour of the discomforts. The story was taken down from William Watson, tenant of Claongart, by the Rev. Daniel Kelly,

10. A surviving section of the old coastal track from Machrihanish to Carskey, south of Inneans Bay, which is visible in mid-picture. George McSporran and Judy Martin are walking ahead of the photographer, A. Martin. Summer, 1988.

around 1838, and concerns the Rev. John Cunison, who had been minister of Kilbride in Arran until 'outed' for nonconformity around 1663. Following his expulsion, he retreated to Kintyre and occupied a 'miserable dwelling', Clach-fhionn, in Strathduie Glen, not far from the present reservoir at Lussa. For seven years, according to tradition, he subsisted largely from 'the fishing of Strathduie water'. One day, a gentleman (*duine-uasal*) from his native Atholl visited him.

> 'As his house had neither window nor chimney, the smoke proved so annoying that Mr Cunison and his friend had to retire from the house and rest on a bank outside, while a few trout which the minister himself had caught for their repast were making ready. Mr Cunison, thereupon, told his guest that on his return to Atholl he was to tell his relations there that his house possessed one door, which had to serve for entrance and way of egress therefrom, and also for the smoke to escape and the light of heaven to fall on his table when Providence supplied him with a dinner. A Covenanter with humour, surely, this genial divine, who could discourse facetiously amid surroundings so comfortless, and circumstances so depressing. We can imagine a twinkle in his eye, as he points out to his friend, from the bank on which they recline, that the door of his poor abode was more serviceable by far, owing to the variety of its uses, than that of the stateliest mansion.' [55]

Surprisingly, given the Duke's 'practical knowledge of agriculture'[56], his Kintyre instructions contain very little on the main crops of the time, oats (or 'corn') and barley ('bear'), though his concern to encourage the growing of wheat is recurrent.

Potatoes are not mentioned at all, yet, as Eric R. Cregeen states in his Introduction (p. 7), the 'yields of potatoes' was one of the Duke's personal interests. The potato was still a newcomer to the Highlands in the latter half of the eighteenth century, but its ascent would be rapid and by the early nineteenth century it had become a vital cash-crop. It was a boom time for local farmers. Visiting smacks shipped cargoes not only at Campbeltown – one writer, in 1853, remembered counting sixty-eight cart-loads of potatoes being driven to the harbour in a day c. 1829 – but also all around the coast, at Peninver, Southend, Largieside, and Gigha. [57] Upwards of 50,000 bolls (approximately 3,175 tonnes) were exported annually from Kintyre in the early 1840s, mainly to Ireland, where, during the famine years of that decade, a great demand for seed-potatoes existed. [58]

By the early 1850s, however, 'potato blight' had arrived and 'permeated throughout Kintyre generally'. The export market declined to insignificance and the three starch factories, at Muasdale, Auchaleek and Machribeg, temporarily ceased to operate. [59] The markets recovered, but the twentieth century brought a slow decline in commercial potato-growing. At present only a few Kintyre farmers cultivate modest crops for local sale, on a buy and collect basis.

To what extent the 5th Duke, notwithstanding his formidable command of the affairs of his estates, understood the outward lives of his tenants, let alone their dreams and aspirations, remains debatable. His was naturally a luxurious life, beyond anything his tenants could begin to imagine. It is highly improbable that he ever resorted to knocking limpets off a rock with a stone to put food in his belly; a wet summer, which ruined the harvest of peats, would not have deprived him of heat and the means of cooking; his military service was not calculated to allow him to send a little money home to his family; he never committed an act of extreme violence or murder in order to protect a few gallons of illicit whisky from the attentions of Excisemen, and in so doing ensure that the rent for a dilapidated hut might not go unpaid; and he never pulled on a patched pair of breeks in the morning.

Comparisons could be multiplied with ease, but in the final analysis he lived the life into which he had been born, as the most vociferous of his detractors might have been content to do had that birthright been theirs; and, as Eric R. Cregeen has argued, as landlords went at the time, he was by no means the worst. Finally, to his passion for control and understanding, a debt is owed by historians and genealogists, for without the censuses, maps, and reports which he commanded be delivered to his office at Inveraray Castle, our knowledge of Argyll in the late eighteenth century would be vastly the poorer.

In July 1955, the Argyll Estate in Kintyre was sold by the trustees of the late 10th Duke, Niall Diarmid (1872-1949), to pay death duties. The auction, conducted by Messrs Knight, Frank and Rutley, London, was held in the Town Hall, Campbeltown, and lasted three days. An unknown bidder had offered £174,000 for the entire 28, 857 acres, but the 145 lots – including 78 farms and holdings, 63 of them milk-producing – were sold separately, predominantly to the sitting tenants, and raised a greater sum. Present at the sale were the chamberlain of Argyll, R. M. Hamilton, and the factor for the Kintyre estate, C. Calder. That auction effectively ended the Argyll Campbells' eventful association with Kintyre extending back to 1607. The last word went to an elderly, unnamed tenant, who exulted: 'We're all lairds now!'[60]

Instructions to the Chamberlain of Kintyre

[Editorial note. The numbered insertions in SMALL CAPITALS correspond to the Commentaries which follow. Text in square brackets signifies editorial intervention.]

October 1785.

1. You will cause enter this in a Book which bring with you every year to the meeting for settling Accounts and as soon as you arrive give it to me with your Report upon it that I may have time to consider it and think of fresh Instructions.

2. By the Lease of the Coal I am entitled to a share of the produce or the fixed rent in my option but I have never been informed what the produce is. You will therefor procure Abstracts of the Accounts & report to me the import of them.

3. As the Trustees have not given any Lintseed to my Tenants in Kintyre for two years past there is no occasion for my being burdened longer with the Flax dresser who may therefore be dismissed.

1: Flax

4. Enquire how far it will be agreeable to the Tenants to pay a certain price yearly in time coming for the Teind Meal and Bear and Multure meal payable by their Leases such as 16/ for the Boll of Meal and 18/ for the Boll of Bear and report.

2: Rents

5. You may advance to the Town of Campbeltown £150 to enable them to bring in the Backs Water to the Milns taking security for its being repaid to me by installments of 10 P Cent yearly in terms of their Memorial to me on that subject.

3: Backs Water

6. You must apply to the Justices of the County for liberty to alter the line of road at Turners Farm so as to encourage his inclosures unless you can settle the matters with Colonel Campbell by yourselves or with the assistance of some of the Neighbours. He proposed to submit it but as I understand the law is clear in favour of the alteration desired and am informed that the Colonel is not truly injured by it I trust he will be advised to withdraw his opposition. If not the law must take place.

4: John Turner, Tonrioch

7. As formerly signified I am well inclined to prolong the Leases to such of my Tenants as are industrious and deserving without receiving any additional rent but then I expect that they in return are to begin to make some solid improvements and when any application is made to you for a Prorogation you must consider deliberately what improvement is best adapted to the particular Farm and turn and situation of the Tenant and report to me that I may decide upon it. In general I consider Stone dykes to be the

first improvement but as these cannot be made on every Farm other articles must be thought of such as draining, ditch, & hedge &ca.

Signed / Argyll

You must pay attention to the marches of my property with other Heritors in Kintyre, and get them ascertained and settled, where there is any doubt or dispute.

Signed / Argyll

Answers to Instructions October 1785.

1. Done
2. Done
3. Done
4. The Tenants have agreed.
5. Done
6. Colonel Campbell beg'd delay until he would apply to your Grace.
7. Done in part.
8. I have enter'd into submission with Ugadale about the march between Cuilundune & Killeonan and a very long proof is taken upon both sides but the Arbiter Mr. Maxwell has not decided the case. Besides the above there is dispute about marches with Ugadale at least in three other Farms.

5: MACNEALS OF UGADALE
6: UGADALE ESTATE AND BROOCH
7: LOSSIT HOUSES

There is some Ground contraverted between a Farm or two of your Graces and one of Sanda about nineteen acres disputed.

8: MACDONALDS OF SANDA
9: MACDONALDS OF LARGIE

With Cariskey there is contraverted ground in two parts but not considerable.

10: MACNEILL OF CARSKEY

There is a large piece of ground in controversy with the Baron Mc Oshenaig of Lephinstra.

11: MACSHANNONS

It is probable there may be more of that kind tho' not yet come to the Chamberlains knowledge excepting in Straduie with Kildallaig there is some Ground disputed.

12: CAMPBELLS OF KILDALLOIG
13: CAMPBELLS OF GLENSADDELL
14: CAMPBELLS OF SKIPNESS
15: CAMPBELLS OF STONEFIELD

Instructions October 1786.

1. Inform Mr. MacDowal that on account of the expences which at present attend his Coal operations I do not mean to take the share of the produce last year which I observe is more than double the fixed Rent. But that in time coming he must lay his account with paying what shall become due to me according to the Lease.

16: CHARLES MCDOWALL

2. I observe you have settled with the Tenants to take money from them in time coming in place of Multure meal and Teind meal and Bear and I am satisfied with what is proposed.

3. Colonel Campbell having signified to me his inclination to do what is agreeable to me with regard to the dispute betwixt him and Turner about turning the road you may tell Turner that he will meet with no more disturbance on that head provided he pays to the Colonel the half of the value of his dyke which is reasonable and which you must see done.

4. Colonel Campbell having intimated to me an Assignation in his favour of the Inn at Campbeltown which was built by John Watson on a Lease from me you may let him know that I have no objection to his taking possession of the house in order to recover his money out of it only that it must be used as an Inn and sett to a proper person to be approved of by me and who must keep the house and serve the public as prescribed in the Lease.

17: COLONEL CHARLES CAMPBELL

5. You will make the enquirys about the proper stance for a Light house upon the Mull of Kintyre and other particulars regarding that matter pointed out in Sir James Hunter Blairs Letter and correspond with him on that business and also report to me upon it.

6. Archibald McDuff has applied for a renewal of his Lease which I will not give at present as he is in such bad circumstances. But in order to encourage him I agree to allow the great arrear of £103. 13. 11 to be given up in payment of his Claim for buildings & meliorations by his present Lease and to continue him in possession at the present rent upon a new Trial. If he does well and pays his rent regularly for two or three years to come I will then consider of giving him a new Tack.

18: ARCHIBALD MCDUFF, GARDENER

7. You must encourage the cultivation of Wheat and enquire into the knowledge and skill of the Miller and Bakers as to the grinding

and dressing it and try to get them instructed in the art of making good flower.

/signed/ Argyll

Answers to Instructions October 1786.

1. I have acquainted Sherrif MacDowal that hereafter he is to pay the share of the produce of the coal agreeable to his Lease in place of the £30 he has been hitherto charged with.

2. The Tenants have for Crop 1786 paid money for their multure Meal and Teind meal and Bear at the rate of 18/ for the Boll Bear and 15 Shillings the Boll Meal excepting the Meal payable out of the Milns which they paid in kind and have been dispos'd of to advantage. I have no doubt the Millers would also agree to pay the above price for their Meal were it proposed to them but I am rather disposed to think it is safest they be continued to be made to pay the Meal some of them being weak in circumstances and might misapply the money were they to sell the meal.

3. The Road on Turners Farm is changed and the half value of the dyke paid Colonel Campbell by your Grace but is to be paid back by Turner.

4. Colonel Campbell has been told that your Grace agrees to his geting the Assignation in his favours of the Inn at Campbeltown which was built by John Watson he being bound that it be used as an Inn and to perform the other conditions of the Tack.

5. The Stance of the Light house has been fixed upon and the house is near built.

19: MULL OF KINTYRE LIGHTHOUSE

6. Archibald McDuff has been told that he is not to get a Tack of his possession at present on account of his poverty but he has got credit for his great arrear of £103. 13. 11. Sterling and he has discharged any claim he has had for building his house and other meliorations made by him.

7. I have made enquiry with respect to the grinding and dressing of Wheat by conveening the Magistrates of Campbeltown some of the English Farmers the Miller & some of the Bakers all of them agree that the flour made of the Kintyre Wheat is dark in the colour and unfavourable for the Bakers to use. They alledge that much of the wheat is musty and say that washing it is the only remedy for that, but the Bakers say that washed Wheat never makes good flour and all agree that justice is not done to it at the Miln and that the

Miln is hurt by its being sometimes used in making Piligrass. On the whole from what I heard reasoned amongst them I imagine the cause of complaint is owing to the Farmers threshing their Wheat too soon and to the Milns not being kept in good order.

20: BARLEY AND ITS MILLING

8. I have settled with Caradale about the march between the Town Common and Moy also between the common and Drummore and the marchdyke built.

9. I have settled with Ugadale about the march between your Graces Farm of Strone and his farm of Kerameanish [Keramenach] also between Kerameanish and your Graces Farm of Mucklich [Mucklach]. The great question about the march between your Graces Lands of Kilenan [Killeonan] and now Ugadales Lands of Cuilindown is not yet decided tho' a long tedious proof has been long since taken on both sides. The reason of their not being decided is that Ugadale cannot be got to close his proof. From the Proof hitherto taken I think your Grace should prevail. The ground in dispute is considerable.

(Signed) Dug Campbell.

Instructions October 1787.

1. You are now to charge Mr. McDowall with the full Coal rent for last year.

2. As I understand from my Agent that the Fewars of Campbeltown have no right of property in any of the mosses in that neighbourhood only the priviledge of taking peats and that a Process is depending before the Court of Session for having this point ascertained you must give notice to Mr. McMath that I cannot after this explanation go on to make the proposed exchange which proceeded upon the idea that he had property to give for property. And I desire that Mr. McDowall may proceed to continue the Canal thro' these mosses without ceremony as I am resolved to support him in doing so.

3. I am pleased with your activity in trying to prevent the shameful attacks upon wrecked vessels and bringing the transgressors to punishment. But something more is still necessary to check such abominable practices and I desire that you will be at pains to find out some of the most active on the late occasion and point them out to me that I may take every opportunity of showing my disapprobation of their conduct by refusing to prorogate [extend] their Leases and otherways and in future I desire it may be condition in all Leases that if the Tacksman or any of his family are convicted of plundering any wreck'd vessels or goods he shall forfeit his Lease and this to be publicly intimated to all my Tenants by Advertisements on the Church doors.

21: SHIPWRECKS

(Signd) Argyll
23 October 1787.

Instructions to the Chamberlain of Kintyre
October 1788.

1. Enquire for & recover the Instruction books of the two last Chamberlains and bring them to Inveraray next October and give them to me as soon as you arrive that I may have time to look into them while you are here.

2. If you do not find the matter of the repairs to Mr. Robertsons Manse explained in these Instructions try to recover the correspondence which Kintarbert had with me upon it and send me a copy to Roseneath that I may reconsider it and give directions for executing the work next summer. By the by it is a matter in which the other Heritors [rate-payers] are concerned as well as me as they must pay their shares and if they have not been already consulted their approbation must be procured or Application must be made to the Presbetry to visit the Manse and order the Repairs.

22: Rev George Robertson and Glebes

3. I am satisfied to pay my share of ten pounds yearly for a Helper to the Minister of Southend he contributing ten pounds yearly himself which with the School sallary and perquisites will make nearly £50 yearly to the Helper.

4. The fines to be levied from the Wood Cutters along with the expences. The half of the fines to be given to the Informers and the rest to be accounted for.

5. I approve of your proposal of exacting a small duty for every boat laid up upon the ground near the shore betwixt Limecraigs and Kilkerran.

6. You will attend to the finishing the exchange of a part of the Farm of Crossibeg for Mr Smiths Glebe at Kilmichael.

7. I approve of having the house and offices at Limecraigs repaired and a dyke built around the orchyard, you may get Estimates of the whole expence and send them to me.

8. I approve of your remitting my Rents to my Receiver General at Edinburgh by bills at short dates from the Agent for the Paisley Bank.

9. As the Lease which I have of Mr. Campbell of Ascomilns Lands in Kintyre expires partly at Candlemass 1790 and the rest in the course of that year it is necessary you intimate to him my resolution to give up the possession at the end of the Lease and warn

the subtennants in proper time to remove. You must also consider how the great Arrears which they owe me is to be best recovered.

23: ASKOMIL

10. The four Lists of Arrears of rents & feudutys due to me out of the Estate of Kintyre for the year 1786 & preceedings given up by Kintarbert and the four Lists now given up by Mr McGibbon for the year 1787 and preceedings are all herewith given to you in order that you may immediately attend to the collecting of what is due.

11. As Mr. McGibbon gets the whole sallary for this last year I agree to allow you sixty pounds for the time, part which you may charge to my account.

Answers to Instructions 1788.

1. The only Instruction Book I have been able to recover is the one to which this now added.

2. The Heritors having all agreed that these Repairs &ca should be executed the Estimate is lodged with Mr. Robertson & a Tradesman engaged to do them.

3. The Minister has got a Helper and he has been paid his Graces proportion of the £10 per annum.

4. Fines for Wood cutting accounted for.

5. Directions have been given to the Tenant of this piece of ground to exact the Duty which he says he has done.

6. The Minister has advanced new Claims that have retarded the settlement of this matter.

7. The mansion house of Limecraigs has been repaired wherever it has been found necessary in order to render it habitable. The Dyke around the Orchyard as not being so material has been delayed.

24: LIMECRAIGS HOUSE

8. Observed.

9. Intimation given to Mr. Campbell of Ascomiln and the Tenants all warned, there is a great deal of Desperate & nominal Arrear on this possession which has been particularly noted in the Arrear Rolls. The rest is in a fair way of being recovered.

10. Every possible exertion has been made to recover payment of these Arrears; a circumstantial report has been made on the arrear rolls now given in.

11. Charged.

Signed Hum^y Graham.

25: HUMPHREY GRAHAM

Instructions October 1789.

1. The proposal of the Arbiters to allow Mr. Smith an equivalent for one half of the bit of disputed ground at Kilmichael Glebe seems to be a reasonable one and should be gone into. But the Minister has no right to exchange the burying ground and therefore nothing can be given him in return for it. It should be inclosed and all cattle shut out from it.

26: Rev. Dr John Smith
27: Kilmichael burial ground

2. You have been very successful in diminishing the arrears and must continue your exertions till they are totally done away which will be a great ease to yourself in future and a good thing for the Tenants themselves who never thrive till they are brought to pay regularly.

3. A considerable part of the present arrear is evidently desperate and a separate list of that part may be made up and given in with next Account that his Grace may authorise your droping it out of your Books where it is only a useless incumbrance.

4. Mind to recover the Heritors share of the 12/ paid for advertising the Kirk of Killean.

5. As you have explained that the Election Dinner bill this year was higher than usual owing to some strangers being about the place you may pay the ballance and charge it in next 6. account in place of making the Town pay for it as you proposed.

6. Your Stationary and Postage expences to be stated each in one article in future accounts so as the total of each may at once be seen.

7. Your Salary to be charged under the head of <u>Annual</u> Burdens in place of Arrears as in this years account.

8. The <u>Ballance</u> to be stated under the head of <u>Cash</u> Payments in future in place of Arrears as in this years account.

9. In order that new Leases may be granted with deliberation you must let it be known in the country that unless Proposals are given in to you before the 1st of August that they will not be taken under consideration till the following year in order that you may have time to consider and report upon them.

10. You should recover from Largie the ballance of his Bond with the Interest due on it.

(Signed) Ja: Ferrier.

Inveraray 23 October 1789.

11. Enquire what is the reason the Town of Campbeltown are not paying back to the Duke the £150 lent them in 1786. See Instructions 1785 No. 5 and recover the Installments that are due.

12. Notice what is said in the Answers to that years Instructions and at the end of the Answers to the Instructions 1786 in regard to disputed marches.

13. Notice to recover from Turner the money which his Grace advanced for him to Colonel Chas Campbell. See Article 3d of Answers to Instructions 1786.

J. F. [James Ferrier]
23 October 1789.

28: JAMES FERRIER

Answers to Instructions 1789.

1. A piece of ground equivalent to the Glebe at Kirkmichael and half the disputed Ground has been marked off at Crossibeg and the Minister has been in possession of it this last year; but he has not removed his Tenant from Kirkmichael Glebe who has a Tack from him and refuses to remove till it expires.

2. For reasons already known the arrear could not be much diminish'd this year.

3. Done.
4. Done
5. Done
6. Done
7. Done
8. Done
9. Done

10. Done as to the principal but Largie refuses to pay the Interest. his reasons are mentioned in his Letter delivered.

11. The Town of Campbeltown have been obliged to lay out some money in necessary repairs of Streets &ca & in building a Market house which has prevented them paying up any of their debt but probably next year their circumstances may afford a payment.

12. Some small matters regarding Marches have been settled but there are some material questions which it will be necessary to authorise the Chamberlain to employ the Sherrif Substitute in geting determined.

13. Done.
Signed Hum^y Graham

Instructions to the Chamberlain of Kintyre 1790.

1. Altho Mr. Smith cannot give the natural possession of the Glebe exchanged till the expiry of the Lease upon it you can draw the Rent of it and as I suppose he took the highest rent he could get there can be no great loss on that score.

2. I agree to your employing young Langlands to point out the proper improvements on Farms and to oversee the execution of them and let me know what Salary he will expect for that work.

29: LANGLANDS FAMILY
30: LAND VALUES

3. I approve of your streighting the march betwixt Leigh Kileonan and Ugadales Lands near the Bridge.

4. The designation of Mr. Robertsons Glebe I understand was originally very irregularly gone about and the after exchange seems also to have been conducted in a very loose manner but as I wish to have no disputes with Mr. Robertson the decayed trees surrounding his Glebe which have been already cut you will sell to the best advantage at his sight and give him the money and I desire that no more may be cut unless such as are evidently decaying the price of which may also be given to Mr. Robertson.

5. Without entering into the minutiae of the other dispute about the hutt which he is rebuilding you will observe that by Law he is entitled to a barn a byre and a stable as Offices to his Manse and if he has not these independent of the house in question either it or some other must be given to him and consequently it seems to be of little moment to dispute his title to this particular house.

6. You will charge me with the Premium which I promised you for the recovery of old arrears in your next Account.

7. You may treat with the Tenants of Laggan & Gartgralan [Gartgreillan] about giving the ground necessary for establishing a bleachfield and the deductions of Rent to be allowed them.

(signed) Argyll

Answers to Instructions 1790.

1. The Tenant of the Farm of Kirkmichael has agreed to draw the Rent of the Glebe from Doctor Smiths Tacksman for the remainder of his Lease.

2. The Chamberlain has given William Langlands Twenty Guineas on account untill your Grace is pleased to say what Sallary

he ought to have which he expects to be not less than £30 p. annum as he is obliged to keep a horse.

3. Done

4. Attended to.

5. Ditto

6. Ditto

7. The Bleachfield being laid down in another part of the country it was not necessary to do any thing in this matter. It ought now to be had in view to reserve a part of these Farms in case a Cotton work should be established about Campbeltown as it is probable this would be found the fittest situation for such a business.

31: BLEACHFIELD
32: LINTMILL

signed Hum^y Graham.

Instructions to the Chamberlain of Kintyre October 1791.

1st I agree to allow William Langlands Thirty pounds Sterling yearly from Martinmas last for directing and overseeing the improvements in Kintyre on condition that his Father give him his advice and assistance where necessary without any further charge to me.

2. Consult Simson my Carpenter and Bruce the Gardiner here as to the Timber which can be given from this place for houses in Kintyre and make trial of a cargoe of it. A vessel may be sent from Campbeltown with coal and carry back the Timber but concert the proper time so as there may be no unnecessary detention of the vessel at Inveraray. At the same time that this trial is made of my own timber I desire that you will contrive to get some foreign timber upon the easiest terms which I suppose is by geting it at first hand from the Baltic. Keep a fair account of the expence of the one and of the other of these cargoes and the uses they are put to and give a view of the difference so as the best mode may be followed in future in procuring Timber from Kintyre. It is common in the Forth and probably in Clyde to send out vessells to the Baltic loaded with coal and to bring back timber. I cannot engage myself in such a trade nor desire to employ you in it but you may perhaps find a Merchant in Campbeltown willing to try it by sending out a cargoe of coals at his own risk and bringing home a cargoe of Timber you engaging to take a certain quantity of Timber at the prices current for the time in the Clyde. In this way I should save the freight of bringing Timber from the Clyde or Air [Ayr] to Campbeltown and the Merchant at Campbeltown ought to have the profit besides employing a Campbeltown vessel in place of a Clyde one.

33: Timber for building
34: Rural buildings

3. Endeavour to satisfy Dr. Rowat for the damage which he says was done him by opening the new Street and finish the exchange of his old moss Rooms which are in the way of the Canaal for other moss but let this be done in such a way as that he is to have no claim to the property of the solum of the moss after it is cut away.

35: Dr Charles Rowatt

4. Inform yourself and Report the quantity of Kelp made upon the different farms belonging to me in Kintyre and the prices which have been got for it of late years.

36: Kelp

5. Find out also the number of people upon my Estate and Report to me after this Form.

Parish   Farm   Age   Men   Women   Children

37: Census of 1792

Answers by the Chamberlain of Kintyre to Instructions of October 1791.

1. William Langlands conform to the first Article acts as overseer of your Graces Improvements in Kintyre. His father has made up a small charge for his own trouble in some particular cases which amounts to about £4. 14.

2. A vessel or two was sent from Campbeltown by Mr. Graham late Chamberlain for Timber from Inveraray for building tenant houses in Kintyre, and the same as far as necessary regularly distributed. Foreign Timber at the rate of Sales in Campbeltown would become high for common tenants houses, as a thatch roof requires timber of a particular square or thickness neither is green planting of any dimensions thought proper for tenants out houses where it is not preserved by smoak, or laid over with tarr, Peeled oak and ash timbers is thought the best for this purpose. No Merchant in Campbeltown could be found to embark in the proposed scheme of sending a loadening of Coals to the Baltic & returning with a Cargo of timber for the purposes mentioned.

3. Many fruitless attempts have been made to get Doctor Ruat to settle his claims with regard to the alledged damage he has sustained in opening the new Streets, In fact he has reaped advantages, Therefore the Doctors backwardness in this matter can only be accounted for as proceeding from a Selfish motive of withholding the Feuduties due to your Grace as long as possible already considerable. The Dispute as to the Mossroom by which he retarded the cuting of the Canal was settled with him in November last by his Accepting of an equivalent of moss in Moninaclive, where your Graces Tenants & Feuars of Campbeltown cut their peats.

38: Coal canal and moss rooms

4 & 5. The Returns of Kelp, and Number of people required by these articles of the Instructions have been made and now presented to your Grace.

(Signed) Dun Stewart.
October 24th 1792

39: Duncan Stewart, new Chamberlain

Instructions to the Chamberlain of Kintyre [1792].

Octr 1792.

1. Attend to the 2d of Instructions of last year with this variation that when timber is again wanted for houses a simple way of coming at the comparision wanted is to buy foreign timber for one house and to build another with my own timber keeping an exact account of the quantity and quality of the latter and the freight and other charges attending it so as to compare with the cost of the foreign timber used in the other house.

2. The third Instruction of last year is Continued.

3. The Tenants to get notice that they are not in future to cut Kelp and the whole kelp on my Estate under your charge to be advertised to be sett for 3, 7, or 19 years. Proposals to be given in to you or to Mr. Ferrier – the tenants have hitherto been allowed to cut the kelp only by indulgence and therefore have no right to be continued in possession of it nevertheless I will allow them during the years to run of their Leases deduction yearly of what they have been in use to draw from it. But in new Leases the Kelp to be reserved to me without any such deduction and the tenants to be informed of this when they make their proposals – the reservation to begin with the Leases to be granted this year.

N. B. This countermanded for the present Qu: a part to be allowed for manure.

4. Consider of a plan for having the hedges and ditches regularly cleaned and dressed in Kintyre and notice not to suffer the hedges to be too much clipped.

5. The Charity School and the house for the master to be made comfortable so far as not already done.

6th I agree to be at the Expence of building two School houses in the parishes of Kintyre in the places most convenient for my tenants the Expence of each not to Exceed £50. also to allow to each of the Schoolmasters £5. Sterling yearly to purchase milk and fuel with a bit of ground for potatoes and Garden stuffs. the Christian Society will probably give Sallarys and the Inhabitants who take the advantage of the Schools must pay reasonable School fees. If more schools are necessary for the parishes the other Heritors will no doubt furnish them.

40: SCHOOLS

7. The Bond of the Town of Campbeltown to me for £150 dated the 19 July 1786 bearing interest from Whitsunday preceeding is herewith delivered to you to operate payment.

8. Unless Mr. Maxwell can be got to determine in the Submission about the disputed marches with Ugadale you must raise a process before the Sherriff for having it settled & March fences raised. Any other marches with Ugadale to be settled either by Submission to Mr. Maxwell or by such process.

41: JAMES MAXWELL

9. The piece of ground part of Drumlemel [Drumlemble] near the Bleachfield which has been possessed by Colonel Charles Campbell by some tollerance from my tenants must be taken back and given in possession either to the tenants in Drumlemel or the Bleacher.

10. Specimens of the soapy earth to be sent to Glasgow, Liverpool & Bristol and to be advertised for sale Offerers to specify what they will give for it a ton or to be invited to Establish a pottery at Campbeltown.

Inveraray 24 Octr. 1792.

N. B. Consider of the best mode of having trees raised in different parts of Kintyre to answer the demands of the Country for Timber – also Salleys.

After the foregoing Instructions were made out the Chamberlain received the following Letter from Mr. Ferrier relative to the Kelp Shores.

Copy. Dear Sir Since you left this the Duke of Argyll has changed his mind as to taking the Kelp making into his own hands immediately or rather the selling of it, and resolved only to reserve power in all new Leases to take possession of the Shores and Kelp growing thereon and to manufacture and carry away the Kelp on allowing to the Tenant the value as stated in your late report of the Rent. This reservation you will please add to each of the Leases not yet given out before you deliver them.

I am Dear Sir
Your most Obt Svnt
(Signed) Ja Ferrier.
Inveraray 26 Oct. 1792.

Answers by the Chamberlain of Kintyre to Instructions of October 1792.

1. An experiment of the difference of the Cost or expence of building Tenants Houses with Inveraray Timber and that of Foreign Timber has been made in building two Houses in the Farm of Cristolach and the Account thereof now produced.

2. It was reported last year that Dr. Rouat had allowed the Canal to be cut through his Moss room and an equal quantity of new moss marked out to him upon the north side thereof, below the Lands of Drummore, but he still refuses to enter into any writings upon this transaction nor will he condescend to make any satisfactory answer to repeated applications made by the Chamberlain respecting the opening of Argyll Street and opposes the completing of the new cross Street from Kirk Street to the new Schoolhouse.

3. This Instruction is answered by Mr. Ferriers Letter of the 26th October last, copied above, the orders there given being regularly complied with when Leases on Shore farms occur.

4. The best plan the Chamberlain can think of as to keeping the Hedges and Ditches clean is contained in proposals made by John Kell Tenant in Ballebrunan, offering to keep all the Hedges on your Graces property in Kintyre in good order for nine years, the first three years at the rate of three pence per fall, the next three at two pence per fall, and the last three at one penny or three half pence per fall, the Tenants to maintain him as occasionally employed. These proposals are partly signed by the Tenants, but as some of them have refused to sign the transaction is not yet complete. If approved off and completely agreed to, Kell means to fetch his Uncle from England to assist him.

42: JOHN KELL, BALLYBRENNAN

5. The House and Schoolhouse for the Master of the Society School at Campbeltown are put in complete repair. Vide Accot [account] of Outlays.

6. Two new Schoolhouses are built in a substantial manner roofed with slate, the one in the parish of Kilchousland at Links of Peniver, the other in Glenbreckry Parish of Kilcolmkill.

7. It being far advanced in the Season and the Sherriff Court nearly up before Mr. Maxwells final answer was received, declining the Arbitration proposed, Ugadales Marches must lye over till next Spring.

[8. omitted.]

9. A removing from the piece of ground belonging to Drumlemble occupied by late Col. Charles Campbell was brought on and opposition given, but Comby the Factor on the Colonels Estate [probably D. Campbell of Combie in Nether Lorn, a noted stock-breeder] requested to be continued for one year having previously sett that piece of ground to the Tenants of Machrihanish, to which he said that Mr. Ferrier had consented.

10. Specimens of the Soapy Earth have been sent as directed. No returns has yet been obtain'd from Liverpool and Glasgow, a fair trial of its quality was made at Bristol, as may be seen from Mr. Lanes Letter on that subject from which it is fear'd that Earth will not turn out to what was expected. The Letter is now produced.

11. A Report pointing out the best situations for planting on His Graces property in Kintyre is herewith produced, and the Chamberlain conceives that this can only be brought to effect by enclosing, and by having a Gardiner or Nurseryman there for raising young Trees, and constantly overlooking the plantations. The best situation for such a person, is the Lower part of the Farm of Little Kilkerran.

Signed Dun Stewart.
17 October 1793.

Copy Letter from John Lean Bristoll to Mr. Stewart.
Bristoll 6th May 1793
Duncan Stewart Esq. ,
Sir

In reply to your esteemed favour of the 28 Janry last accompanyed by the recommendation of our Friend Mr. Daniel Fleming I need only say that I received of Capt Agnew the Box of Clay therein mentioned part of which I delivered to a Pottery where all kinds of white & cream colour'd stoneware are manufactured and part to another Pottery where all kinds of Coarse brown stoneware such as Jarrs Mugs, Jugs &ca are made, both of these Houses have given it a fair trial, and find that it will not stand the heat of their Kilns, when taken out it is run into a mass without shape or form partly exhausted and spongy. Both of these Houses say that for their use it is not of any value. I need add no more than that

I am &ca
Signed John Lean.

Situations in Kintyre most adapted for raising Trees upon.

Kilcolmkill Parish

Laigh Remuil	A very steep Glen easily enclosed from any trespass of Cattle and south Exposure.
Feochaig	Several small Glens easily enclosed from any trespass of Cattle & south east exposure.
Corrylach	Along the stone dyke to be built alongst the water side very fit for planting & lyes low.
Brecklate	Some small corners of Ground easily enclosed & south exposure very fit for planting.
Keperigan	Several small corners of ground easily enclosed south exposure very good for planting.

Kilblaan Parish

Killervan	Some small Glens may be easily enclosed & south east exposure.
East Kildavy	A very steep Glen between the said Farm and the west being the march very fit for planting.
Glenmuril	Several Glens easily enclosed very fit for planting south east exposure.
Knocknagrain	Some Glens and corners of ground very easily enclosed fit for planting south east exposure.

Kilkivan Parish

Lagnacraig	A very extensive face and Glens some small corners easily enclosed very fit for planting south exposure.
Auchanslishaig	Some small Glens easily enclosed from any trespass of Cattle south west exposure.
Lecknacroive	Several Glens & corners very easily enclosed some of the Glens already planted and thriving well.

Kilkerran Parish

Balnbraid	Several Glens easily enclosed very fit for planting south exposure.
Balinatunie	Several Glens and corners part of which already planted and thriving well south exposure.
Arrinascavach	Some Glens & corners easily enclosed south exposure.
Little Glenramiskill	The march Glen betwixt said Farm and Big Glenramiskill very good for a few plantings.

Kilchousland Parish

High Ballemeanoch	A brae face very easily enclosed with stones south east exposure, fit for planting.
South Peninver	A narow deep Glen betwixt said & mid Peninver requires no enclosing.
North Peninver	A small piece of ground below Samuel Galbreaths Houses mostly enclosed already N. E. exposure.
East Laggan	Several small Glens easily fenced from any trespass well shelter'd east exposure. The march Glen betwixt said Farm and Mid Laggan very fit for planting.
West Laggan	Some small Glens easily fenced from any trespass well shelter'd, North East exposure. The march Glen betwixt said Farm & Killipole called Ault more Killipol it is very deep & long full of Brush wood well shelter'd fit for planting. ['Killipole' is the farm now known as Calliburn, and the march – or boundary – glen 'Ault Mor Killipol' clearly refers to the burn running through the glen, *Allt Mor*, 'Big Stream', a previously unrecorded place-name, which, by the distinguishing terminal specific 'Killipol', suggests another stream of the same name in the locality.]
East Drumgarvie	A small holm along the waterside fenced by the water on the one side & a ditch may be cut on the other side, it being marshy and wet.
West Drumgarvie	A holm upon the point opposite to the foot of Aultmore Killipole very easily enclosed fit for planting. In Do a small spot of ground along the big water side called Dailchoran can be easily enclosed south exposure. The march Glen betwixt Drumgarvie and Gartgrallan [Gartgreillan] is a long deep Glen south exposure requires little or no Fencing. ['Dailchoran' is another hitherto unrecorded place-name.]
East Gartgrulan	Several small Glens easily fenced from any trespass, south exposure number of Trees may be planted about the Kail yards.
Ballochgair	A space of an acre or so lying betwixt the march of Ardnacroish and the back of the Houses of Ballochgair easily enclosed shelter'd & south exposure.

44: Wood and woodlands
45: The Rowan

Instructions to the Chamberlain of Kintyre [1793].

October 1793.

1. As it appears from the trial that has been made, that it is my interest to give my Tenants in Kintyre Timber from Inveraray for their buildings, rather than foreign Timber, especially at this time when Foreign Timber is so dear, You must let Mr. Graham know in time what Timber is necessary for the Buildings of next year, specifying, as near as you can, the size and the kinds wanted, and concert with him the best & cheapest method of geting it transported either by your freighting a Campbeltown Vessell and sending her to Inveraray with coal and to take back the Timber or by his freighting an Inveraray vessel and loading her with timber and you sending back coal.

2. It does not appear to be necessary to have any writing with Dr. Rouat about the moss, as I have no objection to his geting Peats, where they can be conveniently given him, and since he does not choose to have his Claim liquidated for the alledged damage done to his property, by the new Street, I think it unnecessary also to press him on that head But if he continues to withhold his feuduties upon these or any other pretences he must be forced to pay by legal dilligence.

3. As I do not want the Hedges to be clipped especially when young all that is requisite is to clear them of weeds once or twice in the year, and to throw up about the Roots the loose earth at the bottom of the ditch which at the same time serves as a scouring to it. This is what every Tenant can easily do either with his own hands, or by his Servants, and is what they must be taught to do. In the same way when any part of a fence falls down or is broke down and when an open ditch fills up, every Tenant must be taught to repair such fence and scour such ditch and William Langlands whose business it is to be constantly going round overseeing and directing the Improvements must attend to these articles & see them done, and when a Tenant is obstreperous or negligent, he must inform you, and you must employ a person to execute the work, and pay him for it, and recover the expence from the Tenant in terms of the clause in their Leases which obliges them to pay such expences. If this is strictly followed out, a very few instances will be sufficient to shew the Tenants that you are in earnest, and that they must not trifle with you in these matters.

4. Look out for two Schoolmasters for the Schools that have been built and converse with the Tenants of the Farms where they are stationed as to the best mode of supplying them with milk and feuel and communicate to my Agent at Edinburgh that he may represent to the Christian Society and try to get some encouragement from them. If they will give none, then the Tenants must either make out amongst them what is sufficient to encourage the Schoolmasters to take up the Teaching or the Scheme must be laid aside altogether and the Houses turned to some other use.

5. I insist on your recovering from the Town of Campbeltown £15 yearly until I am repaid the £150 which I lent them, on their solemn promise that it should be paid after that rate. But you are out of the bygone interest to allow them £50 which I agreed to give them to help to build the new Schoolhouse.

6. Enquire what will be the expence of fitting up the Miln as a Wheat Miln and how far the Town are desireous to have that done as I am willing to contribute towards it.

7. Inform yourself fully before next Meeting and state in writing the nature and extent of the Disputes with Ugadale about Marches, that I may consider what is to be done since Mr. Maxwell has refused to proceed in the submission to him.

8. The same as to the dispute with Mr. McAllister of Cur.

72: McAllister of Cour

9. The easiest and best method of raising a Plantation of Trees upon every Farm appears to be by adding a piece of ground to each of the Gardens and making the Tenants enclose it sufficiently and remove that part of the present fence betwixt the Garden and the addition and then filling up the addition with young Trees, whereby the Tenants will be obliged to protect and save them from Cattle for the sake of their Gardens.

10. Such of the old Ash Trees as appear to be decaying should be pollarded, which will save
and recover them as I have experienced in many instances.

11. The pruning of young Trees, often does harm, and therefore should be very little practiced.

12. You must be at pains to recover all the Plans of my Farms in Kintyre and send the whole here with a List of them, as I think I can get copys made on much easier terms than those you mention. You must also return to me the Book containing the description of Farms in Kintyre which was sent to Limecraigs to be copied.

46: Farm plans

13. You must let George Langlands and his son William know that I am not pleased with their conduct in the Sett of the Farm of Balibrunan as I see clearly that by the undervaluation of the Father and Improper interference of the Son I have been led to lett that Farm at £40 yearly below its value. The son must be told explicitely that while he remains in my service in his present station which ought to occupy his whole time and attention I will neither give him a Farm nor allow him to possess one under any other person. If he chuses to give up his present employment and to become Farmer I shall have no objection to his offering for every Farm of mine until he is accomodated but while he holds that employment I will not agree to his becoming a Farmer, because it is only by going constantly through the country and directing others that he can be of any essential use to me and that I cannot expect him to do after he gets possession of a Farm of his own.

14. You must recover from the late Mr. Thomsons Heirs the half years Stipend paid them by mistake and now paid a second time to the Synod.

15. The Tenants must pay interest for the expence I lay out on the march dykes with Saddell.

Answers to the preceeding Instructions

1. The Timber necessary for the Kintyre Tenants last season was got down by a Campbeltown Vessell at a moderate back freight, being loaded up with Meal and Beans for your Graces use.

2. The Instruction with regard to Dr. Rouat has been complied with, He has not yet paid up his Feuduties, but daily promises, his Letter on that subject is presented herewith.

3. The charges in this Instruction have been punctually notified to the Tenants, and William Langlands has accordingly employed men to finish the Improvements on the Farms of such as are most backward viz Brecklit, Darlochan, Durry, and Crosshill. Mr. Mcneill of Cariskey has been frequently spoken to about building his share of the marches with Muckloch and Auchinsavill adjusted and excambed, with him last year, p. signed plan thereof, but he has hitherto put it off.

4. The Instructions respecting the Charity Schoolmasters in the parishes of Kilchousland, and Southend, have been complied with, and Gardens of two acres for each are now about being inclosed,

one of them already finished, with a dyke of five feet high, so as to insure the safety of the planting proposed p. Mr. Ferriers Letter of the 12th April last.

5. The moiety payable of the Town of Campbeltowns Bond has been received and the £50 allowed by your Grace to the Town towards building a new Schoolhouse has been accordingly given out of the bygone Interests due on said Bond. Vide Genl Accot.

6. A plan and Estimate of an additional or sufficient flower Miln at Campbeltown has been procured and now produced with the Magistrates & Councils opinion thereon.

7. The extent of the disputed ground with Ugadale situated betwixt his Lands of Arnicle and your Graces Lands of Torrisdale and Lephincorrach, is in one plan 30 acres and 30 perches, and in another part of said muir to 26 acres 32 Roods and 36 perches. The Chamberlain has been told that the late Ugadale, and a Baillie Archd Campbell Factor in Kintyre had a Meeting and an adjustment of these marches when two jutting points of Land were ascertained and exchanged. Ugadale marked out the march of the acquired one, but your Graces Managers having neglected to do the like, both are now claimed by Ugadale or his Tenants. Archd McGill now Tenant in Arnicle remembers something of the transaction. There is likewise controverted ground betwixt your Graces Lands of Couilindown which extend to 17 Acres and 32 perches. A Submission was entered into in 1786 by late Ugadale and Your Graces Chamberlain respecting these last Marches, by which the whole was submitted to Mr. James Maxwells decision in 1787 a proof was partly led, but nothing finally done. The proceedings as far as entered into lye with the Chamberlain of Kintyre.

8. The controverted March betwixt your Graces Lands of Craigmore, and Mr. McAllisters Lands of Cour appears to the Chamberlain to have been some considerable time ago adjusted, as a distinct straight and proper Line of march has been struck, and a ditch cut, all the way to the burn marching with Largys Land and there is no vestige of a ditch or march, but for the most part a plain level Muir where Cour now claims. The principal part now claimed by him runs a good way betwixt Largys Lands of Narrachan, and the back of Craigmore, where Cour can have no access to it save at the end of the Ditch mentioned, and would become very auckward and troublesome for the Tenant of Craigmore in the event of Cours

obtaining it. This being observed to Cour he alledged that when this ground was given up by his predecessor, and the ditch, or present march made, that a servitude of three soums[*] of Cattle was imposed on Craigmore in lieu of the ground now claimed. Should this be proven it will be more eligible to give Cour a few acres of the Shore of Barmollach marching with his Lands of Amadell[**], than to give the muir claimed the extent of which is 38 acres, 3 roods & 31 perches.

[*A 'soum' was a unit of grazing reckoned sufficient to keep a cow.
** This place-name is unrecognisable.]

47: BOUNDARIES

9. Where the situation admits of it, Instructions have been given to the Tenants to prepare Gardens as mentioned.

10. Several decayed Ash Trees have been pollarded this last Season, and many of them spring well, more shall be done in the same way this season.

11. The article of pruning has been & shall be attended to.

12. The plans of such of the Kintyre farms as are now a letting could not easily be dispensed with at the time. All the other plans would have been sent up as desired, but that the Chamberlain had been informed that the Schoolmaster of Inveraray appointed to copy them had been called away from thence.

13. This part of the Instructions was distinctly read and made known to George Langlands & his son William.

14. The half years Stipend advanced to the Synod of Argyll has been received from the late Mr. Thomsons heirs.

Vide Genl Account.

15. The Tenant of Laigh Ronachan is charged in next Marts Rent with the Interest of the money expended by your Grace on the March dyke with Saddell.

Signed Dun Stewart
1794 October 11th

Instructions to the Chamberlain of Kintyre [1794].
October 1794.

1. Articles 1. 2. 3. 5. 9. 10. 11. 12 & 15 of last years Instructions to be attended to.

2. Nothing can be done I see at present as to erecting a Wheat Miln in Kintyre as there is not wheat enough raised in the Country to answer the Expence.

3. You may propose to Ugadale and Cour to submit the disputed Marches to Mr. Campbell of Comby.

4. Get an Estimate made of the Expence of sending a Ton of Marle from Laggan to Inveraray & Roseneath and send it to me.

5. Keep Cariskey in mind to build the march dykes. He writes that if you or Langlands can find persons to make the dykes he will pay for them.

6. Get an Estimate made of the Expence of enclosing a piece of ground at Limecraigs for a Sheep park for your own better accomodation there.

7. The allowance for an assistant Minister in Southend must now be discontinued.

Answers to Instructions 1794.

1st. Has been and is duly attended to.

2. Requires none.

3. Ugadale and Cour agreed to submit the disputes relative to their marches to Mr. Campbell of Comby, who by his Letter to the Chamberlain agreed to act accordingly, but he has not yet taken any steps in that business. Cour is impatient and despairing of Combys proceeding in the matter, requests that your Grace may be pleased to appoint Mr. Duncan Campbell Sherrif Substitute as Sole Arbiter as to his marches.

4th. The Carters of Campbeltown after repeated solicitations, declined giving in an Estimate of driving the Marle to Campbeltown by the Ton they generally charge three Shillings per day for a Horse and Cart, and their Carts being bad and small, all that they could take at a time, might be about a quarter of a Ton weight, and two rakes a going is the most they could drive at that distance, so that the Ton would come to 6/ the distance being above five miles, one of which being extremely steep and bad road. The Marle would require being dug, and thrown from the Pit, a month before the driving of it, as otherwise it becomes soft, and liquid by the motion of the Cart.

5th. Has been complied with.
6th. The Estimate required is herewith produced.
7th. Complied with.

Instructions to the Chamberlain of Kintyre [1795].
October 1795.

1. It has been said that the tenants of Kintyre gave up the raising of Wheat Crops from the want of a Kiln to grind Wheat, but this was no good reason as they could easily have sent their Wheat to the Clyde Market, and it is probable that the true reason was their discovering or supposing other Crops to be more profitable. Be at pains to find out the true cause and inform me.

2. I have no objection to Mr. Duncan Campbell being the Arbiter for settling the March betwixt my property and Mr. McAlister of Cour.

3. Consider whether a Road from the Marle pit to the nearest shore and a small Quay there can be made at a moderate expence.

4. I am sensible that the Ministers of Campbeltown ought to have their Stipends augmented, if there were free Teinds [tithes] in the parish, and as I understand there are no free Teinds I desire you will propose to the other Heritors to give them a voluntary contribution of £15 or £20 each during their incumbency, but to be done in a way that will not oblige us to continue it to their Successors.

5. You must prevent the proprietor of Ardnacross & his Tenants from fishing opposite to my Lands.

6. I agree to give the Salmon fishing and Red Herring House to Carradale for seven years at five pounds yearly the House to be delivered to him under comprisement, and he is to understand that he is to have no right to take any part of my Woods for his operations.

Signed Argyll

Answers.

1st. The most intelligent Farmers have been conversed on this subject the reasons assigned by them are 1st That the sending of their wheat to the Low Country subjects to risks and reduced price, from Freight & Agency. 2d Those in the Low grounds or Laggan of the Country alledges that the winter storms from the Atlantic Ocean burns up & hurts the Brand. 3d That some years ago a considerable quantity was raised in Kintyre which took the Blight, and being sent to Market was returned on their hands. 4th that such risks, and accidents do not attend a Barley Crop, which affords them an equal profit, ever since the Licensed Stills have been allowed to work.

2d Mr. Duncan Campbell the Arbiter is now upon the marches with Cour.

3d An Estimate of the Road from the Marle pit, and of the expence of a Quay on the Lands of Ardnacroish, the only practicable place for such is now furnished.

4th This article is answered by the Ministers having commenced a process of Augmentation before the Court of Teinds.

5th The proprietor and his Tenants have been debarr'd from fishing beyond the limits of the Farm of Ardnacroish, and they have hitherto acquiesced.

6th Carradale having died before the term of entry to the Red Herring House, the Family decline being concerned, letters on that subject are produced. Messrs [Daniel] Clark & [John] Campbell [Jnr.] the late Tenants thereof have hitherto paid no attention to Your Graces orders for their paying the apprised value for the Experiment Wherry, alledging that they have lost much by the concern. The deficiency of the Houses, are this year apprised against them, or removing Tenants.

51: Red Herring

Instructions to the Chamberlain of Kintyre [1796]

October 1796.

1st. To bring the Rental of the Estate to the yearly accounting as it is often wanted.

2d To simplify the State of Augmentations so as to render the examination of them more easy in one of the two ways which has been described.

3d To send yearly to the Receiver General a month or six weeks before the accounting a List of the augmentations that are to be brought on that he may have it in his power to compare them with the Copys kept by him of the Leases.

4 To keep in view that the Duke is to reserve the Kelp from the Leases in future.

5. The apprised deficiency of repairs to the Herring house must be recovered from Messrs Clerk & Campbell.

Ja: Ferrier.

Answers

The Rental is taken up. The Augmentation state sent at the proper time.

Messrs Clark & Campbell have been summoned in order to recover the apprised Deficiencys, and a second or 3rd Reclaiming Petition from them is now presented.

(Signed) Dun Stewart.

October 1797

Instructions to the Chamberlain of Kintyre [1797].

October 1797.

1st As I understand that the People of the Parish of Campbeltown are very impatient to have another Church built in place of the Highland one now in ruins. I agree to give ground for the Stance of it at the head of the New Street opposite to the new Quay of Campbeltown, I geting the Stance of the old Church in return without the Walls which will be wanted for the New Building, and you will signify to the Ministers that I approve of their bringing forward this measure as soon as possible either by a voluntary consent from the other Heritors, or by a Decree of Presbetry, taking it for granted that after the great expence occasioned to the Heritors by the building of the other Church that this second one will be erected upon as frugal a plan as can be. As I understand the Ministers Manses want some Repairs these should be given at the same time and proper dykes ought also to be built around the different Burrying Grounds in the Parish which are said to be in a very ruinous and neglected state.

52: THE HIGHLAND PARISH CHURCH

2nd I do not approve of the Minister of Southends taking possession of the Schoolmasters Croft & keeping him so long out of it, and I desire that measures be immediately taken for restoring the possession to the Schoolmaster.

53: THREE MINISTERS OF SOUTHEND

3d I must also express my displeasure at George Langlands pretending to consider me as bound to give a new Lease of his Farms at an undervalue and without having the least information as to the extent of the favour which I am thus to bestow. Langlands may have been a useful person in the Country, but in every instance where he has done any thing for me, he has taken care to be amply paid, and I feel no obligation upon me to renew his Lease without enquiring into the value of his Farm, and geting an adequate Augmentation from him. I therefore desire that these Farms be advertised for Sett next year, and that you examine them minutely and give your own opinion as to the value.

4th William Langlands having disregarded the Notification which was given to him in 1793 and interfered in the Sett of many of my Farms, since that time, you may give him notice that I do not chuse to depend upon his services after next Whitsunday, and if you think it necessary to have some other person in his place, look out for one & correspond with Mr. Ferrier on the subject.

5th The Farm of Laggs to be advertised for sett but you may inform Scipio Campbells Widow that I will have in view to allow her some advantage from it.

54: Captain Scipio Duroure Campbell

6th The Farm of Inenbeg and Inenmore to be also advertised for Sett.

55: The Inneans and the sheep invasion
56: Learside settlements

Inveraray
19th October 1797

Supplement to the foregoing Instructions
received when at Edinburgh in February 1798.

7. The Books of the Farming Society where should they be kept, and who should have the charge of them.

8. A Report of the Mosses on the several Farms under your Charge specifying the quality viz. Depth, whether they appear rich and easily improved, whether fit to be used as a Manure or compost mixed with other substances for the Improvement of Gravely or Dry ground. These circumstances to be attended to in future Leases, and the Tenant to be obliged to cultivate part of the Moss and also to make trial upon a small scale of Moss composts formed according to the new method.

9. What has been done this year in the article of Planting within the fence of the Kail yards.

57: Tree-planting in kailyards

10. A Report to be sent in writing of the General success of the Herring Fishing mentioning the parts where it has been carried on, and the different proceeds of its commencement in each place.

58: Seditious stirrings in Southend

Answers to Instructions 1797.

1st A Decreet of Presbetry has been awarded against the Heritors and intimated to them for building the New Church. A Committee of the Heritors was likewise appointed for corresponding and entering into Contract with Mr. Russell at Edinburgh for building the same, but no progress has been made therein from the place appointed for the Stances being under Lease to a Mrs Fergusson, who has subset the same to Collector McKenzie and who could not be brought to come to a point. Another situation is now thought on at the Lochend, pointing the Harbour and Island Davar much approved off by severals at present the Houses in that place are part ruinous and now under Lease, so that if my Lord Duke approves of it there can be no hinderance to the commencement of the work in that respect.

2d. The Schoolmaster of Southend was last year put into possession of the Croft mentioned.

3d George Langlands Farm has been advertised and offers for it now given in.

59: BALINATUNIE AND THE LANGLANDS FAMILY

4th Intimation was given to William Langlands by reading this Instruction to him, he afterwards wrote a penitential Letter to your Graces Commissioner and has been continued for a year, some person of that kind is necessary.

5th The Farm of Laggs has been advertised and offers now given in.

6th As has likewise the Farms of Inenbeg and Inenmore possessed by Donald Campbell.

7th The Books of the Farming Society are at present kept in Mr. Hugh MacKays office, who is Clerk to the Society, to whom every Member grants receipt for every Book taken out and pays twopence for Booking such.

60: KINTYRE AGRICULTURAL SOCIETY

8th A List or Report of Mosses in different Farms is herewith produced.

9th There were no plants or young Trees got from Inveraray since Spring 1797 a number of these being weakly and young were put into a Nursery in McDuffs Garden in Spring 1798. A number of them were planted in a belting that runs betwixt the March of Crosshill, and the Sheep park built at Limecraigs.

10th A particular Report of the Success of the Herring Fishing was sent to His Grace last March specifying the quantity and where cured.

61: HERRING-FISHING

Signed Dun Stewart

Report of Improveable Moss in different Farms in Kintyre.

[In the table below, the abbreviated measurements are:
'A. ' = 'Acres', 'R. ' = Roods and 'P. ' = Poles.]

	A.	R.	P.
North Christaloch	9.	3.	23.
Moss from 2 feet deep to 6 feet with a sandy bottom all improved and under Crop.			
High Gartloisken	30.	1.	37
Moss from one half foot deep to 5 feet all improved and under Crop.			
Balligroggan	59.	3.	8
Moss from 5 feet deep to 10 feet & very soft unimproved.			
Killonan	39.	0.	32
Moss from 2 feet deep to 7 feet all improved but 5 acres for Peats.			
Aross	200.	0.	32
Moss from 4 feet deep to 12 feet, & some parts more very soft of grayish colour, in this Moss a great number of His Graces Tenants cut peats yearly.			
Knockriochmore	1.	2.	13
Moss from 2 feet to 4 ½ feet deep improved and under Crop			
Backs	176.	2.	6
Moss from 2 feet deep to 10 feet, some part very soft of grayish colour 30 Acres of it improved, and under Crop. Peats cut here the same as in Aross.			
Skeroblingorry	28.	1.	25
Moss from 2 ½ feet to 6 feet, with a clay bottom 16 Acres improved and under Crop.			
Kirkmichael	18.	3	4.
Moss from 2 feet deep to 7 feet with a whitish clay bottom improved and under Crop.			
Achinleck	1.	1.	36
Moss from 3 feet deep to 7 feet a clay bottom improved and under Crop.			

	A.	R.	P.
Darlochan	369	0.	25

Moss from 4 ½ feet deep to 10 feet, part a clay, part a gravely and sandy bottom great part green and rough some brush wood, <u>five</u> acres only improved & under Crop.

Durry	143.	0.	28

Moss from 2 feet deep to 9 feet, part a clay and part a sandy bottom. 10 acres improved and under Crop. Still a great quantity of peats and haggs on this Farm.

Clochkill	122.	1.	11

Moss from 1 ½ feet deep to 6 ½ feet, with a sandy bottom unimproved.

Laigh park	20.	1.	37

Moss from 2 feet deep to 7 feet with a clay bottom improved and under Crop.

Beachmore	11.	3.	31

Moss very deep and blackish coloured this all in the Mountain.

Ballochgair	1.	1.	21

Moss from 2 feet deep to 4 feet, with a clay bottom improved and under Crop.

Achinbrack	16.	1.	16

Moss very deep of a brownish colour high up in the Mountain.

Craigmore	17.	1.	34

Moss very soft, brownish colour high in the Mountain, part of this was in dispute with Cour and most of it allowed to him by the Arbiters.

Drumlemble	145.	3	16
Strawbeg	87.	1.	9.

This is mentioned Muir in the Survey Books but is really moss, part easily improved, particularly what falls to the shore of East and West Drumlemble.

62: PEAT-CUTTING AND DRAINING OF THE MOSSES

Instructions to the Chamberlain of Kintyre [1798].

October 1798.

1st You will attend to the first Instruction of Last year in so far as regards the New Church which may be built upon the situation at the Lochend which you describe incase you are compleatly satisfied that the other Stance is under Lease and that the Lessees cannot be treated with easily for a Stance for the Church. Previous to which it will be proper that you see the Lease said to be granted and examine if it allows subsetting, which appears to have taken place.

2d. William Langlands to be put in mind to give in his quarterly Reports regularly, and to mention the state of each of the young plantations, at least once in the year; and what is doing as to the improvement of Moss.

3d. The Improvements to be executed upon the Farms, which have been let at this time to be specified and sent to Edinburgh along with the Memorials without loss of time in order that the Leases may be made out.

4th I desire your immediate attention towards recovering payment of the heavy Arrears which have been allowed to be incurred by the Tenants, and which are upon the whole no less than £1600 Sterling above those of last year.

You must employ an Agent at Campbeltown to raise Actions of Removing before the Sherriff upon the Act of sederunt 1756 against such of the Tenants as do not immediately settle for the Rents of Crop 1797 & proceedings.

63: RENTS AND REMOVALS
64: 'CLEARANCES'

5th. Report as to the last Herring Fishing, and when and where the Fish go and the Prices as near as you can.

6th. When any Payment is made in future, in consequence of a Deliverance or Instruction, these must be produced or referred to as Vouchers of your Accounts, when they come to be examined.

Signed Argyll

Inveraray 17th October 1798.

[In Eric R. Cregeen's transcript, which follows the page numbering of the original manuscript, pages 192 and 193 are left blank, suggesting that the Duke's instructions for 1799, replied to below, were not copied. Page 200 of the transcript, between the instructions for 1801 and 1805, was also left blank.]

Answers to Kintyre Instructions 1799

1st The Ministers of Campbeltown were informed of this part of the Instruction. The Heritors have agreed to advertise for a Contractor for building a Church and an advertisement for that purpose has been sent to Mr. John Ferrier to have inserted in the public papers. But there still exists a dispute about giving up the stance of the old Church for a new one, in terms of the Instruction of October 1797. the Clergy and Elders alledging that an Aile [aisle] formerly built to the old Church belongs to the Poor, and which they now let to Carpenters and refuse to give up with the other part of the Stance. The Session have been called upon to shew their rights to this Aile, which it is believed they have some difficulty to establish.

2d Notice was duly given to William Langlands of this and he has complied therewith.

3d. It is feared the Arrears may still appear large but every exertion and prosecutions have been used.

Signed Dun Stewart.

Limecraigs October 1800.

Instructions to the Chamberlain of Kintyre [1800].
October 1800

1. I will have no dispute about the ground of the old Church. If it is not given chearfully and thankfully for the stance which I have offer'd for the New Church, then I will keep my ground and let the New Church be built upon the stance of the old one.

2. Speak to or correspond with Mr. Graham about sending the Woodman from this place to Craigmore & Achnabreck at the proper Season to inspect and value the Timber and woods mentioned in your Memorandum that I may thereby be enabled to give further directions in regard to them. The large Trees should be numbered and measured and the Tenants should be made answerable for any that shall be cut without authority. I shall never cut Trees for the sake of preventing their being cut down and stolen by other people while there are Laws to protect them.

65: Craigmore and Auchnabreck

3. Let me knew what is doing by the Farming Society in Kintyre, what books they have got, and where they are kept and how managed. I have been and am willing to give Premiums upon being informed how it can best be done.

4. I cannot think of giving my Limestone at Crosshill to be sent out of the Country as Ballast to Ships for the paltry consideration of five or even Ten pounds yearly, but consider how it can be wrought so as to be useful at home in building and as manure and I will be ready to encourage the working of it, by giving the liberty desired on reasonable terms which I conceive must be so much for the Ton, not any fixed sum in money.

66: Limestone
67: Crosshill Farm

5. The Ministers of Campbeltown having never drawn any thing in consequence of the fourth Instruction anno 1795 I desire that you will pay them my proportion for bygones and in time coming until they obtain legal Augmentations taking receipts from them separate from the Receipts for Stipends, and bearing expressly that they are Bounties from me and are not to be considered as Stipends.

6. I agree to the proposed exchange of thirteen acres of Moss belonging to my Farm of Little Straw now disjoined from it by the Coal Canal for fifteen acres of moss belonging to Mr. Campbell of Barbrecks farm of Stramore disjoined from it by the Canal and laid into Little Straw and authorise you to pay Mr. Campbell the

difference as it shall be settled betwixt you taking my Tenant bound to pay Interest for it.

68: Little Straw

7. I cannot agree to grant any priviledge to any person taking Wattling or any thing else from my Woods, as I have long found it necessary to seclude my own Tenants from taking any thing of the kind at their own hand, But if Wattling can be spared from my woods I have no objection to its being given to Mr. Campbell of Barbrecks Tenants by my Chamberlain in any way that will not fix a servitude upon me which must be carefully guarded against.

8. Consider of planting Willows in the Meadows at Limecraigs and other proper places. I find them profitable at Roseneath from the vicinity of Greenock, and think they would be so in the Neighbourhood of Campbeltown.

69: Willows

9. Look out as soon as you return for some Meal Barley and Oats to be sent here soon and advise me what quantity of each I may expect and the prices.

Signed/ Argyll.
20 October 1800.

Answers

1. From the War with Denmark, and the high price of Timber no Contract is yet enter'd into for building the Church.

2. The woodman was sent down and no doubt has made his Report. Where no regular Wood Ranger is, it is a difficult matter to make legal detections particularly as these depradations are uniformly committed under the cloud of night generally by handsaws to prevent noise.

3. I have repeatedly required Mr. McKay Clerk to the Farming Society to give me a particular detail of their operations and daily expect it. They have held out some Premiums, particularly for the greatest quantity of wet [?] mowsley land drained in a proper manner, likewise for these shewing the best specimens of compost Dunghills. Two Farmers in Kintyre have bought oxen at the late Lord Stonefields sale with a view of gaining the Premium offered by your Grace for that mode of husbandry. I have likeways been in correspondence with a John Campbell Farmer in Bogside Airshire who has agreed to send one of his sons for sometime to Fife or

Aberdeenshires to acquire a thorough knowledge of the Vaccinian husbandry and to become bound to use no other Cattle provided your Grace will prefer him to a Farm for that purpose.

4. The Quarrier who wished to take the Limestone quarry last year was killed in the Town quarry and no other has yet offered.

5. The Ministers of Campbeltown are paid your Graces bounty agreeable to your desire.

6. This article was intimated to Mr. Clark Barbrecks Factor who Reports that Mr. Campbell will not accept of the difference in money but in Land from the adjoining farm of Dalvaddy.

7. This respecting the Wattles shall be carefully attended to.

8. The Meadows being long drained and improved make a very good return and is generally alternately under Potatoes and Oats. Mr. Campbell of Kildaloig had a piece of marshy ground planted with Willows but found it necessary, it is believed from the licentious depradations of the rabble in Campbeltown to root them up, he has drained it, and has this year a famous Crop on it. But loads of Willows might be planted with advantage in the different farms along the Inclosures and ditches in marshy and mossy Lands. It there makes a tolerable fence and of use to the farmer who will study to preserve them from their utility to himself.

9. The Barley and Meal were shipped according to Orders.

Signed Dun Stewart

Limecraigs 8th October 1801

Instructions to the Chamberlain of Kintyre [1801].
October 1801

1. I cannot admit that my trees and woods must have Wood rangers to protect them. The Law obliges every Tenant to preserve what are upon his possession and to make good the damage unless he can shew that it was done by another person and the law must be enforced.

2. I agree to pay my share of £100 Scots yearly to each of the Ministers of Campbeltown for Communion Elements for the year 1796 and subsequent years.

5. Insert in this Book the List of Tenants who were convicted of Distilling last year that they may be taken notice of when their Leases expire. The Arrears due by Carradale stated in your List together with a payment of Stipend which I have been making for him to the Minister for some years back to be settled, as soon as he comes of age and when that is done I shall have no objection to pass from the article of £2. 18. -. for the Red Herring house.

5. Let me know the price of Beans.

6. I would rather have my own Tenants led to plough with Oxen than bring a stranger from Airshire as proposed by you.

7. A List must be made up and authenticated of the Machinery Engines Tools &ca. which have been delivered at my expence to the Coal Company and are to be redelivered by them at the end of their Tack.

Signed Argyll.

Instructions to the Chamberlain of Kintyre [1805].
October 1805

1. Consider what proper mark of approbation I ought to confer on such Tenants as have fully complied with the conditions of their Leases in regard to Improvements.

2. Let me know which of the Tenants are most proper to be mark'd for neglecting to execute the improvements undertaken by them and if the best and most regular punishment will not be to charge them with the additional Rents specified in the Leases.

Signed Argyll

Commentaries on Instructions

1: Flax

Flax and lint are the same. Crops were grown on many Kintyre farms until the latter half of the nineteenth century, but processing of the crop was time-consuming and messy.[1] In 1775 the flax-dresser or 'heckler' (comber) in Campbeltown was James Wilson, employed by the Board of Trustees for Manufactures and Improvements in Scotland. In that year, an apprenticeship indenture was drawn up between him and Dugald McCallum, son of Duncan McCallum, Kilkerran, to learn the craft of flax-and hemp-dressing.[2] This was part of the Duke's strategy for the pacification of his tenantry, particularly in the northern parts of his estates, such as Morvern, where the spirit of Jacobitism lingered sullenly. By the establishment of localised industry, it was 'confidently expected that the inhabitants would be wooed from their disaffection by the manifest benefits of the new times'.[3]

2: Rents

This instruction, to which the Chamberlain's response was, 'Tenants have agreed', clearly signals the end of rents being paid partly in money and partly in produce and services, and the beginning of a wholly monetary arrangement, which was doubtless much simpler to administer. One example will suffice to illustrate the old system. In 1776, the two-merkland farm of Corphin, with its pendicle Blarferne, was leased to John and Lauchlan McIsaac Jnr. at an annual rent of £25 2s, plus I boll multure meal, 2 bolls teind bear (tithe barley), 5 bolls oatmeal, and 24 'carriages', or packhorse loads. When the lease was renewed in 1799, the payments in kind and services had disappeared and the rent was set at £44.[4]

These services, or 'servitudes' as John Smith termed them, involved the carting of peats and hay, and also an obligation to labour at seed time and harvest. By 1798, when Smith's book on the agriculture of Argyll was published, rents on the 'larger estates' – of which the Argyll Estate was certainly one – were being paid entirely in money, but on 'lesser estates' continued to be paid in kind. Smith recommended the total abolition of services, in favour of rents' being 'formed into one sum of money, including public burdens, such as minister's stipend, schoolmaster's salary, road-money, etc. '. [5] See also the present writer's observations on 'The Leasing System' in *Kintyre Country Life*, pp. 7-8.

3: Backs Water

The Backs Water runs parallel to the A83 road, past Craigs, before looping south into the Laggan and joining with 'Machrihanish Water' to enter Machrihanish Bay. ('Machrihanish Water', however, is apparently an Ordnance Survey name: the entire water-course is universally known as 'The Backs Water'.) It was a vital channel in the drainage of the Laggan mosses and its course was modified to that end. 'Backs' is from Gaelic *bac*, 'bank', probably referring to peat-banks, and two Laggan farms have the name 'Backs', East and West. [6]

The plan was clearly to divert part of the flow into Campbeltown to power the meal mill there. Four years later, in 1789, the Duke's agent, James Ferrier, was enquiring of the Chamberlain why Campbeltown Town Council was 'not paying back to the Duke the £150 lent them in 1786', and urging him to recover the overdue instalments. The Chamberlain's explanation (No. 11) was that the Council had been obliged to lay out money on 'necessary repairs of Streets' and in 'building a Market house', but that 'probably next year their circumstances may afford a payment'. The issue of that debt would reappear.

The meal mill at Campbeltown was demolished in 1939 and the last millar there, Archibald Revie, died in 1941. The mill is commemorated, however, in the names Millknowe, Miller's Park, Mill Street and Mill Road. The dammed lade – an extensive body of water where the playing field opposite Hillside Road now is – was drained in 1938, but the name 'Mill Dam' survives. [7]

4: John Turner, Tonrioch

'Turners Farm' must be Tonrioch near present-day Stewarton. John Turner was one of the northern English farmers brought into Kintyre by the 5th Duke 'in hopes of introducing a better mode of agriculture'; but, according to John Smith in 1798, 'they have generally adopted, rather than changed, the customs of the place'. [8] Turner, who was from Newton, near Carlisle, received his lease of

11. Backs Water from Parkfergus bridge, showing the straight line of the cut. Photograph by A. Martin, December 1995.

12. Campbeltown meal mill, c. 1905. From A. Martin's collection.

13. The Mill Dam, c. 1935. Carol McCallum watching a family of mallard on the lade. The visible houses are at the west end of Dalaruan Street and the white gateposts mark the entrance to Drumore House. Photograph from the late Carol McCallum Timms.

14. Carved stone in outbuilding behind Low Tifergus farmhouse. The inscription is evidently dated August 1677 and commemorates Lachlan MacNeill of Tirfergus, whose arms are represented. The panel, and two carved human heads, also incorporated into the outbuilding, are believed to have originally adorned MacNeill's house at Tirfergus. Photograph by A. Martin, 1996.

Tonrioch in 1775 and had it renewed – for 21 years – in 1787, at the original rent of £75. [9]

Colonel Campbell was Charles Campbell (p. 102), who had leased 15 acres from the Argyll Estate in 1776. That lease was for 57 years, at three times the norm of 19 years an unusual length, which generally signified a commercial enterprise which the Duke wished to encourage. This must have been the piece of land – detached from Drumlemble farm and 'near the Bleachfield' (p. 121) – affected by the realignment of the public road which was to help Turner fence his fields to better effect. Drumlemble had been divided into East and West in 1780. [10] The road realignment went ahead, as the Chamberlain's reply confirms. The Duke reimbursed Colonel Campbell for his half of the expense of rebuilding the roadside dyke, but the sum was to be repaid by Turner.

5: Macneals of Ugadale

'Ugadale' would have been Hector Macneal, proprietor of that small estate on the east of Kintyre. He was descended from Lachlan MacNeill Buidhe (c. 1611-1695) who acquired Tirfergus and Largiebaan in 1660, followed by Lossit, Knockhanty and Glenahanty in 1668. Lachlan married twice, had 14 children and at least 80 grandchildren. Three of his sons settled in the north of Ireland and the remaining five became lairds in Kintyre: of Tirfergus, Lossit, Ugadale, Kilchrist and Machrihanish. This widely extended family, which ultimately adopted the spelling 'Macneal', was thoroughly researched by A. I. B. Stewart, whose studies were published in the *Kintyre Magazine*, Numbers 15, 19, 20 and 21.

'Cuilundune' or Cullindoun was a smallholding about a mile south-east of Knocknaha. The steading, which latterly housed a shepherd, is now ruinous. Since Kilchrist was held in feu by the Macneals, [11] Cullindoun was presumably then attached to that holding and bounding with Killeonan, which was the Duke's. When the Jacobite Rebellion broke out in 1745, Lachlan McNeill was laird of Kilchrist and into his third term as Provost of Campbeltown. He commanded the company of Militia which was raised in Campbeltown in March 1746, took it to Inveraray and thence into the Highlands. He was succeeded as provost in 1748 by Neil Macneal, laird of Ugadale; a third member of that family, Torquil of Ugadale, was earlier – in 1717 – appointed provost, and served two terms. [12]

A Macneal appears in another, later dispute in that same area. In 1819, George McNeal, who had just succeeded to Knocknaha Mill on the death of his father, Captain Hector, raised an action in the Court of Session against Charles Rowatt of Kilkivan (p. 132), alleging that Kilkivan estate was thirled (bound) to his mill and that Kilkivan tenants were abstracting the multures, or miller's payments. [13]

6: Ugadale Estate and Brooch

Ugadale Estate was acquired by the Macneals of Lossit in the late seventeenth century and sold in 1975. Even within the Macneal family, the belief persisted that the property had come to the family through marriage, but A. I. B. Stewart discovered that the last male in the Ugadale line, Donald Mackay, had died bankrupt and that Torquil Macneal bought the estate from his trustee and thereafter married Catherine Mackay, a twin daughter of Donald's. [14] The earliest plaque in the Macneal enclosure in old Kilkerran graveyard commemorates Torquil, who died in 1728 aged 75. Subsequent Macneal lairds tended to marry outwith the Kintyre landed families, with the exception of Captain Hector (1822-1905), whose wife Constance Glencairn Campbell (1839-1912) was a daughter of Colonel Walter Campbell of Skipness.

With Ugadale and Arnicle, or perhaps, more correctly, with Catherine Mackay, came the splendid silver 'Brooch of Ugadale' with its centrepiece of magical crystal, which so fascinated Queen Victoria, when she saw it, that she desired, and secured, a replica. According to tradition, the brooch was presented to Farquhar Mackay in 1306 by the fugitive Robert Bruce, whom Mackay had helped cross Kintyre to safety. When Bruce became King of Scotland, he granted the Crown lands of Ugadale and Arnicle to Mackay. The original title, written on a scrap of sheepskin, was lost, but a replacement was issued during the reign of King James IV. The brooch was hidden by the Macneal family during the alarms of the 1745 Rebellion and remained missing, believed lost, until the original Lossit House was demolished in 1824, when it fell from behind a panel and was noticed and saved by one of the workmen. [15]

15. Knocknaha Mill c. 1900. Courtesy of Mr Murdo MacDonald.

16. The Ugadale Brooch, photographed by A. Martin, 1996.

17. Frontal view of Lossit House, photographed by A. Martin, 1996.

7: Lossit Houses

Despite the family's standard designation 'of Ugadale', its main, and most substantial, residence was at Lossit, Machrihanish. According to Colonel Hector Macneal, who died in 2009, the old house at High Lossit had been burnt in an accidental fire before its demolition. When the foundations were being dug for Lossit Cottage, he said, the foundations of the old mansion were found. A wall to the south of the cottage and a section of wall at the roadside are all that remain of the original building. The present Lossit House was built between 1820 and '26 by George Macneal, but was extended in the late nineteenth century and then reduced in the mid-twentieth century, by the demolition of two wings. [16]

8: MacDonalds of Sanda

'Sanda' was probably Archibald MacDonald, an Advocate at the Scottish Bar who died in 1795 at Greenock on his way to Argyll. The issue of the disputed ground was no doubt settled in a civilised manner, but the ancestors of these two men, Campbell of Argyll and MacDonald of Sanda, were for generations bitter enemies. As Clan Donald's power declined from the fifteenth century on, so Clan Campbell's power increased.

Archibald Mor MacDonald of Sanda commanded the Royalist force trapped in Dunaverty Castle in the summer of 1647, and was executed in the ensuing massacre, which was observed by Archibald Campbell, Marquess of Argyll, who, under the overall command of General David Leslie, led a regiment in the campaign to free Argyll from the grip of his nemesis, the legendary warrior Major-General Sir Alexander MacDonald, otherwise known as 'Alasdair MacColla'. Archibald Mor's son, Lieutenant-Colonel Archibald Og MacDonald, was killed later that year along with MacColla in the Battle of Knocknanuss in Munster, Ireland.

In 1650, three years after the massacre, the Marquess of Argyll successfully raised an action to have the Sanda estates forfeited on grounds of arrears of feu-duty and rebellion. The parties called as defenders were Angus MacDonald, son of the slain Archibald Og, and Archibald's widow Christeane Stewart. However, the Restoration of the Monarchy in 1660 reversed the Marquess of Argyll's fortunes and he was convicted of treason and executed in 1661; so, the political tide which carried Archibald Campbell out of the world also carried the MacDonalds back to Sanda, and in the same year Ranald MacDonald was restored to the lands of his grandfather. This Ranald, according to local tradition, had been smuggled to safety by his nurse, Flora MacCambridge, before the massacre at Dunaverty, and was now head of the family, his brother Angus – heir in 1650 – having presumably died.

Ranald was succeeded by Archibald, Archibald by John, and John by Archibald the Advocate, during whose time the family fortunes entered a decline. When the estate was sold in 1799, four years after his death, only Sanda itself and the mainland farm of Gartnacopaig remained from the Lands of Saint Ninian, which had originally belonged to the Priory of Whithorn and included Macharioch, Blasthill, Eden, Knockmorran, Penlaughton, Kilmashenachan, Pennysearach, Acharua, Balegreggan and Drumorenabodach. The much diminished estate returned to the MacDonald family in 1825 but was finally sold in the 1920s.

The Sanda family was founded by Angus MacDonald, a son of Sir John Cathanach MacDonald of Dunnyveg, Islay, who famously, in 1494, hanged King James IV's governor over the walls of Dunaverty Castle, in sight of the King, and was himself executed for treason two years later. [17]

9: Macdonalds of Largie

The other important cadet branch of the MacDonalds in Kintyre, that of Largie, descends from Ranald, a son of John Mor and Marjory Bisset of Antrim, and a grandson of John of Islay, 1st Lord of the Isles. The tenth laird, Angus, supported the Royalist cause during the Civil War, as a consequence of which Largie was forfeited, and Dugald Campbell of Inverawe – known as 'The MacConachie' – was granted a lease of 53 merklands of the estate in 1652. At the Restoration in 1660, however, the family regained the estate. According to tradition, John, 14th laird of Largie, attempted to join Prince Charles Edward Stuart's rebellion in 1745, but only got as far as Clachan, where a scalding incident with a punch-kettle disabled him, fortunately as it transpired. [18]

Of Largie Castle, it has been remarked: 'One could easily be forgiven for thinking that this house was a slightly altered Scottish castle of the early 17th century . . . ' In fact, it was built between 1857 and '59, and described in 1861 by the Rev. Edward Bradley

18. The Island of Sanda from Polliwilline Hill. Photograph by A. Martin, July 1997.

19. Largie Castle, by Rev. Edward Bradley ('Cuthbert Bede'). From *Glencreggan* (1861).

as 'arranged and fitted up in accordance with the comforts and luxuries of modern life', and 'well situated in a finely-wooded park, containing timber of large growth'. Largie Castle was demolished in 1953 and when Michael C. Davis visited the site in 1981, 'not one stone was found upon another'. The stable block and a walled garden of 'substantial proportions' were all that remained. The earlier castle Bradley described as 'merely a fortified house, strong but plain in character, and of small size; and the little that remains of it forms a portion of a farm-house'. [19]

10: MacNeill of Carskey

'Cariskey' would have been Lieutenant-Colonel Malcolm MacNeill, died c. 1824, a grandson of Malcolm MacNeill, who secured a charter to Carskey Estate in 1700 from the 1st Duke of Argyll, though MacNeills were in occupancy there as early as 1505 and ranked as one of the leading families of Kintyre. [20] The Kintyre MacNeills safely distanced themselves from the political and religious strife of the seventeenth and eighteenth centuries. Southend historian Archibald McEachran records a tradition that in 1647 Neill MacNeill of Carskey 'took no active part in assisting the defenders of Dunaverty'. [21]

The present mansion-house at Carskey, built in 1905 by James Boyd and Catherine Coats, is the third on the site. The 'handsome commodious house' completed by Lieutenant-Colonel A. Forbes Mackay – the last laird of MacNeill descent to occupy Carskey – fewer than thirty years earlier, was demolished to make way for the larger and more opulent present building. The earliest known MacNeill house – 'a square keep with one or more wings built on' – which Mackay demolished to build his house, is believed to have stood west of the present driveway. [22]

11: MacShannons

'Mc Oshenaig' is one of many variants of an old Southend name, now fixed as 'McShannon' in Kintyre. Macoshenags were harpers to Clan Donald. In 1505 – the first certain record – Muriach McMaschenach, 'citherist', had substantial rent-free lands in Southend for his services. Descendants, who changed the family name to 'Shannon', were proprietors of Lephenstrath estate from 1701 until 1819. [23] In 1771, Mary MacShannon emigrated

20. Carskey House, c. 1925. Reproduced from postcard in collection of Mrs Maureen Bell.

from Southend with her husband Hugh Montgomery, sailing from Campbeltown to Prince Edward Island, Canada. Their great-great-grand-daughter Lucy Maud Montgomery would write the international best-selling novel *Anne of Green Gables*. [24]

12: Campbells of Kildalloig

Kildalloig Estate forms the south-eastern portion of Campbeltown Parish and includes Davaar Island. The Campbell family of Kildalloig, which later succeeded to the Baronetcy of Auchinbreck in Cowal, descended from Sir Duncan Campbell of Lochow, by his second wife, Margaret Stewart, daughter of Sir John Stewart of Blackhall, natural son of King Robert III. [25]

When the 1st Marquess of Argyll set about the plantation of Kintyre in the mid-seventeenth century, he brought in many Lowland lairds and their followers – industrious Protestant stock – but he also brought in men of his own clan and of other clans of proven loyalty. Among those who received tacks between 1666 and 1669 were George and John Campbell in Kildalloig and in other widely dispersed holdings. [26]

John Campbell of Kildalloig married Elizabeth or Elspeth, daughter of Lachlan McNeill of Lossit, in 1660 and died c. 1706. He was the Duke of Argyll's Chamberlain in Kintyre[27] and among the members of the first town council of the newly constituted Royal Burgh of Campbeltown which met in June 1700, all of them appointed by the 10th Earl of Argyll, Archibald Campbell. [28] Successive generations of the family are buried in Kilkerran graveyard, Campbeltown.

The last member of the family prominent in Campbeltown was Katherine Mary Edith, born in Edinburgh, the only child of Sir Louis Campbell, 9th Baronet of Auchinbreck. Orphaned in early childhood, she was brought up largely by her maternal grandparents in Canterbury. She died in Campbeltown in 1906 at the age of 31. By her charitable disposition and innate kindness, particularly towards needy children, she endeared herself to the people of Campbeltown, and especially to the fishing community, which raised funds for the erection of a memorial fountain – since removed and its whereabouts unknown – at the head of the New Quay. It bore the inscription: 'Erected by the Fishermen of Campbeltown in affectionate remembrance of their friend Miss Katherine Mary

21. Miss Campbell of Kildalloig. Reproduced from the *Campbeltown Courier*, 10/8/1907.

Edith Campbell of Kildalloig, who died 22nd August, 1906, aged 31 years. ' Kildalloig Estate was sold in 1925 to Edward Dudgeon, brother of Mrs Macalister of Glenbarr, and the present house was built by him to plans drawn up by James Miller (1860-1947) and dated 1926. [29]

The Valuation Roll for 1751 showed the following Campbell estates, in addition to Kildalloig and, of course, the very extensive lands of Archibald, Duke of Argyll, himself: Archibald of Stonefield, Colin of Skipnige, John of Glensaddell and Dugald of Glencarradil.

13: Campbells of Glensaddell

Although Glensaddell is scarcely mentioned in these instructions, that estate, in the eighteenth century, impinged more upon the affairs of Campbeltown than any of the others, because its laird was the largest landed proprietor in the district next to Argyll himself: Drumore and Dalintober both belonged to him. Dalintober came into existence as a planned village in the 1760s and was the creation of John Campbell of Glensaddell. His idea was to offer a harbour where traders were exempt from payment of landing and shipping dues, and the proposal proved an attractive one. In 1766, merchants began buying up plots of land on which to build dwelling-houses and warehouses, and the quay at Dalintober was built about the same time.

The initiative, however, was resented by the magistrates of the Royal Burgh of Campbeltown, who saw it as unfair competition which would reduce their harbour revenues; but since Dalintober was still in the parish of Kilchousland and outwith the burgh boundaries, there was little they could do in the short term. But in 1844, the village's special status ended when the town council, after four years of litigation, established that goods landed or shipped at Dalintober were not exempt from harbour dues. [30]

Ironically, perhaps, the first Provost of the Royal Burgh of Campbeltown, in 1700, was John Campbell, eldest son of the Laird of Saddell, who succeeded his father in 1707. The last laird, John MacLeod Campbell, was a writer and amateur archaeologist who died in 1936. He was born in India and educated at St Andrews University. He inherited the estate at the age of twenty-one from his grandfather, Colonel J. N. Macleod, a brother of Dr Norman Macleod of the Barony (p. 144). Indeed, there were eminent divines

22. The foreshore at Dalintober, c. 1900, looking east. The village ring-net skiffs are beached for the annual spring clean and behind them stand the net-drying poles. The Dalintober fleet ceased to exist after World War II and the quay – from which this photograph was taken – has gradually become derelict. From the MacGrory Collection, courtesy of Argyll & Bute Library Service.

23. Saddell Castle, c. 1920. It has since been restored and converted into holiday accommodation. Reproduced from postcard in collection of Mrs Maureen Bell.

24. John Campbell, last laird of Saddell, at entrance doorway to tower of Saddell Castle, c. 1920. Reproduced from postcard in collection of Mrs Maureen Bell.

on both sides of his family. The theological doctrines of his paternal grandfather, Dr John MacLeod Campbell of Row, were judged to be 'so far in advance of his times' that he was deposed for heresy by the General Assembly of 1831. [31]

Like many old Scottish castles, Saddell – which was built around 1508 – is reputed to be haunted. Certainly, it was the setting of many violent events, from its burning by the raiding Earl of Sussex in 1558, to the burning to death, in 1902, of Marion McLean, a housemaid whose clothing caught fire while she was lighting an oil-lamp at the head of the stair. [32]

14: Campbells of Skipness

The second Provost of Campbeltown was also a Campbell laird, Walter of Skipness, a family which descended from the second son of Archibald, 2nd Earl of Argyll, who received the lands of Skipness from the Crown in 1502 and was killed on the battlefield at Flodden in 1513. The best known of the Skipness Campbells in Kintyre history was Mathew, who served in the wars of Gustavus Adolphus (1594-1632), king of Sweden and militant champion of Protestantism. Major of the Marquess of Argyll's regiment, Mathew Campbell was killed at Dunaverty in 1647 during an attack to cut off the besieged Royalists' water supply, and buried in the old Gaelic churchyard of Lochhead. [33] The Campbell family sold Skipness estate, with its imposing medieval castle, in the mid-nineteenth century.

15: Campbells of Stonefield

The Campbells of Stonefield, who became lairds of Tarbert after the MacAlisters, took their name from an earlier family estate on the shores of Loch Etive, Auchnacloich, which translates from Gaelic as 'Stonefield'. According to Dugald Mitchell, the Stonefield connection with Tarbert began c. 1716 with the purchase from Campbell of Blythswood of lands 'to the south and west of Bardaravine Burn'. During the '45 Rebellion, Archibald Campbell of Stonefield was Sheriff of Argyll. He died in 1777 and was succeeded by his son John, Lord Stonefield, an eminent judge.

Lord Stonefield's second son, Major John Campbell, was 'the hero of Mangalore, the soldier whose memorable defence of that [Indian] town from May, 1783, to January of the following year, first arrested the victorious career of Tippu Sultan . . . ' 'Shattered in health', he soon afterwards quit the army and died in Bombay, a Lieutenant-Colonel, on 23 March 1784, at the age of thirty. [34] The big house 'Mangalore', on Langlands' map of 1801, roughly where the present Glenreasdell Lodge stands, was clearly named in his honour, presumably by his father, who died in 1801.

16: Charles McDowall

'Mr MacDowal' – later referred to as 'Sherrif McDowall' – was Charles McDowall of Crichen, which was the family estate in Wigtonshire. [35] He became an advocate in 1734 and was later appointed Sheriff of Renfrewshire, but he clearly had an interest in mining prior to his being granted a 27-year lease of the Campbeltown coal and salt works in 1771 by the 5th Duke of Argyll. [36] He took over the saltworks at Pans – at the western end of the present Machrihanish village – and began trial borings for coal. Having secured a new lease, allowing him greater scope, McDowall established a mine at West Drumlemble, from which he would ultimately construct a canal to Campbeltown. In 1779, as 'Sheriff McDowall', he is shown as lessee of Balligreggan, Dailquhasan and Marypans. He died in 1791. [37]

McDowall's memory endured in two place-names. Crock Crichen is a knoll on the landward side of the road at Lossit Gate, opposite the house which McDowall built for himself and which later became an inn, since demolished. 'Crichen's Dam' was used occasionally to denote Killipole Loch, which McDowall dammed and directed into Rhudal Burn, c. 1770, to drive a water-wheel which powered the pumps in the Drumlemble mine. The dam was raised c. 1790 to supply water to the coal canal (p. 140) and raised further in 1905 by Lossit Estate which used its water to generate electricity at the Home Farm. That innovative plant supplied power, by overhead wires, not only to the Estate but to Machrihanish village. The water was led to and held at Loch an t-Soluis (Gaelic, 'Loch of the Light'), a pond at the head of Lossit Glen. In taking the water west, however, Rhudal Burn was denied a share and reduced to little more than a ditch. [38]

25. Salt Pans, from the Duan, by James Stewart, from William Smith Jr.'s *Views of Campbelton and Neighbourhood*, 1835.

17: Colonel Charles Campbell

'Colonel Campbell' was Charles Campbell, a representative of the Campbell family of Barbreck, an estate in Craignish, Mid Argyll. He acquired a number of lands in Kintyre, including Tangy and Glenbarr estates, and was appointed Provost of Campbeltown in 1771. He was clearly a wealthy man, but generous with it for the good of the town. That he owned one of the eight four-wheeled carriages then existing in Argyll, was considered a measure of his wealth. [39] He also leased and sub-let farms. In 1779, he held Lecknalarach in Kilchenzie Parish and Laigh (Low) Blary and Kilmaluag in Killean Parish from Argyll Estate. All of these properties are listed without a resident 'tacksman'. [40]

On 20 May, 1796, following the Colonel's death, his effects were sold by public auction. The 'roup roll' survives and provides a fascinating insight into the furnishings – library included – of an eighteenth century Kintyre laird's house. [41]

Peter MacIntosh's *History of Kintyre*, published in 1857, contains many tales from oral tradition, including one which clearly relates to Colonel Campbell. Like most such tales, it contains elements of both truth and legend. It begins with a 'young man named Charles Campbell' finding a 'poor man lying in a ditch by the wayside, who had fallen in a state of exhaustion, and unable to extricate himself, and would undoubtedly have very soon perished'. Young Charles pulled the man from the ditch, took him to the nearest house, saw that he was well clothed and fed, and left orders that he should be looked after until his strength had recovered and he could go on his way. 'The old man gave many thanks to Charles, and prayed to God that he might be proprietor of the lands surrounding the part to which he carried him; which afterwards took place.' According to MacIntosh, Charles joined the army, went to the East Indies, was promoted to the rank of colonel, 'accumulated great riches' and 'purchased a large estate', which included Glenbarr, Tangy, Machrihanish, Lochsanish, Trodigal and Killeonan. [42]

18: Archibald McDuff, gardener

In 1769, Archibald McDuff, gardener to the Marquess of Lorne at Rosneath, was granted a lease of the lands of Whitehill, at Witchburn, on the outskirts of Campbeltown. He set up a kitchen garden with fruit trees, pot herbs and roots as well as a nursery for

26. Surviving hedgerow on east (left) side of farm-track to High Tirfergus. The hedge is typically mostly hawthorn, but with some crab apple trees in it. Photograph by A. Martin, 2/2/1995.

27. Gnarled and wind-bent old hawthorn forming part of hedge at Tomaig. Crosshill Reservoir and Davaar Island in distance. Photograph by Hartwig Schutz, 13/4/2006.

thorn trees. [43] In 1789, 150,000 'quick thorn' plants were imported from Ireland and tended at MacDuff's nursery 'for the use of His Grace's Farms in Kintyre'. To this mass importation Father James Webb, in 1952, attributed that 'feature of South Kintyre . . . roads are bordered and fields divided by thorn hedges'. [44] Certainly, this is no longer so much the case, since many hedgerows have since been uprooted, particularly in low-lying areas; but hawthorns – and blackthorns, too, though to a far lesser degree – remain intrinsic features of Kintyre landscapes.

In the Kintyre Estate Census of 1792, Archibald and his wife Marrion Bruce were among 24 inhabitants of Whitehill, the road to which was known as 'Duff's Walk' into the twentieth century. [45]

19: Mull of Kintyre Lighthouse

The lighthouse alluded to was at the Mull of Kintyre, on the Duke's land. After Kinnaird Head, it was the second lighthouse erected by the Trustees for Northern Lighthouses, which was formed in 1786, and one of whose members was the Provost of Campbeltown, James Maxwell, who was also the Duke's chamberlain in Mull and Morvern (p. 144). Construction proved difficult, owing to problems of accessibility by both sea and land, but the lighthouse, designed by Thomas Smith, the board's first engineer, finally became operational in 1788. [46]

The first lightkeeper at the Mull was William Harvey, shipmaster in Campbeltown, who in 1790 petitioned the Duke for better arable ground, complaining of the exposed nature of his house and garden. [47] New dwelling-houses were erected in the nineteenth century. William was followed as keeper by his son Mathew, who died in 1867. [48]

20: Barley and its milling

'Piligrass' = Scots 'peelygrass', which is barley with the husks removed (to produce a kind of pearl barley). Traditionally, barley, or 'bear', would be milled in a 'knockin stane', a chunky rock – sometimes naturally outcropping – with a hole incised in the top of it. Some water would be poured into the hole and the barley carefully agitated with a wooden pestle, so that the husks and residual weed-seed floated to the top and could be poured off, leaving the pearl barley. This 'knockit bear' was a major ingredient

28. Mull of Kintyre and Lighthouse, c. 1910. Reproduced from postcard in collection of Mrs Maureen Bell.

29. Presumed knockin stane in rock outcrop at Auchenhoan, photographed by A. Martin, 31/3/1999. Camera lens cap provides scale.

in kail dishes and was commonly served as an accompaniment to meat. [49] A few of these stones may still be seen in Kintyre. There is one, *in situ*, at the remote ruin of Innean Dunain, near Largiebaan.

21: Shipwrecks

Concerning the Duke's threat not to extend the leases of those of his tenants, or their families, convicted of looting shipwrecks, the outcome is unknown. Nor is there evidence that forfeiture of lease for conviction of plundering was made a 'condition of all leases', but a clause was certainly incorporated into the lease of Clochkeil (1795), Polliwilline (1803) – both farms with coastal boundaries – and Lochorodale (1803), which is well inland. The clause was as follows: 'If the tacksmen or any of their families shall be convicted of plundering or pilfering from any wrecked vessel or goods which may happen to be cast on the shores of Kintyre or of resetting any such goods knowing them to be stolen, then the present lease is to cease and be at an end.'[50] Tradition, reliable or otherwise, maintained that 'a respectable farmer named McWilliam, who found a cask of rum on the shore and kept it, lost his farm for doing so'. [51]

Plundering of shipwrecks was universally engaged in on the coasts of Kintyre, as elsewhere. The morality of looting was not, in the fervour of the occasion, much considered. Poverty dictates its own moral codes, and, for poor folk, the arrival of a ship's cargo, or her wreckage, on a shore close to home, represented a bounty not to be spurned. For many folk, it was definitely a case of the more the merrier, though it has to be said that there is no evidence of deliberate wrecking of ships. It should also be said that there are many accounts of the dangers to which witnesses to shipwrecks exposed themselves in the rescuing of seamen.

The general scarcity of trees in Kintyre, and the expense of buying imported wood, made the beams and timbers from a broken ship irresistible, not least for building purposes. When the brigantine *Saltcoats* stranded below Ballevain on 15 December 1815, her cargo was salvaged and her hull sold to the Coalwork Company of Campbeltown. A few days later, however, 'she was broke in pieces by a violent storm, and a great quantity of the timbers belonging to her were drove on shore'. The company employed a squad of men to gather the wreckage, but other men were gathering on their own initiative, and a heap of that timber was discovered at Mid

30. Knockin stane, containing rainwater, in front of doorway at Innean Dunain ruin, photographed by A. Martin, 19/1/1997.

Darlochan, a farm belonging to the Duke. When a warrant was issued for the arrest of the tenant John Kelly, he incriminated his sons Hector, Archibald, Robert, Peter and John; but the outcome of the case is unknown. [52]

Undoubtedly, the most famous of the innumerable Kintyre shipwrecks was that of the *Charlemagne*, a three-masted iron-hulled clipper which, on 19 March 1857, ran aground in fog at Feochaig, outward bound from Greenock to Australia on her maiden voyage. Two reasons explain the endurance of this shipwreck in local memory – a ballad, sung to the tune of 'Hey Johnny Cope', was written about her, and her general cargo included a large quantity of superlative whisky. As she broke up, the barrels of whisky were washed out of her hold and cast ashore on beaches from Feochaig round to Largiebaan. [53] Few, it may safely be assumed, were ever delivered into the hands of the Receiver of Wrecks.

When the present writer was recording oral traditions and folklore in Kintyre in the 1970s, another wreck which recurred in stories was that of the Anchor Line steam barque *Macedonia*, which, inward bound from New York to Glasgow, ran aground in fog north of the Mull Lighthouse on 30 May 1881. Most of her cargo was salvaged, but, when the weather deteriorated, attempts to save the ship herself were abandoned and she broke up. [54] Her cargo included flour, and Duncan Sinclair (31/3/1977) was told that people walked to the wreck from as far distant as Drumlemble and carried bags home. Calum Bannatyne (12/6/1977) was told that bags were washed ashore as far north as 'the Killean coast'. The outer layer of flour had been spoiled by sea-water, but once that crust was broken, the flour within was perfectly dry, and his mother baked scones with it.

The Duke's interest in shipwrecks and in valuable goods washed on to the shores of his estates was not essentially proprietorial. He was hereditary Vice-Admiral of the Vice-Admiral Court of Argyll, and the Admiral Courts in Scotland had jurisdiction in civil and criminal cases relating to the sea and the tidal zone. [55]

Wrecks might also attract the interest of Collectors of Customs and insurance agents. In 1826, William Watson Jnr. in Kirk Street, Campbeltown, represented Lloyds of London & Liverpool, the Sea Insurance Company of Scotland and the Glasgow & Liverpool Underwriters. [56]

31. Shipwreck on the Kintyre coast, c. 1900. From the MacGrory Collection, courtesy of Argyll & Bute Library Service.
Flotsam from the vessel has been washing ashore. Convictions for plundering were rare, but in 1869 Thomas Sharp and his wife Mary McCaog, at Corphin on the Learside, pled guilty to the theft of a black coat and 1½ yards of Coburg cloth, property of Charles Morgan, master of the schooner *Clyde*, which was wrecked on that coast several months earlier. Thomas was sentenced to thirty days' imprisonment.

Shipwrecks and their salvaged cargoes were generally sold locally, usually by auction at the scene. In 1856, two 'sales of wreck' were conducted at Carskey Bay, Southend. The sale of the brig *J. G. Hall*, which included her stores 'under bond', was conducted by an agent of her owners in Yarmouth, Nova Scotia. Mr Gowdie, Lephenstrath, paid £16 for her hull and £5 for her coals; rigging, spars, etc. were bought by other parties. The schooner *Success* of Belfast realised about £80, including stores, coals, etc. [57] The *J. G. Hall* was on passage from Ardrossan to Corfu with a cargo of coal and the *Success* from 'Mary Pans' – an alternative name for Salt Pans (p. 101) – to Belfast, also with coal, when they were caught in a severe storm earlier that month. [58] In the following month, an oak log 'containing 83 cubic feet' was advertised for public auction at Oragaig, and a 'considerably damaged' 19-foot-long ship's lifeboat at 'First Water'. [59]

Looting, notwithstanding its romantic aspects, was not a victimless crime. Ship-owners stood to suffer heavy losses, especially when a wrecked vessel was uninsured, and the effect on ship-masters may be imagined, having suffered the trauma of losing a vessel, and perhaps also crew-members, then having to witness scenes of plundering.

There is a story that 'the late Dr William McDonald, the laird of Pennyland', Southend, took a corpse in his carriage to the Duke's factor in Campbeltown, and said to him: 'Here is a dead body for you that has been washed ashore; you had better claim it like everything else, and bury it. '[60]

22: Rev. George Robertson and Glebes

The 'Mr. Robertson' referred to in connection with repairs to his manse was the Rev. George Robertson D. D. (Glasgow), minister of the Lowland Church. He was born in Alness, Ross-shire, and graduated M. A. from King's College, Aberdeen. In 1757, he was appointed teacher at George Heriot's Hospital, Edinburgh, after which he went to Campbeltown as assistant teacher at the Grammar School. He then studied theology at the University of Edinburgh, was licensed by the Presbytery of Kintyre in 1761, became assistant minister of the Highland Church in Campbeltown, and was ordained two years later as minister of the Lowland Church. Nominated by the 4th Duke of Argyll, his 'call' was signed by only three members of the Lowland congregation, one of whom was the

32. Smack aground on sea-lashed rocks north of the Battle Isle, Tarbert, an oil painting by William J. McCallien, reproduced by permission of Archibald K. Smith.

Duke's chamberlain, and he was so unpopular that the majority of his congregation seceded and founded Longrow Church in 1767.

In 1761 he had married Mary Stewart, daughter of the Rev. Charles Stewart of the Highland Church. They had one child, Annabella, born in 1776. In 1799 she married Laurence Mackenzie, Collector of Excise, Campbeltown, who is mentioned in Duncan Stewart's 1797 report (No. 1) on negotiations to secure the site for the new Highland church. Rev. Robertson died on 8 August 1820, having, by all accounts, improved his ways and rebuilt his congregation. [61]

There was further discussion in 1790 (Nos. 4 & 5) concerning the Rev. Robertson, his glebe, and a 'hutt' which he was rebuilding. A glebe was the portion of land assigned to a parish minister in addition to his stipend, or salary. Rev. John Smith remarked in 1792 that there were two glebes in the parish, one 'distant and partial' and the other 'under the legal extent'.

The former glebe was his own at Kilchousland, attached to the Gaelic or Highland charge, to which in 1789 four acres were added from the adjoining farm of Crossibeg, as a kind of 'trade-in' for the disputed glebe lands at Kilmichael, which Smith had sub-let (see No. 6 and p. 119). There is a persistent tradition that Smith also occupied the nearby holding of Drumchrottan, also known as North Smerby and now a ruin on the farm of High Smerby, but Rev. A. J. MacVicar could find no documentary evidence of this, [62] nor could the present writer.

The Lowland glebe, popularly known as the Gownie Park, Scots for 'Daisy Field', was that belonging to the Rev. Robertson. Its location is preserved in the name Glebe Street in Campbeltown. The higher, parallel, Dell Road took its name from the road, known as The Dell, to Gallowhill Farm. There were no houses built in that area until the 1870s. [63]

Robertson and Smith each received a stipend of '3 chalders 8 pecks of bear' (barley) and £36 13s 4d sterling. A chalder consisted of 16 bolls, and a boll today is 10 stone. In those days, however, volume measure was the norm, since weights had not been standardised and grain-weighing machines were rare; but these measures varied from place to place.

Smith evidently considered the glebe a liability to ministers who lacked private means. 'A minister who occupies his glebe must keep a horse, (besides hiring another occasionally), a man, a maid, and a herd. The whole produce of four acres will not maintain them, so that he is a loser of more than the full amount of their wages.' [64]

23: Askomil

The Duke here is intimating his intention to give up the leases of Askomilbeg, Askomilmore and Auchalochy, granted by Archibald Campbell of Askomil when the Duke was still John, Marquess of Lorne. These lands, on the north side of Campbeltown Loch, have been extensively built over since the nineteenth century, but in the eighteenth century Askomil basically comprised the farming townships More and Beg (Gaelic *mor* and *beag*, 'big' and 'little'). There was earlier a fortified house of some description, known as Castle Moil or Askomel House, which was outrageously burned in 1598 by Sir James MacDonald, with his father and mother inside it, though they survived the blaze. A later fortification was built on Askomil land in 1639 against the possibility of an invasion by the MacDonald Earl of Antrim. It was garrisoned by some four hundred men under Sir Duncan Campbell of Auchinbreck (who would be executed without trial on the battlefield of Inverlochy in 1645). That fortification was not stone-built, but was an entrenched camp equipped with cannon. Its existence is commemorated in the place-names Fort Argyll and Trench Point. [65]

As Marquess of Lorne, John was leased Askomilbeg in 1770, Askomilmore in 1771, and Auchalochy in 1783, all timed to expire in 1790. He displaced John McStalker, Archibald McMillan, John Curry, Donald McSporran, Robert Smith, James Watson, James Alexander, and others, who shared the tenancy. The annual rent for Askomilbeg was £96 3s, for Askomilmore £84 7s 10d, for Auchalochy £23 17s, and £15 2s 2d for the limestone quarries on Askomilmore, which, by the terms of the lease, could be exploited commercially as well as for the needs of the farms. [66]

The Duke himself, of course, was not in the least actively involved in either farming or quarrying. The lands and quarries would have been let to sub-tenants, who were now to be given notice to quit and whose 'great Arrears' were to be somehow recovered. See answer which follows.

24: Limecraigs House

Limecraigs House in Campbeltown dates from the early eighteenth century and formerly stood within its own policies, of which the orchard would have been a part. Its most notable resident was that 'formidable figure', Elizabeth Tollemache, who died there in 1735. After she separated from her husband, Archibald, 1st Duke of Argyll, and during her widowhood, she lived mainly at Limecraigs, attending to the Kintyre estates and interesting herself in local affairs. Her sons John and Archibald were successively 2nd and 3rd Duke of Argyll, but neither left a male descendant and the title passed to a first cousin, John Campbell of Mamore, father of the 5th Duke. She was buried within the old Lowland Church in Kirk Street, Campbeltown – since 1904 the Highland Church Hall – and is commemorated in the arms of the Royal Burgh of Campbeltown by the Tollemache family of Suffolk's arms, at bottom right. [67]

Limecraigs House still stands, but has been sub-divided into individual dwellings, and the private tree-lined driveway, which led up to it from Kilkerran Road, is now a public road serving Campbeltown Grammar School and the housing developments which now occupy the former grounds. Few venerable trees remain, but in 1843 Limecraigs House was described as being 'embosomed in trees', consisting of ash and plane, and some of them 'upwards of 150 years of age'. [68]

When Gerry and Pat Nugent had the main part of Limecraigs House in the late twentieth century, they found a rusted eighteenth century flintlock pistol concealed in a wall of the building. [69] In the former gamekeepers' house, on the west side of the building, naturalist and author Dugald Macintyre was born in 1870. His father, also Dugald, was a gamekeeper with Argyll Estates for fifty years and 'saw the commencement of game preservation' in Kintyre. [70]

25: Humphrey Graham

Colonel Humphrey Graham, 'an able man of agreeable personality', succeeded Donald Campbell of Sonachan as Chamberlain of Argyll in 1792. [71] The Humphrey Graham who was Provost of Campbeltown, 1789-1791, must have been the same man.

33. Limecraigs House. Photograph by A. Martin, 2011.

26: Rev. Dr John Smith

'Mr Smith' was the Rev. Dr John MacLullich Smith, born in 1747 in Glenorchy, North Argyll. His middle name, MacLullich, ought to have been his surname, but his Jacobite father, having escaped from the battlefield at Culloden in 1746, became an outlaw and changed his name. [72] Dr Smith was minister of the Highland Parish Church, Campbeltown, from 1781 until his death in 1807. When Smith came to Campbeltown in 1781, his church was ruinous and his manse, in Kirk Street, dilapidated. He repaired the manse at his own expense and lived there until about 1796, when he moved with his family to a new house, likewise built at his own expense, in Kilchousland Glebe.

Smith did not live to preach in the new Highland Church – for which he had campaigned stubbornly – but died in the year of its completion, 1807. His funeral cortege from the new church to Kilchousland was said to have been the largest ever seen in Campbeltown. He was buried in a walled enclosure within the ruin of Kilchousland chapel. The marble memorial tablet was erected by his widow, Helen MacDougall, who survived him by some thirty-six years. The inscription says: 'He was a man of great piety, talent and learnings, and discharged every duty of the sacred office with distinguished ability and faithfulness. Zeal in the cause of the Redeemer animated his whole life. '

Smith was a prolific and diverse author in both Gaelic and English. Some of his works, such as his *Statistical Account of the Parish of Campbeltown* (1792) and *A General View of the Agriculture of the County of Argyll* (1798), continue to be read and quoted. As the Rev. Angus J. MacVicar remarked, Smith was 'in the opinion of many, the ablest minister we ever had, not only in Campbeltown, but in Argyllshire – a man of whom the people of Campbeltown and Kintyre should be for ever proud, and whom they should never forget'. Smith 'respected character, wherever he met it, whether among the rich or among the poor' and 'feared nobody'. [73]

27: Kilmichael burial ground

The 'Kilmichael' referred to is the old parish church at NR 698 227, beside the A83 road north of Campbeltown. Both Kilmichael and Kilchousland parishes were united with Kilkerran parish in 1617, after which their chapels fell into disuse. By the beginning of

34. Kilchousland Church, by T. P. White, c. 1865; reproduced from his *Archaeological Sketches in Scotland, District of Kintyre*, Edinburgh 1873.

35. Kilchousland, looking north-east. Photograph by A. Martin, 27/2/2011.

36. Memorial tablet to Rev. Dr John Smith in Kilchousland Chapel, (below) photographed by A. Martin, with, left, Smith's portrait, reproduced by permission of the Highland Parish Church.
Smith's mother Mary Stewart was a sister of 'James of the Glens', hanged for the murder of Colin Campbell of Glenure in Appin in 1752.

the nineteenth century, Kilmichael chapel had been demolished and its stone removed, and no structural remains survive. At the time of the correspondence, the glebe at Kilmichael was obviously still extant and had been let by Dr Smith for another to cultivate, hence the wrangling, which continued. This may have been one A. Beith, who was tenant of Kilmichael Glebe until it was 'excambed and joined to Kilchousland Glebe' (p. 112), and who subsequently went to Lochgilphead. [74]

A memorial in 1792, from Daniel McMillan, tenant in 'Kirkmichael', refers to the houses on the farm having been built on the burial ground there. [75] In 1806, the lease of South Kirkmichael, when granted to Sheriff Duncan Campbell, required him to enclose the churchyard with a 4-ft. -high stone dyke to keep out cattle and to 'preserve the same for cutting grass'. [76]

In 1838, 'old D. McMillan, tenant in Kilmichael', recollected when the church walls were still standing; he was in the habit of climbing them to harry sparrows' nests. He also claimed to have witnessed 'one of the largest funerals that was ever seen in the country going into the kirk-yard'. In 1838, a 'trough stone' could still be seen on the grave of 'John McNab, laird of the Moy', but the inscription had become illegible. In McMillan's house there had been a small window, 'round at the top', but it was given away by Sheriff Campbell's manager to a mason for a house he was building in Millknowe, and Sheriff Campbell used the stones from the church in the building of the Kilmichael farmhouses. [77]

28: James Ferrier

James Ferrier (1744-1829), Writer to the Signet, was the 5th Duke's agent and receiver-general, whose 'loyalty to the Duke and his great abilities made him indispensable to the Duke, who was influenced by him probably more than by any other individual'. He was a son of John Ferrier of Kirkland, Renfrewshire, and in 1767 married Helen Coutts. From 1802 to '26, he was principal clerk of the Court of Session. The novelist and close friend of Sir Walter Scott, Susan Edmonstone Ferrier (1782-1854), was the youngest of his ten children. [78]

29: Langlands family

'Young Langlands' was William, son of George, the Duke's improver and surveyor. In his instructions of the following year, the Duke agreed to an annual salary of £30 for William Langlands, which was the minimum Langlands expected to receive, since he was 'obliged to keep a horse'. The engagement, however, was conditional on Langlands Snr. 's giving William 'his advice and assistance where necessary' without any 'further charge to the Duke' – in other words, training the son in his own time. William was dismissed from the Duke's service seven years later, but the Chamberlain relented on receipt of a 'penitential Letter', and he was retained for a further year.

George Langlands arrived in Kintyre c. 1773. His job was to advise on land division and rotation of crops, and other improvements. In addition, he surveyed and mapped individual farms and also completed an admirable map of Argyll in 1801. According to Andrew McKerral, 'Lieut Langlands' surveyed the Duke's estates in acres, consigning to history the 'pennylands' and 'merklands', and their multiples and fractions, by which system land was valued in money rather than in physical extent. [79] See 'Land Values' below.

Langlands had married Sarah Kitchen on 17 June 1764 in Chollerton, Northumberland. [80] They had nine children, most of whom married into the local community, and descendants of whom remained in Kintyre into the twentieth century. Arthur and Matthew Langlands, Glenbarr Mains, were acquitted on charges of sheep-stealing after a lengthy trial in 1933. [81]

Two sons, at least, had military careers. Roger was a Lieutenant in the Royal Navy when in 1818 he married Mary Taylor, daughter of Lauchlan Taylor in Auchinchoirk (Oatfield), and a Captain when his daughter Mary was born on Sanda in 1832. [82] Major George Langlands, who died in 1851, at the age of 81, in London, served in the 74th Regiment of Foot, 'under the Duke of Wellington in India and on the peninsula'. [83]

It seems likely that Langlands was instrumental in the leasing of south Kintyre farms to farmers from Northumberland and Cumberland in 1775 and 1776, but of that there is no evidence. John and Richard Langlands – from Northumberland, like George – were given the lease of Balnagleck in 1775, [84] but there is no evidence of kinship, though that too must be considered a possibility.

30: Land values

Although the monetary valuation of land was abolished during the 5th Duke's time and replaced with valuation by acreage, separated into 'arable', 'grazing', etc. , many tenants were reluctant or unable to adopt the new system. One of the enumerators in the 1841 Census of Saddell and Skipness Parish appended to his returns the following submission: ' . . . the farmers in the District appointed for him can but in few cases give any tolerably accurate information as to the No. of Acres they possess and no assumed Nos. have been attempted. ' Twenty years later, the Rev. Edward Bradley commented: 'They don't know much in Cantire about the acreage of their farms, and describe them according to their rental. Thus when you ask a Cantire farmer what is the extent of his farm, he will tell you it is a two-hundred pound farm, or whatever its value may be. '[85]

31: Bleachfield

The 'Bleachfield being laid down in another part of the country' would appear to be a reference to the business established by George Langlands (p. 120), to give employment to his eldest son, Ralph. In the 1790s, almost £2000 worth of flax, or lint, was exported from Campbeltown in the form of yarn; yet fifty weavers were employed in and around Campbeltown working cotton yarn received from Glasgow. Most Kintyre farmers, however, chose not to take their lint crop to Langlands' mill, owing to the high cost of having it processed – 2s 6d per stone, or about a quarter of its value.

The mill itself was built in 1792, and an associated bleachfield, for the bleaching and drying of the cloth, was established two years later with the 'encouragement and aid' of the Duke, whose commitment to the project was expressed in the exceptionally long lease – of 38 years – which he gave to Langlands. That field was originally a part of the farm of Strathbeg, and was detached at an annual rent of £9. Langlands was also given, at an annual rent of £4, a pendicle, detached from Drumlemble farm, which had been leased by Colonel Charles Campbell, by then deceased. Strathbeg no longer exists in name, and the whole farm is called Bleachfield.

In 1797, Ralph complained to the Duke that his house was built over the mill and that 'when the whole machinery is at work the noise is so very great that those in the dwelling-house can scarcely hear each other speak'. He requested help to build another house. The mill, which was powered by water drawn from Chiskan Burn by means of a lade and dam, was converted to wool-production some time prior to 1814. When Ralph's 38-year lease of Bleachfield expired in 1833, it passed to Humphrey Langlands, but five years later Humphrey was evicted and his belongings sold by public auction. He lost a cow, twenty-one stacks of oats, three stacks of barley, two stacks of beans, eight sacks of oats, potatoes – both stored and still in the fields – and all his household goods. The sum of £244 16s 4d was raised for the Duke of Argyll. [86] In the Killean and Kilchenzie Census of 1851, Humphrey, described as an annuitant, aged 58, was living at Muasdale with his wife, children and a servant, Effy McKay.

In 1861, Samuel Mitchell in Strath was advertising at Lintmill a 'complete set of machinery for spinning and other branches of woollen manufacture', in addition to carding and dyeing facilities. [87]

32: Lintmill

That industrial settlement became a small village, known as Lintmill, by the roadside west of Stewarton. Its houses could be reached by external stone stairs leading down to them from the main road. In its heyday, Lintmill could boast a cartwright's and joiner's workshop, a grocer's shop and an inn (whose keeper in 1841 was Donald McNish). Wool production ceased about 1910, after which the population of Lintmill began to decline and the unoccupied buildings to fall into disrepair. The ruins were finally demolished in the late 1950s to facilitate road improvements, and the rubble was removed for re-use. [88] Only a broken wall now remains to mark the site of a once-thriving community.

The population censuses give some indication of the character of the village. In 1851, there were 15 households and 59 inhabitants, including a wool-carder, Charles McFarlane, a wright, John Revie, and a farina (potato flour) manufacturer, John Greenlees, with the rest agricultural labourers. In 1901, there were nine households and 45 inhabitants, including a road-contractor, James Kerr, a wool-spinner, Duncan Ramsay (born in Tillicoultry) and a joiner and cartwright, Duncan Mauchline (born in Pollokshaws). Architect H. E. Clifford (1852-1932) had a Lintmill connection. His mother Rebecca Anderson's father John was a wool-carder at Lintmill and appears there in the Census of 1841.

37. Remains of the Lintmill village. Photograph by Judy Martin, 2011.

After Lintmill village fell into disuse, the site was occupied by families of Travellers, or 'tinkers' (from their original occupation as itinerant tin-smiths). In a census of Travellers taken in April 1964, John W. Townsley and George Townsley and their families were camped there; and later that year, John and Isobel Townsley and family. William McKerral, who farmed Bleachfield from 1961 until his retirement, remembered Townsley families at Lintmill in the 1960s, when they forked sheaves at harvest, and into the 1970s, when their labour changed to building bales behind the baler.

The last Travellers there were Anthony Stewart, his wife Jean Townsley, and their family, who occupied two caravans on the hard standing of the earlier public road. On the afternoon of 11 January, 1984, while attempting to secure a caravan against a sudden gale, 32-year-old Mrs Stewart was killed when the caravan blew over on her. This tragedy appears to have ended the Travellers' association with Lintmill, but in that decade, in any case, camping ceased among the Kintyre families, which were all allocated public housing in Campbeltown. [89] See this writer's *An Historical and Genealogical Tour of Kilkerran Graveyard*, pp. 37-39, for a brief account of the history of Travellers in Kintyre and the main familes – Townsleys, MacPhees and Williamsons – associated with Kintyre.

33: Timber for building

Timber and trees were seldom far from the Duke's thoughts. In the above instructions, he is considering ways of obtaining roofing timber for his Kintyre tenants at as little cost to the estate as possible. In his reply, the Chamberlain noted rather vaguely that 'a vessel or two' brought cargoes of the Duke's own timber from Inveraray to Campbeltown, but that no merchant in Campbeltown was willing to risk shipping a cargo of coal to the Baltic and bringing back a cargo of timber. The coal would clearly have been mined at Drumlemble, and therefore – as acknowledged throughout the history of coal extraction in Kintyre – of inferior quality. The coal-timber trade from certain East Coast ports was a thriving concern. That trade survived at Bo'ness until the mid-twentieth century, but, as Robert W. Smith points out, 'Bo'ness is advantageously close to the Baltic, Campbeltown anything but'. [90]

There would have been Campbeltown vessels capable of voyaging to Baltic ports such as Danzig, but the prospect of a

38. A Travellers' camp in Kintyre, c. 1935. Photograph by Dugald Semple. Semple, who died in 1964, was a pacifist, vegan, author, lecturer, naturalist and photographer, well known in his day as the 'Apostle of the Simple Life'. He was a frequent visitor to Kintyre and became friendly with the last laird of Saddell, John MacLeod Campbell (p 96), who allowed him to camp on his land and then build a hut at Port na Gael in Saddell Bay. Campbell, too, shared an interest in Travellers. According to his obituary, he had 'made a special study of the lore of the tinkers and other nomads'.

potentially hazardous passage round the Mull of Kintyre, through the Minches and northabout between Orkney and Shetland on a venture from which the Duke stood to save on freight costs while the commercial risk was the merchants' alone, probably dissuaded them from committing themselves.

In the instructions for the following year, 1792, the Duke asks his Chamberlain to compare the costs of building a house with Inveraray timber and one with foreign timber. The Chamberlain reported that an 'experiment' had been conducted at Christlach, Southend, where two tenants' houses were built. He submitted an account of relative costs, which clearly demonstrated that home-grown timber was more economical, prompting from the Duke, in 1793, a further set of instructions concerning the ordering of timber from Inveraray and the cheapest means of shipping it – either a Campbeltown vessel could take a cargo of coal to Inveraray and return with timber, or an Inveraray vessel could take a cargo of timber to Campbeltown and return with coal.

Argyll Estate supplied the couples and rafters for house-building or repair directly to tenants, though occasionally, if a tenant found, or was asked to find, his own timber, he would be paid the 'comprysed value' of it. Existing timber would, as far as practicable, be re-used, an economy which the Estate naturally encouraged. From a contemporaneous estimate for the building of a dwelling-house 30 feet by 16 feet, it is clear that timber was the most expensive item, accounting for £13 5s of the total £30, or 44 per cent, even without the wood necessary for doors and windows, which are not specifically costed. [91]

The main roofing component was the 'cruck-frame', which rested not on the wall-head, but at floor level or a little above floor level. Until the nineteenth century, the prevailing turf or turf-and-stone walling of common dwellings was too weak to carry A-frames. The cruck-frame could be formed of a single piece of timber, with a natural bend, or of two pieces pegged together. [92] From the Tiree chamberlain's report three years previously, an idea of the quantities of timber emerges, though dimensions are not specified. John McArthur in Hillipole, for example, was supplied with 8 'couples' (cruck-frames), 8 'pantrees' (ribs) and 100 'kabbers' (the timbers laid over the ribs of a couple, from Gaelic *cabar*). Other tenants' allowances varied, but all timber was supplied from the 'woods of Lochsunart', [93] the Duke's own plantations in Morvern.

Larger country houses – such as those belonging to lairds – and some town houses were constructed of mortared stone and roofed with slate. In 1744, the 3rd Duke offered leases of exceptional length – i. e. , of 57 years – to those of his tenants in Campbeltown who were prepared to build two-storied houses with slated roofs, and short leases – of 14 years – to those unable to slate theirs. [94]

34: Rural buildings

In the mid-nineteenth century, an improved model of farm steading was generally adopted. These are the steadings which can be seen to this day: two-storied farmhouses built of dressed and mortared stone and with well-pitched slated roofs, now looking positively elegant beside the bungalows which have sprung up around them. These steadings were usually built in a square, with byre, barn, and workers' accommodation joined to the house, and the courtyard entered through an opening known as the 'close'. The erection of these more substantial steadings was no longer the responsibility of tenants, but of local masons contracted to estates. On 14 March 1855, for example, a notice appeared in the *Argyllshire Herald* inviting contractors to tender for 'a Farm Steading to be erected on the Farm of Clochkeel', plans and specifications available for consultation in the office of the Argyll Estate chamberlain.

Earlier steadings were crudely and haphazardly built. Even the best of them were relatively primitive: long, narrow, one-storey structures with thatched roofs. They tended to be draughty, leaky, smoky and gloomy within. Windows were few and small, and, in the more basic of these dwellings, the fire – which provided heat, a little light and the only means of cooking – was placed on the floor.

Two pre-improvement Learside steadings in close proximity to each other demonstrate a contrast. The one at Glenmurril, on the south side of Balnabraid Glen, represents the oldest type of stone building and may belong to the late eighteenth century. It was constructed in three small compartments under one roof and is without mortar and lacking a fireplace and chimney. Balnabraid, facing it across the glen, is a more substantial structure, probably from the early nineteenth century, and has lime-mortared walls and a fireplace and chimney in one of the gables. Both were deserted in the latter half of the nineteenth century. [95]

The houses belonging to the cottars or 'day labourers' were even more primitive. This class was the most numerous of the rural

39. 'Mainland coast, Argyll' thatched cottage, 1946. Reproduced from *The Thatched Houses of the Old Highlands*, Colin Sinclair, Edinburgh 1953.

40. Glenmurril ruin at bottom right. Balnabraid ruin is on the opposite side of the glen, amid trees. Photograph by A. Martin, 1987.

41. Balnabraid ruin in 1986, with sycamore growing through the floor. The fireplace lintel in the surviving gable collapsed several years afterwards.
Photograph by A. Martin.

42. 'Interior of a West Highland Cottage, Cantyre', drawn in 1859 by Edward Bradley and published in his *Glencreggan* (1861). In the upper left-hand corner, fish – probably small saithe – hang to dry, and in the lower right-hand corner peats are piled ready for use in the chimney-less fire, above which a pot-hook hangs.

inhabitants. Three or four families, typically, would congregate on one farm – the bigger the farm, the more cottars, generally. The Rev. Donald MacDonald, minister of Killean and Kilchenzie Parish, described these cot-houses in 1843 as 'wretched hovels, rudely constructed without any mortar, one division of which is occupied by the family, and the other converted into a kind of byre, and often no partition in the hut to separate the human from the brute creation'. These houses were held from year to year, typically at a rent of £4 or £5, 'and the tenants, who are their landlords, can dispossess them at pleasure'. Along with the hut went a small kail garden, 'scanty' pasture for a cow, and a patch of potato ground on the outskirts of the farm. Rents were paid from the earnings of their children, whom they hired out as servants throughout the district. [96]

The great artist William McTaggart was born in 1835 at Aros, the son of just such a cottar, Dugald McTaggart, who earned a living variously as labourer, illicit whisky-distiller and peat-carter. The family left or was evicted from Aros a few years after William's birth and moved to another smallholding at Flush, on the outskirts of Campbeltown. William left no record of his childhood within a poor, Gaelic-speaking family. Perhaps he preferred to forget or obscure the worst of it. Certainly, when he married Mary Holmes in 1863, he described his father's occupation as 'farmer', which was rather stretching the truth. [97]

Yet he never repudiated his heritage, even at the height of his fame and prosperity. On the contrary, his Gaelic upbringing in Kintyre enhanced his art, and, although he never settled back in Kintyre, he returned year after year to paint its seascapes. The question of his birthplace is one which arises repeatedly, but the reality is that even if the precise location had been recorded – and he could probably have done that himself in his own lifetime – it is unlikely that any trace of the building will have survived, at least above ground. The bulk of it was probably turf.

Even such a substantial steading as Lochsanish, which stood in the Laggan to the west of Aros, has disappeared. After the buildings were abandoned, they were demolished and the rubble used to fill in four craters left on Parkfergus farm after a Luftwaffe bombing raid on 6 November 1940. [98] The site is entirely cleared now, and unless one knew where it stood, Lochsanish – which compared in scale with nearby Parkfergus – could not be identified on the ground.

43. Nineteenth century Kintyre farmhouse and steading. A sketch, dated 1987, by Mackean Stewart, published on front cover of *Kintyre Magazine* No. 21.

35: Dr Charles Rowatt

Dr Charles Rowatt (1732-1826) belonged to an old Lowland family in South Kintyre. His ancestor, Alexander Rowatt, factor to the Dowager Countess of Argyll in Kintyre, was taken prisoner in the aftermath of the Earl of Argyll's Rebellion of 1685, questioned by the Scots Privy Council, acquitted and released. [99]

Dr Charles, who was tangling with the Duke on two fronts, was a well-known physician in Campbeltown. He was proprietor of Kilkivan, near Machrihanish, [100] but had a house on the Castlehill, Campbeltown, which was known as Rowatt's Close. In 1819, George McNeal raised an action in the Court of Session against Rowatt concerning his Kilkivan tenants (p. 86). Dr Rowatt, who appears not to have married, was a founder member of Longrow Church and evidently established the town's first lending library under the auspices of the church. Daniel Mactaggart, founder of the Campbeltown legal firm, named a son, Charles Rowatt Mactaggart, in the doctor's honour, and that son himself became a medical practitioner. [101] A plan of Argyll Street and the projected new street, showing Dr Rowatt's feu, is in the Argyll Papers, Bundle 3057, dated 1792.

That Rowatt was an eccentric character is clear from a nineteenth century description: 'Look at him, shuffling along the street, dressed in slouched beaver, black silk cloak, with tippet, velvet knee breeches, black silk stockings, and shoes with large silver buckles. He was a unique figure. Dr Rowatt's name was a household word, for he claimed acquaintance with very many of the community on their introduction into the world.' [102]

36: Kelp

With this instruction, the Duke signals his intention to cut himself in on the profits of the kelp industry. Kelp – the term applies both to the seaweed and to its product when burnt – was used in the manufacture of glass, soda and soap. Kelp-making had begun early in the eighteenth century and prospered from the final quarter of that century into the early nineteenth century, when alternative and cheaper sources of industrial alkali began to corner the market. The work, which was dirty and demanding, involved gathering and then burning seaweed in kilns built on the foreshore. 'Kiln' is the accepted term, but it rather glorifies what was generally a shallow

44. Main Street of Campbeltown looking towards Castlehill, by James Stewart, c. 1835. From *Views of Campbelton and Neighbourhood*, William Smith Jr., Edinburgh 1835.

rectangular pit, crudely bordered with rocks. The present writer, in the mid-1980s, surveyed stretches of the Kintyre shores and identified a small number of kilns, but some of these now elude his efforts to rediscover them – presumably they have disintegrated or been covered by storms. Wrack, when burned, melts; and when the molten mass had cooled, it would be broken up and stored until a quantity sufficient for sale had accumulated. When Tarbert-born geologist Professor William J. McCallien visited Sanda in 1925, he noted an 'old kelp store on the shore of the northern bay'. [103]

The Duke's request for particulars on the Kintyre kelp industry was answered that same year, but the report, regrettably, was not preserved with the correspondence. In the following year, it is clear from his instructions (No. 3) that his intention was to claim ownership of the seaweed and so exercise full control over the industry. His tenants were to be given notice that in future they were not to cut kelp – their previous freedom had been 'only by indulgence' – and instead the resource was to be leased for periods of three, seven or nineteen years; but those tenants who had been accustomed to making kelp would be compensated until expiry of their leases. The edict had scarcely dried on the paper, however, when it was 'countermanded for the present', and another afterthought jotted in the margin, 'Qu: a part to be allowed for manure', this latter note an acknowledgement of the necessity of seaweed as fertiliser.

After these instructions were written, the Kintyre Chamberlain received a letter from the Duke's principal agent, James Ferrier, confirming that the Duke had 'changed his mind as to taking the Kelp making into his own hands immediately or rather the selling of it, and resolved only to reserve power in all new Leases to take possession of the Shores and Kelp growing thereon and to manufacture and carry away the Kelp on allowing to the Tenant the value as stated in your late report of the Rent. This reservation you will please add to each of the Leases not yet given out before you deliver them'.

The 'reservation' took the following form, as in the lease of Mid Peninver, granted in 1817: 'Reserving also the sea ware or wreck growing, or that may happen to grow, or be driven on the shore of the said lands fit for making of kelp ...'[104] (As an aside, on I October 1819, the tenant in High Peninver, James Greenlees, wrote to the

45. Kelp-kiln on Island of Gigha, 1987. Photograph by Judy Martin.

Chamberlain complaining that his neighbour in South Peninver, Duncan Stewart, had hindered his men when they were gathering, for fertiliser, 'Drift Seaware' which had washed on to Stewart's part of the shore. [105])

The outcome of the Duke's efforts to control the kelp industry in Kintyre is unknown, but in other parts of his estate – notably Mull – his plans met with such resistance that in the end he was forced to continue to allow his tenants to sell their own kelp, and to take his share of the proceeds through increased rents. [106]

The only published account of kelp-making in Kintyre was written by 'Cuthbert Bede' (Rev. Edward Bradley), who noted that about a sixth of the market value of the kelp made on Glencreggan shore was paid as a 'royalty' to the laird. During the 1859 season, kelp fetched £6 per ton, but it took, on average, 24 tons of weed to produce one ton of kelp. The main market was in Glasgow. [107]

The kelp industry was nothing like as important to the Kintyre economy as it was to the economy of the Hebrides, where the viability of entire crofting communities hung on the fluctuations of markets. In Kintyre, for a start, crofts were rare and farms substantial. The generality of tenant-farmers in Kintyre would have had no physical involvement in kelp-burning, which was left to sub-tenants – the cottars and their families.

The present writer, while collecting Kintyre oral history in the 1970s, recorded a woman who remembered seeing the last of the kelp-burners at work, the smoke of their fires burning late into the summer evenings as they raked the kilns. She was Margaret Littleson, born Margaret Black at Dalkeith Farm in 1881. Her few memories of the kelp-burners are preserved in the present writer's *Kintyre Country Life*, which contains an account of the industry in Kintyre; but the last word should go to Edward Bradley, whose observations were recorded no great distance from Margaret Black's birthplace, in a little bay below Glencreggan. Bare-legged women, 'dressed in their oldest clothes tucked up to the knees', are pulling wrack from the tidal rocks where it grows.

'When they have gathered a lapful, [they] carry it to the shore, or lay it on heaps upon the rocks, from whence it will be transferred to the cart. The kelp-cart is made to perform many journeys backwards and forwards from the half-sunken rocks to the shore; and the horse plunges through the breakers and up the loose shingle, scattering

46. Kelp-making near Glencreggan, Kintyre, drawn in 1859 by Rev. Edward Bradley and published in his *Glencreggan* (1861).

the bright wave-drops from him at every plunge, while his driver freely uses the whip and screams at him in Gaelic horse talk. Two other men attend to the fires, turning over the heaps of smouldering kelp, and keeping them in a blaze within their circles of stone, or in shallow pits, while the columns of smoke go up like beacon-fires and are answered by hundreds of others along the coast ...'[108]

37: Census of 1792

This comprehensive survey was conducted, parish by parish, in the following year, and bound in with the Chamberlain of Argyll's Accounts from October 1792 to October 1793, lodged at Inveraray Castle. A. I. B. Stewart (1915-1998), a native of Campbeltown, procurator-fiscal in the town from 1941-1974, and a prominent member of the Kintyre Antiquarian and Natural History Society, painstakingly transcribed the list, which was published in 1991 by the Scottish Record Society as *List of Inhabitants upon the Duke of Argyle's Property in Kintyre in 1792*, and remains a treasure-house of genealogical data.

38: Coal canal and moss rooms

The place-name 'Moninaclive' has not hitherto been recorded, but the location is described in the Chamberlain's answers of the following year as 'below the Lands of Drummore', which places it in the area to the immediate west of Campbeltown, where the townsfolk of the time had their 'moss rooms', or banks for peat-cutting. The first element is clearly *monagh*, Gaelic for moss or peat, while 'clive' could be *cliabh*, genitive *cleibh*, 'creel', 'basket'. [109] This could tie in with earlier names for the farm now known as Gortan: 'Gortancliabh', 'Gortancliach' and 'Gort na Glia'. The location of Dr Rowatt's original peat-bank, which was in the way of the canal's final stage, was also in that area, to the south of Moninaclive.

The dispute was subsequently settled by the doctor's acceptance of 'an equal quantity of new moss marked out to him' at Moninaclive. 'Mossroom' was the name of the area between Gortan and Moy farms, [110] through which the canal passed. Another bogland place-name, which was presumably lost when peat-cutting ceased in that area, appears in a notebook kept by James Watt (see below): 'Culmhor' or 'Kilmore', described as a marsh near Craigs. Ian A. Fraser suggests that it may represent *Cul Mor*, 'the big back place'. [111]

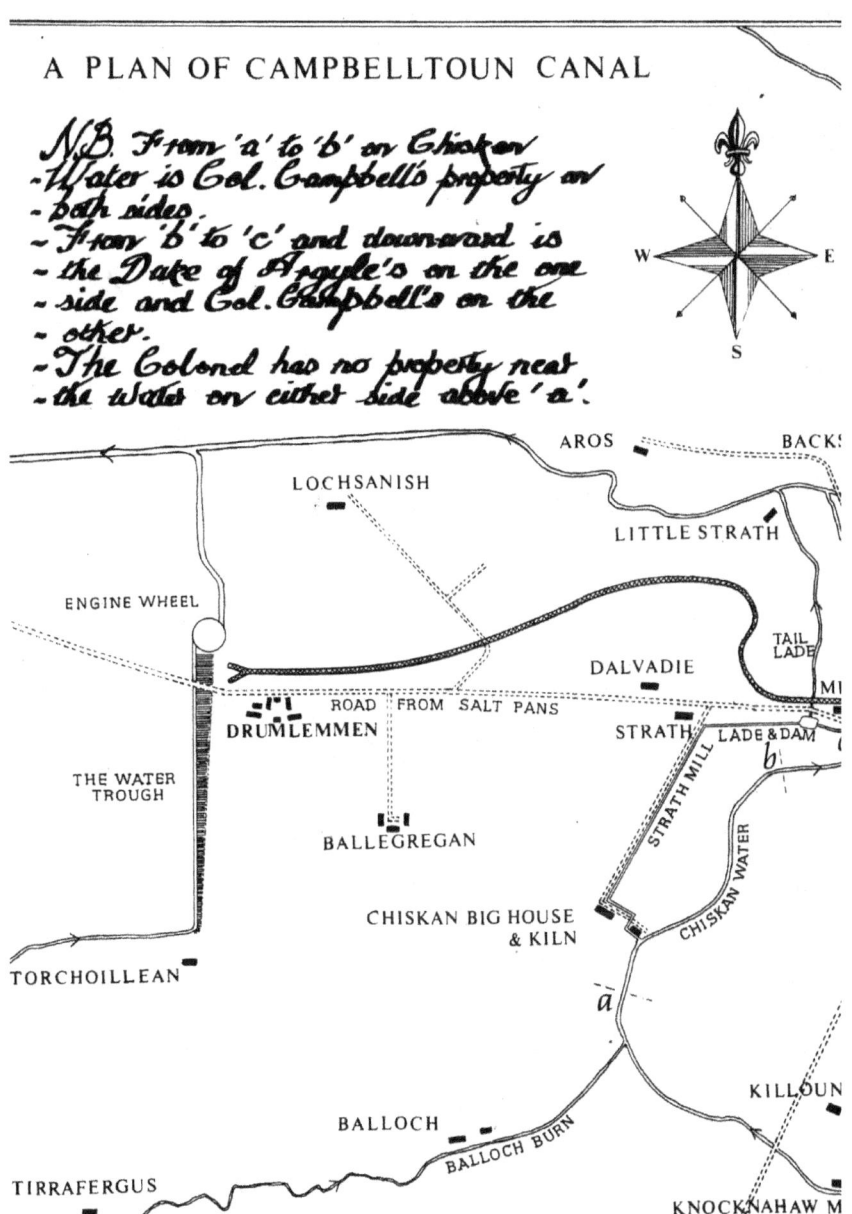

47. Campbeltown canal, c. 1795, adapted from a plan in the Duncan Colville Papers in Argyll & Bute Council Archive, and published in its entirety across the covers of *Kintyre Magazine* No. 41. This reproduction is from the back cover only, omitting the eastern section.

The coal canal project was initiated by Charles McDowall of the Drumlemble Coalworks (p. 100), who brought renowned Scottish engineer James Watt to Kintyre in June 1773 to conduct a preliminary survey. The canal – which, in present-day terms, ran from West Drumlemble farm steadings to the foot of Albyn Avenue – was constructed between 1783 and 1791, and was in use until shortly after the mid-nineteenth century. Coal was transported from the mine at Drumlemble in three horse-drawn barges, replacing pack-horses and carts. Colonel Charles Mactaggart reckoned that coal was used by 'the better class people', but that compared with peat there wasn't a lot of it burned. By the end of the century, about 14 tons of Drumlemble coal were being brought into town daily at a cost of 7 shillings a ton. [112]

That the canal had an occasional recreational value appears in a report in 1851 of the children in John Montgomery's schools in Campbeltown being 'treated to an excursion to Salt Pans on the shore of the great Atlantic, and, in the evening, to a Soiree at Lintmill'. A total of 171 children walked in procession to the coal depot in Campbeltown, whence they were conveyed along the canal to Drumlemble, to complete the journey west on foot. 'The boats started at 11 A. M. , amidst the cheering of the multitude, which had collected on both sides of the Canal to witness the novel, but pleasing sight. As the boats glided along bearing their lively freight, adorned with various flags, fluttering gaily in the breeze, the scene was enlivened by the children singing at intervals some of the lovely hymns taught them in the school, as well as by the beautiful landscape which at every turn was bursting on the view, and the cheers that were ever exchanging as we passed the various groups of people along the banks. '[113]

39: Duncan Stewart, new Chamberlain

Notice the appearance of a new chamberlain. That Captain Duncan Stewart, Esq. , of Glenbuckie, was of Jacobite and Episcopalian stock may appear somewhat anomalous in a servant of the Campbells of Argyll. As A. I. B. Stewart remarked: 'It says much for the Duke of Argyll's generosity that he appointed a Stewart, of Appin blood, as his Chamberlain, so soon after the '45. '[114] Indeed, the 5th Duke and Duncan Stewart's father, John Glas Stewart of Benmore, were both on the battlefield of Culloden in 1746, on opposite sides: Campbell lived and Stewart died.

Captain Stewart married Margaret, second daughter of Duncan Stewart Esq. , of Ardsheal, was appointed provost of Campbeltown nine times from 1792, and in 1798 purchased the estate of Knockrioch, near Stewarton, which village took its name from the family.

When Duncan Stewart was appointed Chamberlain in 1790, his salary was £140 with an allowance of £8 for travelling to Inveraray to settle accounts. By 1803, his salary had increased to a pre-taxation total of £195 10s, which included £8 for attendance at Inveraray and £5 for coals. [115]

Duncan's son, John Lorne Stewart (1800-78), was born in Kintyre and on the death of his father succeeded him as Chamberlain of Kintyre in 1829. He married Mary Campbell of Ardmore, Islay, and with her had three sons and two daughters. Like his father before him, he was provost of Campbeltown, for six years from 1835. He was instrumental in the foundation of Saint Kiaran's Scottish Episcopal Church in Campbeltown in 1848. Having sold the estate of Glenbuckie in 1856, he purchased the island of Coll, where he died. He was a noted agricultural improver, farming Glenahervie, Tomaig and High and Low Knockrioch, and was not without his admirers; but he had his enemies too.

He fought a duel in 1827 with Captain Frederick Campbell (p. 166), and in 1852 was the subject of an anonymous verse satire, 'Bubly Jock', which distressed him so much that he engaged a Campbeltown solicitor, David Colville, to investigate the publication. Suspicion ultimately fell on Captain Charles McKay, a retired seaman with business interests, and a frequent contributor of prose and poetry to the *Campbeltown Journal*. Stewart's character was attacked on many fronts, including grinding the poor, raising rents of farms and eviction of cottars. It was supposed that McKay's father, or grandfather, had been evicted from a Largieside farm, hence his contempt for Stewart.

The poem runs to eleven verses of six lines each, is Burnsian in style and is a creditable piece of literature, except that it is highly allusive and localised. A 'bubbly jock' in Scots is a turkey, and the quotation which heads the composition rather sets the tone: 'Bubly Jock, your mother's a witch/ And a' your weans are warlocks. ' (The version which R. W. Smith's mother knew was, 'Bubbly Jock, yir mother's a witch, she wears an auld mutch and lives in a ditch', and this would be chanted by children whenever they encountered a turkey. [116])

141

See A. I. B. Stewart's exemplary analysis of the poem's content and background in 'Bubly Jock', *Kintyre Magazine* No. 27. [117]

The fifth and last laird of Knockrioch, Lorn MacNeill Stewart, died in Campbeltown in 1927 at the age of 68. He was the eldest son of Captain Duncan Stewart of Knockrioch and Margaret Farooza MacNeill of the Colonsay family. His main interest was in the breeding of black-faced sheep on Tomaig, one of the estate farms. He 'took no share in public work' and died unmarried. [118]

40: Schools

The Chamberlain, in his answer, reported that two substantial slate-roofed schoolhouses had been built, one in Glen Breackerie, Southend, and the other at 'Links of Peninver'. In the following year, 1793, a 'subscription paper' from tenants in Glen Breackerie referred to the 'School House at Culinlongart'. [119] The 'links' at Peninver must have been Traigh Reidh, 'Flat Strand', over which horses were raced, and which is now a caravan site. [120]

In 1819, the Rev. Daniel Kelly, minister in Southend, wrote to the Chamberlain to say that he had applied to the 'Gaelic Schools Society' for a temporary school for the Learside. [121] Three years later, in 1822, a petition was received from tenants on the Learside requesting a cow's grass and kailyard for a Scottish Society for the Propogation of Christian Knowledge schoolmaster; there were about a hundred children in the district. [122] The schoolmaster was Ewan McMaster, who married Flora MacKay, Erradil, one of the Learside farms close to the school, on 9 June 1821. [123] In Keil, Southend, there is a stone erected to Mary Livingston, died 12 March 1836, aged 62, wife of Robert Dunbar, 'late schoolmaster Glenbreckry'.

By 1843, there were four schools in Southend Parish alone, including the one at Glenahervie, to which the Duke of Argyll contributed £4 annually. [124] In the eighteenth century, tenants' rents sometimes included a small sum which went towards the local schoolmaster's salary.

Two of the rural schoolmasters during the 6th Duke's time are known by name from petitions sent to him. John Taylor at Killean in 1808 declared that the old ruinous schoolhouse there was uninhabitable and asked for ground and assistance in building a new schoolhouse. In 1811, John Stewart, Kilchenzie, stated that he had acted as parochial schoolmaster and catechist for 30 years and complained of the lack of a proper dwelling-house and schoolhouse.

BUBLY JOCK.

"BUBLY JOCK, YOUR MOTHER'S A WITCH
AND A' YOUR WEANS ARE WARLOCKS."

YOU miserable miser bitch,
Sin' ye ha'e made me use the switch,
I mean to gie you sic a twitch,
    Athwart the hurdies,
Ye'll wish ye had a thicker breech
    Upon your sturdies.

Your conduct weel deserves satire,
Frae end to end o' braid Kintyre,
For ye've been poutrin' in the mire
    Full forty years;
An how ye're than your maister higher
    The people speirs.

Ye aye ha'e been on mischief bent,
Sin' up amang the craws ye went,
To grind the poor and rise the rent
    O' mony a farm:
The deil his aid has surely lent
    To plot sic harm.

A hundred cottar-bodies poor,
Ye caused to turn outside the door;
And for to make their ruin sure,
    Ye tax'd the peats,
Quist, dried and drawn frae moss and moor
    Wi' toilsome sweats.

The very wreck, by tempest driven
Upon the shore of Skerrie's Riven—
A blessing sent the poor by Heaven—
    Ye e'en must tax,
And a' to Kelp-contractors given,
    To swal your packs.

How many folks ha'e ye brak doun ?
That's seen this day in Campbeltoun
Wi' runty auld nags crawling roun'
    To win their bread,
An shov'd some lousy Lallan loon
    Right owre their head.

Fy ! BUBLY JOCK ! fu' weel we ken
(When ye was laird o' Bucky Glen)
How ye came by the but and ben
    Of Gowan Bank,
And kept somebody in your den
    Till he was crank.

But a' that e'er was said or sung,
Or cramm'd in folks heads to the bung,
Completely in the shade is flung,
    JOCK, by your loups,
When ye contrived to save the d—g
    Frae bodie's doups.

The auld Town-Council interfer'd;
And dang the biggings that ye rear'd,
For every honest body fear'd
    Some plague or trouble;
Aud oh ! but ye was unco sweart
    To burst the *Bubble*.

A hantal mair I ken abont you,
But honest language winna suit you;
The Duke himsel' began to doot you—
    Now—did he not ?
And sairly, man, aboot it put you,
    When he sent S——tt.

Now, BUBLY JOCK ! tak my advice,
Your dealins' ha'e na been sae nice,
Altho' ye hear a *Judas* twice
    Upon a Sunday,
Auld Nick can grip you in a trice
    Upon the Monday.

48. 'Bubly Jock', reproduced in 1990 in *Kintyre Magazine* No. 27, p. 3.

The old schoolhouse had been demolished in 1801 and he asked for a replacement. [125]

There was a schoolmaster in Campbeltown as early as 1622, and a Grammar School was established in 1686, adding Latin, Greek and English Grammar to the existing elementary curriculum. [126] In the Argyll Papers, there is an estimate, dated 5 March 1791, for a schoolhouse and dwelling-house intended to be built in Campbeltown. [127] John Smith, writing in 1792, remarked on a charity school in Campbeltown, supported by the Duke of Argyll and the Scottish Society for the Propogation of Christian Knowledge, which for many years accommodated more than a hundred children, but could 'never receive all the objects', owing to the number of 'poor widows and helpless orphans' annually created by the 'perilous trade' of fishing. [128]

41: James Maxwell

'Mr Maxwell', already mentioned as an arbiter of boundary disputes, was James Maxwell (1758-1829), the Duke's chamberlain in Mull and Morvern. He was born in Kintyre of Renfrewshire Covenanting stock: the family's progenitor, Robert Maxwell, sought refuge among the Lowland planters after the battle of Bothwell Brig (1679) and remained in Kintyre after his freedom was no longer at risk. James was sent to Inveraray to complete his education and there gained a training in law, but, more important for him, he also gained the favour of the Duke of Argyll. He was appointed Sheriff Substitute of Kintyre and in 1786 was elected provost of Campbeltown when only 27 years old.

When appointed chamberlain in 1787, he left Campbeltown and settled in Aros, Mull, of which he received a tack from the 5th Duke. He married Jessie MacNeill (1762-1828), a daughter of Lachlan MacNeill of Drimdrissaig and Elizabeth Campbell of Drumtroon, and had nine children, the eldest of whom, Nancy, married Dr Norman Macleod, minister of the Gaelic Church in Campbeltown. Popularly known as *Caraid nan Gaidheal*, 'Friend of the Gael', he was an influential Gaelic writer. Their son, also Norman, was born in Campbeltown in 1812 and followed his father into the ministry. None of James Maxwell's five sons left any children. James Macdonald, in his *General View of the Agriculture of the Hebrides* (1811), described Maxwell as 'one of the most active and intelligent men in Mull, or indeed in the western isles'. [129]

49. Campbeltown Grammar School, from *Picturesque Campbeltown, Southend and Machrihanish*, c. 1910. The tree in the wall at the school entrance was known as 'Norman Macleod's Tree', after the Rev. Dr Norman Macleod (1812-72), Chaplain to Queen Victoria and a well-known writer and preacher in his time, who was educated at Campbeltown Grammar School.

42: John Kell, Ballybrennan

John Kell was one of the northern English farmers brought into South Kintyre by the 5th Duke to encourage improvement in agricultural practices. He was given a 19-year lease of Ballybrennan in 1775 jointly with Richard Thompson. Both came from Northumberland, Kell from Elrington, Netherwarden, and Thompson from Haltwhistle. The annual rent was set at £39 sterling, along with 24 'carriages' (p. 81) and produce, including 10 bushels of flour, to be milled from wheat grown on the farm, and its value deductible from the rent. [130] A 'fall' is literally the distance over which a measuring rod falls, 6 ells or 6.22 imperial yards, but latterly equivalent to a pole (5 ½ yards). [131]

In the following year, the Chamberlain was instructed (No. 13) to inform George Langlands and son William that the Duke was 'not pleased with their conduct in the Sett of the Farm of Balibrunan as I see clearly that by the undervaluation of the Father and Improper interference of the Son I have been led to lett that Farm at £40 yearly below its value'. The nature of the alleged impropriety isn't clear, unless – merely a guess – favouritism was involved, Kell and Langlands being fellow-Northumbrians. John Kell's lease was due for renewal in 1794, the year after the Duke's complaint. Unfortunately, that lease appears to be missing, but that Kell continued in Ballybrennan is clear from other sources, including the Work Horse Tax of 1797. [132]

When the lease – or leases, since the farm was in two divisions – came up again for renewal, in 1812 the north division went to Archibald Smith, 'late sub-tenant of Bealachanty', replacing John McIlreavie, at a rent of £126, and the south division, in 1813, went to David Andrew, the sitting tenant, at £105. [133] Even considering that rent in kind and services had been abolished by then, the combined rental of £231 represents a hefty increase over Kell and Thompson's £39 fewer than 40 years earlier.

Thompson had been in Ballybrennan for about eight years when, in 1783, he declared that he would have to return to England, since his lands – he was 'proprietor of Low House', Haltwhistle – were to be enclosed. [134]

43: Clay and its exploitation

The letter, rejecting the sample as useless in the manufacture of crockery, is reproduced below. R. W. Smith[135], suggests tentatively that the 'soapy earth' might have been fireclay found in association with coal measures, and the basic material for drain-and sewer-pipe manufacture. In fact, clay of some description was later exploited in South Kintyre. In 1805, Donald Campbell, merchant in Campbeltown, in a memorial concerning the Whin Park – near Whinhill, Witchburn road – referred to the clay soil which had been 'hol'd and hacked after the manner of Pitts some of them very deep for the purpose of taking out clay to make Brick'. [136] An industrial operation, however rudimentary, was clearly in progress. A 'brickfield' and tileworks was established at nearby Drumore, and by 1842 the 'largest kiln' was reported as 'not yet built', but the tiles already manufactured had been of good quality and had sold well. There was also, in the nineteenth century, east of Drumlemble village – on the cleared site of the old school, now marked only by a solitary tree – the 'Kintyre House and Drain Tile Work'. [137] James Ferrier's suggestion (Instruction 10, 1792) that a pottery might be established at Campbeltown, is in keeping with the Duke's concern to encourage new industries.

44: Wood and woodlands

The Duke's enthusiasm for the planting and protection of trees was economy-driven. Woodlands were sparse in Kintyre and timber had to be imported, an expensive business. The solution, therefore, was to grow it, but the best of timber is slow-growing and very much a long-term investment, and while the trees grow they have to be protected, not only from foraging animals but also from needy humans. In his notes to the list (No. 11), the Chamberlain recommends not only enclosure – walling – of the areas selected for planting, but also the employment of a nurseryman for growing young trees and 'constantly overlooking the plantations'. It is unlikely that the Duke would have even considered the Chamberlain's suggestion that a man might be employed to manage the cultivation of trees and maintenance of woods, and in his next set of instructions he recommends that the 'easiest and best method of raising a Plantation of Trees upon every Farm' would be to add a piece of enclosed ground to existing gardens (p. 172).

This principle was embedded in some leases, e. g. that of Milntown farm of Smerby in 1796, where the tenant, Robert McNair, was obliged to 'add a considerable space to the present garden in case the same is found necessary to be planted with trees which are to be furnished by the said Duke'. [138] It would be difficult to ascertain how many of the listed holdings were planted as recommended. In 1795, two years later, the lease of Laigh (or Low) Remuil in Southend, when granted to Hugh McLiver, contained an obligation on him to plant several well-sheltered glens with trees, to be furnished by the Duke. [139] Remuil Hill is now blanketed by coniferous afforestation and its agricultural heritage obliterated.

At a Sheriff Court held in Tarbert on 4 September 1683, among the many prosecutions heard were several involving 'cutting of green wood', i. e. growing trees. Dougald Mcilgoune, John McMurriche and John McAlester in Barmollach, near Carradale, each admitted that he 'cutted wood without libertie not knowing who was his master ...', and all were fined £5 'Scots money'. Neil Thomson in Cregan, Loup, admitted that he 'cut oak timber'. William Buchanan, a prominent merchant and feuer in Tarbert, acknowledged that he 'cuttit Blythswoods* woods but alleged he had liberty from his master the laird of Tarbert'. Donald Moreson and Patrick McFarlan, both also in Tarbert, likewise admitted to the cutting of wood. There is one reference to the 'cutting and peellinge of green wood', [140] which must relate specifically to the collection of bark, which was commonly used in tanning processes. Bark, chiefly of oak and birch, and required in large quantities, was also used as a preservative for fishing nets until the mid-nineteenth century, when replaced by imported cutch, distilled from fragmented trunks of Acacia trees. [141]

From the Duke's 4th instruction in 1788, it is clear that detection of unauthorised wood-cutting was dependent on informers, who were to receive as reward a half of the fines levied, while the other half, plus expenses, was to be retained by the estate. In that year, too, warrants were issued by the Baron Baillie of Kintyre for searching for persons who 'cut down and peel the bark off trees in His Grace's woods in Kintyre'. [142]

*Campbell of Blythswood, who owned lands in North Kintyre, which were sold to Campbell of Stonefield c. 1716. See p. 99.

50. The south end of the now depleted strip of walled-in woodland, known as Bluebell Wood, behind Limecraigs House, Campbeltown. Photograph by A. Martin, 28/2/2011.

45: The Rowan

One tree which is not mentioned at all in any of the instructions – nor does John Smith mention it in the hefty chapter 'Woods and Plantations' in his *Agriculture of Argyll* – is the rowan or mountain ash. The rowan was not particularly useful in material terms, but was – and to a small degree still is – a tree in which great supernatural significance was invested. This is hardly the place to expand on the lore of trees, but close to the door of many ruined steadings an old rowan will be found standing as protection against witchcraft, and there are still country folk who will not cut so much as a branch from a rowan let alone cut one down for fear of incurring some punishment.

Rowans spread vigorously – largely through dispersal of their seeds in bird-droppings – and, since the coniferous afforestation of large tracts of Kintyre and the consequent exclusion of grazing livestock, have proliferated on uplands. They will colonise acidic soil just as readily as the rich soil of gardens, and while they seldom attain more than a few feet in height on windswept hills and moors, they survive and put out their clusters of bright red berries, as they must have done two and three centuries ago in ravines and on rock faces where sheep and goats could not reach them.

46: Farm plans

These plans which the Duke wished to be catalogued and sent to Inveraray for copying would have been maps of individual farms surveyed and drawn by George Langlands or others. The Chamberlain, in his reply, reasoned that the plans of the farms in the process of being leased 'could not easily be dispensed with at the time', and explained that the remainder would have been sent had he not been informed that the schoolmaster of Inveraray, who was appointed to copy them, had been 'called away from thence'.

The necessity of having these plans available when farms were being let is simple to explain. They were used for indicating where improvements were to be carried out, and it would have been George Langlands' job to instruct the tenants in what was required of them in terms of their lease. The lease of Glenmurril to Donald McIlmichael in 1796 will suffice as illustration: '1. To build a stone dyke 3½ feet high and covered with two row of feal [turf] at place marked AB on said plan. 2. To cut a ditch 6 feet wide at top 3½ feet deep and 2 feet wide at bottom but no sallows [willows] to be planted, at BC. 3. To cut a ditch 6 feet wide at top 3½ feet deep and 2 feet wide at bottom but no sallows to be planted, at CD. 4. To build a double feal dyke 5 feet high and breadth in proportion at EF. 5. To build a dyke of the same dimensions at FG. '[143]

The value of farm plans, however rudimentary, was recognised in 1758, when the 3rd Duke, Archibald Campbell, instructed his Kintyre Chamberlain that maps of a number of farms were to be made, 'showing what is arable, greensward and moss'. A surveyor, Alex Ruat (Rowatt), was employed in the following year to survey Limecraigs, Crosshill, Kilkerran and many other holdings in South Kintyre, but he died leaving only his notebook, 'which no-one can understand', therefore no maps were made. [144]

47: Boundaries

One of the Duke's first extant instructions, in 1785, was: 'You must pay attention to the marches of my property with other Heritors in Kintyre, and get them ascertained and settled, where there is any doubt or dispute. ' Disputes over marches, or boundaries, recur in these instructions. These problems were rooted in the fact that prior to the systematic measuring and mapping of land – then in progress – boundaries between properties existed only as landscape features, such as rocks, streams, hillocks, and ridges, augmented perhaps by cairns. These boundaries were generally preserved in local tradition, and, in the event of disagreements among neighbouring landowners or tenants, residents who knew the marches would be consulted before judgement was reached, by an independent arbiter if negotiations had stalled.

As an example of the kind of information it was possible to gather, see boundary cases on Mull in 1786 in the Instructions for Mull, Morvern and Tiree, pp. 138-142. In the Kintyre Instructions, regretably there is no such level of detail, which includes identities of informants, their ages, places of residence, and snippets of personal history. Only an Archibald McGill in Arnicle, Barr Glen, is mentioned above as having witnessed an earlier boundary agreement, for which presumably no written record was made or kept. The Argyll Papers contain witnesses' statements, taken on 14 May 1760, concerning the march between Knocknagreen, Arinascavach and Eleric, in Southend Parish. [145] Also see page 198.

In 1851, when the farm of Low Tirfergus, on Lossit Estate, was offered for let, Robert McLean, thatcher at 'High Drumlemon', had instructions to 'show the boundaries' to interested parties. [146] Later that year, when 'Bealochnahully, near Salt Pans', was offered, Walter McKinlay, 'park-keeper at Lossit Park', was available to 'show the boundaries'. [147] Still later, in 1861, when Upper and Lower Blary on Glenbarr Estate were offered for let, another McLean, Malcolm, 'Ground Officer' at Glenbarr, was the man to 'point out the boundaries'. [148]

As the Duke's leases show, when boundaries were established or new boundaries created by the division of farms, the tenants were obliged to delineate them with dykes or open ditches. Some marches separated the properties of neighbouring landowners, as in 1794 (No. 5) when the Duke instructs his Chamberlain to remind 'Cariskey' – MacNeill of Carskey in Southend – to 'build the march dykes'. Evidently MacNeill had agreed in writing that if the Chamberlain or George Langlands could find men to build the dykes, he would pay for them. Dykes and ditches alike were substantial creations. In 1792, Colin McEachran, Glenahervy 'south shore division', agreed to make a 'new march fence partly with a double fail [turf] dyke 5 feet high and breadth in proportion; in other parts an open ditch 7 feet wide at top, 4½ feet deep and 2 feet wide at bottom, and along the shore to build a stone dyke 3½ feet high to be covered with fail'. [149] In that same year, Donald O Loynachan, Glenahervy 'west division', was instructed to 'streighten the march dyke betwixt said division and the farm of Caintaig with a double fail dyke 5 feet high and breadth in proportion'. [150] March dykes could also be of stone construction, as at Upper Skeroblinraid – Archibald Stewart, 1791 – where the mid and east divisions were to be separated by a stone wall 4 feet high and covered with two rows of turf. [151] Sometimes a thorn hedge was required to be planted alongside a dyke or ditch, as at Upper Rannachan in 1792. [152] All such proposed improvements would be marked on estate plans and perhaps also indicated on the ground by pits dug along the line the march would follow. [153]

These march dykes and ditches remain as features on the Kintyre landscape, along with the 'head-dykes' – which separated the arable land around the steadings from the rough grazing beyond – stock enclosures and sheiling huts. But the physical legacy of land use is far from complete and can never be reconstructed. In lowland areas, agricultural improvements obliterated the evidence of earlier systems, and, in the uplands, hills and glens where crops grew and cattle grazed have disappeared under waves of coniferous plantation.

On and around Knock Scalbert, unimproved landscape – parts of it, indeed, prehistoric – may be walked. To the east of the hill, massive turf dykes still bound and intersect a once-cultivated plain which is now largely marshland, and a haunt of hen harriers and short-eared owls. The coast between Machrihanish and Carskey is virtually unaltered, a few coniferous plantations aside, since farmers moved out and sheep moved in during the late eighteenth and early nineteenth centuries (p. 166). In 2009, Dr Gary Robinson, an archaeologist at Bangor University, Wales, began surveying that coast for evidence of Bronze Age settlement, and the results of his research should demonstrate continuity of land-use from prehistoric times until the present.

48: Marl and Maerl

Marl is soil which consists of clay and lime and was considered a valuable fertiliser. In his instruction, the Duke requested an estimate for sending a ton of marle 'from Laggan'. This was his farm in Glenlussa (not to be confused with 'The Laggan', the plain between Campbeltown and Machrihanish). Indeed, when Laggan was leased in 1778 to Peter Galbreath, Lachlan McArthur and Robert McPhaill, the presence of 'marle of excellent quality on the lands' was mentioned in the lease, and one of the conditions specified was that they 'lay 150 carts of it yearly on the farm'. [154] In the following year, the question of exploiting the Laggan marl-pit for wider profit is raised again, in the 3rd instruction. The proposal to cart loads of marl to Campbeltown has been abandoned in favour of shipment, and the Chamberlain provides estimates for the cost of a road from the pit to the shore at Ardnacross, and the cost of constructing a quay there. Since no more is heard of this proposal either, it must be assumed that the scheme was abandoned.

John Smith, in his *Agriculture of Argyll* (1798), refers to the Laggan marl (p. 197), 'a great quantity ... of which farmers that were near it made some use above thirty years ago, and afterwards gave it up, till within these two or three years that they have tried it again'. He reports their disappointment in the value of the fertiliser and suggests that 'This may be owing to their laying it on too sparingly, to their ploughing it down in a crude state, without allowing it to lie a year on the sward; and to their laying it, not on old ley to which it would do most good, but on poor run-out soil, which required more the application of cow's dung, or some such oily manure, than any calcareous stimulous'. There is no reference to the Duke's earlier scheme to export the fertiliser, which tends to reinforce the conclusion that nothing came of it.

Smith, in his section on 'Manuring' (p. 203), mentions 'coral' washed ashore at Dunaverty. This, he remarks, 'proves an excellent and lasting manure, but the quantity is not so considerable as to be of any extensive service'. In fact, that lime-rich 'coral' was properly maerl – cognate with 'marl' – a coralline algae which is pink or purple in life, but fades to white after death. Its branched nodules can be found not only at Dunaverty, but also below Auchenhoan Head, and perhaps elsewhere on the Kintyre coast; but, as Smith points out, not in useful quantities. Maerl in Southend was known as 'Gillecalum shells' and by Campbeltown fishermen as 'crokers'.

49: Salmon-fishing

Ardnacross is on the east coast of Kintyre, north of Peninver. There seems little doubt that the 'fishing' referred to would have been for salmon, since no landowner could reasonably presume to try to control white or herring fishing off his shores. Salmon born in Kintyre rivers migrate into the ocean, and, when their own time comes to spawn, return to their natal rivers. The fish, in historic times, were at their most vulnerable when migrating along the coast towards their rivers, when congregated at the mouth of the rivers, and when they entered the rivers. The immense economic importance of salmon is clear from the succession of laws for their protection, dating back to the eleventh century. [155]

In the minute of a sheriff court held at Tarbert in 1693, salmon-poaching features prominently. The 'black fish' referred to were recently spawned fish (kelts), while 'red fish' were those which had not yet spawned. These offences were concentrated in the Carradale district, through which, of course, runs Carradale Water, historically the most productive of the salmon rivers in Kintyre. Ewin McEwin in 'the Craig' (presumably Craigmore) 'killed black fish', Donald McMillan in Ronedaill 'killed several black fish', Archibald McMillan in Kilmichell 'killed red fish', John McDowgall in Braikley 'reid and black fish', Niall McArthour and Duncan Mcallum in Auchincreoch 'red and black fish', Gilbert McMillan in Aird acknowledged 'killing fish with nets', Duncan McMillan killed 'reid fish', Robert Buchanan in Auchensale 'black and reid fish' and Niall Mcallum in Auchinbreck 'reid fish'.[156] Fishing methods are not stated, except in the single case of Gilbert McMillan, who used nets, which might suggest that netting was exceptional. The likeliest killing instruments would have been fish-spears.

Recourse to criminal prosecution clearly indicates not only proprietorial interest in salmon, but also commercial interest. There is difficulty in estimating how far back the leasing of salmon-fishing rights extends in Kintyre, but an account from 1759, during the time of the 3rd Duke, suggests at least the seventeenth century. In that year, the Duke was informed of a 'salmond draught or ffishing upon the Dukes ground at the waterfoot of Torasdill near Carradill watter' which had lapsed 'this 30 years past and more'. In the previous summer, Dugald Campbell, laird of Glencarradale, brought in a fisher from 'the North Country' who operated the 'salmond draught' – probably a drag-net, set in a circle and hauled to the beach – at Carradale Waterfoot, but was also carrying his boat, presumably a coracle or the like, at half-ebb to Torrisdale Waterfoot and fishing there until half-flood, catching fish 'without asking liberty for so doing'. The outcome was that the Duke would not allow him to fish at Torrisdale unless Glencarradale leased the fishing.[157]

Stretches of river were also leased. In 1812, a tenant in Laggan, Robert McPhail, applied for a 19-year lease of the salmon and grilse fishing on Glenlussa Water – another major salmon river in Kintyre – at an annual rent of £4. The Chamberlain, Duncan Stewart, offered him a four-year lease at the sum offered, providing he would keep clear of 'Major McNeil's marches'.[158]

By the mid-nineteenth century, salmon-fishing stations – operating bag-nets, staked to the seabed – had been established on the Kintyre coasts at Ardnacross, Saddell, Carradale, Torrisdale, Skipness, Pans, Carskey, and elsewhere. By then, the 'excellent steam boat communications' between Campbeltown and Glasgow fish-market ensured that 'the fish caught in the morning are in good time even for special dinner parties that day'.[159]

50: Wheat cultivation

On the desirability of local wheat cultivation, the 5th Duke was tenacious, but resistance among his tenant-farmers proved insuperable, and that resistance has never been overcome in Kintyre. John Smith, in his *Agriculture of Argyll*, pp. 99-101, believed that the 'true reason' for the rejection of the crop was that 'the demand for bear [barley] to make whisky is greater than even that for bread to eat; and the distillers have a brisker trade and more ready cash than the bakers'. Wheat, he reported, had been 'frequently tried, and found to answer well, particularly in deep loam and strong lands in the neighbourhood of Campbeltown', and Kintyre wheat had been sold in Ayr and in Glasgow, 'where it fetched the highest price in the market'.

The reasons for rejecting wheat, as stated by Smith, were 'the want of enclosures' – i. e. fenced fields – and 'the want of a flour mill'; but, he countered, there were, in South Kintyre, 'a considerable number of enclosures', and, in any case, 'good spring wheat' had been grown 'on fields entirely open'; and 'a little addition to the machinery of the present mill would serve'.

Robert W. Smith disputes John Smith's reasonings and argues that he, the Duke and the Duke's chamberlain 'were all hypnotised by the fact that wheat, as grown elsewhere, especially in the south of England, was the most profitable of all the crops grown in their day'. On the milling issue he remarks: 'Grind wheat, oats and barley on the same stones, and you get wheatmeal, oatmeal and barleymeal, but the profitable end-product of wheat is flour, white flour, and to produce that the outer layers of the grain have to be removed, four of them plus the germ: bran, sharps, middlings, and thirds. Milling and re-milling, with a succession of finer and finer sievings and riddlings. This was certainly achieved in the late 1700s, and for long before that, with a final sieve made of horsehair. "A few additions" with "few" being subliminally associated with "inexpensive"? And never mind the infrastructure of highly-skilled labour involved in the manufacture of these "additions". '[160]

In the promotion of wheat cultivation, the role of the English farmers, brought to Kintyre in 1775 and 1776, was probably central to the 5th Duke's strategy, and Smith quoted one of these improvers, John Turner, Tonrioch, as saying that 'the crop of between eight and nine acres brought him one year above £100; and the crop of four acres another year brought him £50'. Smith estimated that more than £3000 was annually spent importing wheat flour into Argyll, 'which might all be saved, if we would raise wheat of our own'. He promoted, at some length, the merit of wheat in crop rotation, but whisky by the end of the eighteenth century was shaping up to become a major industry in Kintyre, and the master which farmers preferred to serve, not least because many were themselves involved, directly or indirectly, in the illicit trade.

In 1852, in the *Campbeltown Journal,* wheat was reported as being 'little raised in this quarter, but the little is generally good, and the grain is bright and sound; we hear of a partial failure, but the average yield is above mediocrity and is now all secured'. [161]

51: Red Herring

The 'Red Herring House' leased to the laird of Glencarradale, for the relatively short term of seven years, was for the salting and smoking of herrings, which may account for the explicit prohibition of the use of the Duke's woods for 'operations'. As it turned out, the death of the laird of Carradale plunged the project into disarray. In the *First Statistical Account of Saddell and Skipness*, written in 1793, the author, Rev. George MacLeish, remarks on the trading vessels which annually attended the local herring fishery 'for the purpose of salting herrings, or carrying them fresh to the red-herring houses in Liverpool, Isle of Man, &c. and to other markets'. [162] On the Langlands map of Argyll (1801) there is a 'redherring house' marked north of the mouth of Torrisdale Burn and another at Port Crannaig, where the present Carradale harbour is.

The *Experiment* sank in Loch Riddon, where she had sailed for a cargo of wood for the Torrisdale red herring house, and another vessel – unnamed – was also lost, with a cargo of red herrings. Clark, Campbell & Co. of Campbeltown, which managed the business, had written to the Chamberlain on 2 September 1793 asking that the Duke should not demand payment for the *Experiment* on account of all their losses. [163]

The red herring, which has a long history, should not be confused with the kipper, a nineteenth century innovation and term. A kipper is a herring which is gutted, beheaded, split, roused briefly in salt, then smoked for a matter of hours. Gutting aside, a red herring was left entire, steeped in strong brine for months and then smoked for

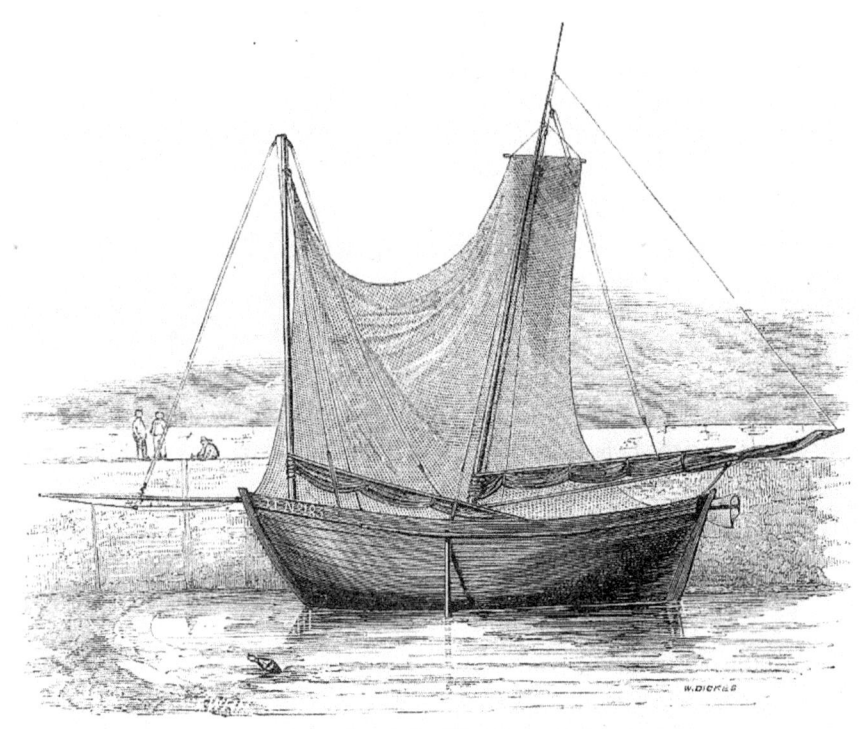

51. A trading wherry, from *Deep Sea Fishing Boats* by E. W. H. Holdsworth (London 1874).

weeks, ending up deep red in colour. Whereas a kipper will keep for only a few weeks, or perhaps a few months, depending on weather, condition of the fish and the care expended on its preparation, a red herring remained edible for longer, a year or more. [164]

52: The Highland Parish Church

This church, to serve the 'Highland' or Gaelic-speaking population of Campbeltown Parish – the Scots-speaking 'Lowland' parishioners had already been provided with a new building at Castlehill, erected 1778-80 – was built in 1803-7 to the design of George Dempster, a Greenock architect, and supervised by Robert Watt, a Glasgow contractor. The building continues in use, as one of the two remaining Church of Scotland properties in town, but is no longer a Gaelic charge.

The site of the old Gaelic church, which was built in 1642 in the form of a Geneva cross, its projections aligned on the cardinal points, was at the head of the New Quay, in the area between the Ardshiel Hotel and Creagdhu Mansions, and is commemorated by a plaque on the triangular walled enclosure there. [165]

That the exchange of the old site for a new site was complicated and acrimonious is clear from the correspondence between the Duke and his Chamberlain, Duncan Stewart. In 1800 (No. 1), the Duke warns that he 'will have no dispute about the ground of the old Church' and threatens to withdraw his offer of a 'stance' for the new building.

53: Three ministers of Southend

The schoolmaster's name is unknown, but the minister at that time was the Rev. Donald Campbell, whose incumbency was brief and ended amid controversy (p. 173). His two predecessors were also Campbells, whose combined ministries covered almost a century – 97 years, to be precise. The first was the Rev. Dugald Campbell of the Kildalloig family (p. 94), who was admitted to Southend in 1696 and died in 1741. His first wife Grizel, a daughter of Baillie Angus Campbell, died in 1705, and he married again, to a daughter of Archibald MacDonald of Sanda, Ann (died 1786). Their first son, John Campbell of Kildalloig, married Mary Campbell, a daughter of the Rev. David Campbell, Dugald's successor as minister of Southend. The Rev. David belonged to another landed family in

52. Highland Parish Church, Campbeltown. From a postcard, dated April 29, 1906, in the collection of Mrs Maureen Bell.

Kintyre, the Campbells of Askomil, and was admitted to the charge in 1742. He was the author of the *First Statistical Account* of the parish, completed two years before his death in 1793, by which time he was practically blind. A fire in his study destroyed the Kirk Session records. In 1755 he leased both Kilblaan and Lochorodale, which were no doubt farmed by others' labour. [166]

54: Captain Scipio Duroure Campbell

Laggs was a 1-merkland holding between Oatfield and Killeonan, into which latter it was absorbed by 1836. In 1775, Laggs was leased to Lieutenant (later Captain) Scipio Duroure Campbell of the 100th Regiment of Foot. He belonged to a cadet branch of the Campbells of Inverawe and married Gilles (for Gaelic *Sileas*, anglicised as 'Julia'), daughter of Captain Archibald Campbell, Limecraigs, of the Bragleenmore family, sometime Chamberlain of Kintyre. [167]

In 1778, during the American Revolutionary War, when Kirkcudbright-born John Paul Jones (1747-92) – 'Father of the American Navy' – was raiding the British coasts in his *Ranger* and causing widespread alarm, as part of Campbeltown's defences a local militia was formed, commanded by Captain Campbell, with his son-in-law Scipio as 'Captain-Lieutenant', or second in command. [168]

Scipio, who was 'born in the Army', and Gilles, born at Limecraigs, Campbeltown, were married at Inveraray on 28 January 1765. They had 13 children, the first, Janet, born at Campbeltown in 1765, and the last, Margaret, born at Gartnacorach (or Gartnagerach), Southend, in 1788. [169]

Lieut. Campbell sub-let Laggs in 1778 and took over the lease of Gartnacorach farm – now Glenahervie – on the southern Learside, from Lieut. Thomas Townley, one of the Northern English farmers (p. 82), but gave that up too, in 1789, and assigned the remainder of the lease to the Rev. William McMillan in Campbeltown, on the grounds that Gartnacorach was too remote from school for his young and numerous family. Lieut. Campbell's stated reason for leaving Gartnacorach may be explained by its distance from Southend village. Some 30 years later, a school would be opened at nearby Glenahervie to serve the Learside children (p. 142). That he and his family were living at Gartnacorach is clear from the above, but, given his social station, it seems unlikely that he was actually working the

53A. Portrait believed to be of Gilles Campbell, wife of Scipio Duroure Campbell (opposite).

53B. Companion portrait believed to be of Scipio Duroure Campbell.

54A. Portrait of Christian Hamilton Campbell (1785-1850), wife of Daniel Mactaggart (opposite).

54B. Companion portrait of Daniel Mactaggart (1786-1859).

land. Many farms were let to merchants, clergymen and landed gentry, but these nominal tenants very rarely lived on their holdings.

By 1797, Captain Campbell was dead and Laggs was to be advertised for let. In 1799, Peter Brolochan was confirmed in the lease, but he and his late uncle, also Peter Brolachan, grazier in Campbeltown, had already been sub-tenants of Laggs since Lieut. Campbell moved out in 1778, and had paid the arrears of rent due by Campbell's widow, [170] to whom the Duke promised 'some advantage' – perhaps that was it.

A daughter of Scipio's, Christian Hamilton Campbell, married Daniel Mactaggart, progenitor of the family of lawyers in Campbeltown, while his son Captain Frederick Campbell served with the 94th Regiment – the Scotch Brigade – which was raised in 1793 and served in India and in the Peninsular War. Captain Frederick had the distinction of having, in 1827, fought one of the last duels in Scotland, an 'affair of honour' which he and his opponent, John Lorne Stewart of Knockrioch (p. 141), chose to settle in Glasgow. After a harmless exchange of shots, as the *Glasgow Herald* reported, Stewart 'advanced towards his antagonist Captain C--------and declared that he considered him a man of honour and a gentleman, which satisfied the friends of the parties'. [171]

55: The Inneans and the sheep invasion

Behind this single line of instruction lies ultimately the story of sheep. The farm to be advertised was originally two holdings, one to the north and the other to the south of a majestic glen which cuts deeply from inland moor to Atlantic coast, mid-way between Machrihanish and the Mull of Kintyre. *Innean* is Gaelic for a cove or amphitheatre-shaped bay. Innean Beag, the 'little' one, is on the north side of the glen, and Innean Mor, the 'big' one, is on the south side, in a relatively sheltered spot through which the Kintyre Way walkers' trail now passes. Each was originally a multi-tenancy holding, communally worked. The terrain is steep and rocky and, in common with all other farms on that coast, cultivation was largely confined to terraces laboriously cleared of stone, and patches of hillside formed into lazy-beds. Existence there was marginal, both geographically and economically, but ongoing archaeological surveys should establish that human settlement there extends back into prehistory.

55. One of the smallest of the structures which shepherds left on the landscape – a 'twinning-pen', for confining a ewe, which had lost her lamb, with a lamb which had lost its mother, to encourage the ewe to accept and suckle the orphan. A young Jimmy MacDonald is inside the structure for scale. Photograph by A. Martin, Largiebaan Glen, 1/4/1984.

The present writer, in *Kintyre Country Life* (pp. 67-69), has examined the gradual transformation of the hills and moors between Carskey and Machrihanish from a string of small 'townships', or communal farms, into several amalgamated holdings for sheep-grazing. This transformation was not effected by 'clearance' of the tenantry in the standard, emotive sense. Rather, expiring leases were granted to consortia of sheep-graziers, typically merchants and members of the professional class, who outbid competition and then employed shepherds to manage their stock. The take-over began to the south, around the Mull, in 1771, and crept northward towards the Inneans.

Even before the coming of sheep to the Inneans, the conjoined farms were clearly being sub-let. The earliest known lease, for 1729, was granted to David Campbell, 'Bailie Deput of the Lands & Bailiary of Kintyre', and signed by Elizabeth Tollemache, Duchess of Argyll. In 1758, another David Campbell, described as 'late merchant in Jamaica, now in Campbeltoun', got the lease, and he was followed in 1777 by Dugald Campbell 'of Auchnabaw'[172]; in 1771, he had expressed the intention of settling in Kintyre to deal 'in grassing black cattle'. [173] Yet another Campbell, Donald, was in possession in 1799, when the lease was acquired by Thomas Train, 'herd in Borgadillmore'. [174] Train was certainly in the business of sheep. In a memorial, dated 26 July 1798 at 'Borgadelmore', he had proposed for a farm and outlined improvements he would make, stating that he had been shepherd at the Mull of Kintyre for more than 20 years and was one of the partners in the Mull Company, [175] a consortium of sheep-farmers. He belonged to the Parish of Carmichael in Lanarkshire, and in 1792 was in Glenmanuill with his wife Janet McKillop and four children. [176]

The shepherds on that coast built no houses, but adapted existing drystone buildings in the deserted townships. In any case, they weren't long on the coast. By around the mid-nineteenth century, with the holdings further amalgamated and under the management of Argyll Estate itself, the herds were concentrated in substantial stone-and-mortar steadings at Ballygroggan and Largiebaan, with a smaller outlier at Balnamoil, above the lighthouse. These early shepherds do, however, have their memorials on the landscape, in the form of stone-built sheep fanks, or 'folds', into which their flocks would be gathered for shearing and smearing and marking.

56. The ruins of Innean Mor township, looking north to Inneans Bay and, on the horizon, the island of Islay. Murdo MacDonald is seated on a wall. Photograph by A. Martin, 28/5/1984.

Both Innean Mor and Innean Beag have a big fank built nearby. The latter was probably constructed of stones taken from the township buildings, of which little remains. Innean Mor was relatively untouched, and, from its ruins may be reconstructed, if only in imagination, the place it was three or four centuries ago – long, low dwellings, thatched and leaking peat-smoke, grouped in a patchwork landscape. On all that stretch of coast between Glemanuill, Southend, and Ballygroggan, Machrihanish, not a soul now lives.

56: Learside settlements

On the directly opposite side of south Kintyre, the Learside, there were distinct parallels. The coast is similar, with headlands, cliffs, and cove-like bays, but on a smaller scale. Inland, as is still obvious to this day, despite afforestation, there was a far greater extent of arable land and a correspondingly greater population, particularly in and around Glenahervie in the south.

Erradil, close to the head of Glenahervie, was particularly noted for its rich arable. John McInnes – 'Dunaverty' in the *Campbeltown Courier*, which occasionally published articles by him – in 1910 had this information on Erradil (which he spelt differently): 'I have it on no less authority than the late Mr Peter McKay of Knockstaple, a gentleman who in his day knew the district well, that the heaviest barley ever known to go into Campbeltown was from the farm of Earadale when it was under cultivation.'[177]

Large scale sheep-grazing came to the Learside, too, but rather later than at the Mull. In 1852, Glenahervie, 'once studded with comfortable homesteads' – the writer numbered them as eleven – was described as 'one monotonous solitary sheepwalk', with 'hardly half-a-dozen acres turned up by the [plough] sock in the whole glen'.[178]

In the 1841 Census, there were three households at Erradil, those of Neil, Donald and Peter MacKay, totalling 22 individuals, including farm-servants. By the following Census, of 1851, the family was gone, replaced by shepherds. Cantaig and Socach were two neighbouring farms, and Glenahervie by 1811 was in four divisions, 'West', 'North-West', 'High' and 'South Shore',[179] with Gartnagerach or Gartnacorach – the present-day Glenahervie – further to the south. At one of these divisions, called 'Old

57. Sheep at the ruins of Erradil, photographed by A. Martin, 27/4/1991.

Glenahervie' or Sheanachie – whose ruins lie next to the road on the brae north from Erradil Bridge – there was said to be an inn as well as a school (p. 142). [180]

As on the Mull coast, the Learside population formed a Gaelic-speaking fringe. In 1792, by which time the initial Lowland Plantation stock was fourth or fifth generation Kintyre-born, the following families occupied the Learside, which, except for Kildalloig Estate to the north, was entirely the 5th Duke's. Among those tenants of his, only three are of doubtful cultural identity: Hendry (Donald, surname likely representing MacKendrick), Fleeming (for Fleming, a Lowland name, but with Gaelic offshoots) and Beith (likewise a Lowland name and likewise with Gaelic offshoots).

Families, north to south:
Auchachoan: McMillan, Walker.
Balnabraid: McKerral.
Ballinatuinne: Olynachan.
Glenmurill: McMichael, Taylor, Conally.
Corphin: McIsaac. McEachran, Stewart.
Erradell: Campbell, McIlreavy, McEachran, McLean.
Succoth: Cameron.
Cantaig: Conallie, Hendry.
Glenaharvy: Olynachan, McEachran, Clark, McIsaac, Fleeming.
Gartnacorrach: McMillan, Thomson, McNeill, Beith. [181]

57: Tree-planting in kailyards

This idea of the Duke's was mooted back in 1793 – Instruction 9 – when he maintained that the 'easiest and best' means of raising a plantation of trees on every farm would be to add a piece of ground to each garden and fill the addition with young trees, the theory being that the tenants, in protecting their gardens from the depredations of cattle, would also be protecting the young plantations. The 'garden' in 1793 had become a 'kail yard' in 1798, but the two were one and the same. Kail, in the eighteenth century, formed a vital element in the people's diet, and was admirably suited to the role, being the only brassica which is able to endure the rigours of winter and to produce a crop from virtually any quality of ground. At that time, it had not yet become a field crop and its cultivation was generally confined to gardens. [182]

Farmers and 'even the poorest cottager' kept a garden, but 'the contents of it are seldom more than a few greens' and 'he is commonly more than an ordinary farmer who has a few roots, and some leeks and onions'. [183] In his response, the Chamberlain reported that no young trees had been received since spring of 1797, and that the young and weak specimens had been transplanted in McDuff's nursery (p. 102), while others had been planted in 'a belting that runs betwixt the March of Crosshill, and the Sheep park built at Limecraigs'.

58: Seditious stirrings in Southend

No reference is made in the 1797 Instructions to a conflict which gripped Southend Parish in that year. Its background was the radicalism and unrest of that period, the ongoing war with France, and a minister who had alienated his congregation and wished to protect his reputation. On 21 January 1797, the Rev. Donald Campbell, minister in Southend, appeared at Limecraigs House, residence of Duncan Stewart, the Duke's Chamberlain, and gave a statement which accused certain of the Duke's 'principal tenants' of having 'imbibed democratical principles' and expressed 'seditious' opinions.

During harvest time 1796, when Peter Campbell was in the parish surveying houses for window tax, Rev. Campbell was proceeding to a christening at the house of Alexander Pickan, Kildavy. Passing through Benton, Pollovulline, he engaged in conversation with William Huie, tenant there, who was shearing at the time. Huie 'made use of very discontented expressions with respect to the House Tax', and had earlier, Rev. Campbell heard, 'made a very Seditious speech to the said Peter Campbell at the time of measuring his Houses'. When Rev. Campbell repeated the gist of sermons he had preached on 'obedience and due submission to the Law of the Country', McMurchy, smith in Kildavy, retorted: 'You may well speak, as you are well paid for it. ' David Reid, another tenant in Kildavy, declared at the christening that 'They have now gone taxing us till we can bear it no longer. ' The war with France, Reid said, was 'ruinous', and the French 'wished peace with us …' Political and religious opinions expressed by John MacKay in Auchadaduie and a son of Hugh MacKerral in Brunerican were also censoriously reported. He had 'observed much more discontent and dissatisfaction with their Superiors among the Lowlanders of his congregation than among any other class of his Parishioners', and following a sermon he preached on submission and obedience to superiors, most of the Lowlanders stayed away from church and had, since a meeting in the house of Thomas Brown, tenant in Machrimore, set about forming a Relief Church. [184]

In that year, 1797, the original relief church in Southend was founded, but the background to the break-away was more complex than the Rev. Campbell was prepared to divulge. In reality, his ministry was deeply unpopular across the entire congregation. Campbell, in the words of the Rev. Angus J. MacVicar, 'indulged too freely at dinners and social functions' – that is, was over-fond of his dram – and was 'careless about his pulpit ministrations and negligent of his parochial duties'. The relief church, Rev. MacVicar remarked, was 'built not by a section of the congregation but by all the Church people of the Parish, and there was no intention at first on the part of the congregation to secede from the Church of Scotland'. [185]

The congregation did later separate, but the split was over the issue of whether the new church would have a Gaelic-speaking minister or not. The Lowlanders carried the majority for an English-speaking minister, and the upshot was that the Gaelic speakers returned *en masse* to the parish church. The first Relief Church minister, the Rev. Alexander Laing, was ordained in 1799. [186]

The Rev. Campbell was a son of John Campbell, tacksman of Scalpay Isle, Skye, and graduated D. D. from the University of Edinburgh. He had come to Southend in 1794, and in 1798, after only four years there, the Duke, his patron, shunted him to the Parish of Kilninver and Kilmelford. But he redeemed himself there and conducted an exemplary ministry until his death in 1843,[187] the year of the cataclysmic Disruption, which split the entire Church of Scotland.

59: Balinatunie and the Langlands family

The Langlands farm was Balinatunie, near Auchenhoan on the northern Learside, and now a ruin. George Langlands received a lease in 1775, for the standard 19 years, replacing John Greenlees and John Muir in the tenancy. He was described in the lease as 'Land Surveyor to the said Duke'. Balinatunie was valued at two merklands and rented annually at £32 5s sterling, plus I boll Multure Meal, 2 bolls Teind Bear and, unusually, 16 Bushels of

58. Parish Church Southend, c. 1900. From postcard in collection of A. Martin.

59. The former United Free Church, Southend, with corn stooks in foreground field, c. 1935. Reproduced from postcard in collection of Mrs Maureen Bell.

'flower', from wheat to be grown each year on the land, and to be deducted from the rent. Despite the Duke's 'displeasure' with Langlands' conduct, clearly expressed in his third instruction for 1797, his surveyor's lease of Balinatunie was renewed in 1799, but with his son Matthew added as joint-tenant. The lease was further renewed in 1818 and in 1837, by which time Matthew was sole 'tacksman' and the annual rent had increased to £75, but without the requirement to part-pay in farm produce. [188]

Matthew had married locally, in 1814, to Anne Campbell of Campbeltown, a daughter of Arthur Campbell, shoemaker, and Isobel Brackenridge. Their daughter Agnes was attacked in 1830, on 'the road leading from Campbeltown to Leewardside of Kintyre', by a youth, John McQueen, alias 'McQuin', born in County Antrim and at the time a farm servant living at Big Kiln, Campbeltown. At the High Court in Inveraray on 3 September 1830, he confessed to 'assault with intent to rape' and was sentenced to seven years' transporation. [189] Since Agnes was born on 22 May 1820, [190] she must have been merely ten years old at the time of the assault. In the Census of 1851, she gave her age as 30 and was unmarried.

In 1850, Matthew got the lease of Dalabhraddan, Southend, and moved there in the following year, after the Census was taken. In 1854, Balinatunie and Auchenhoan were let together as 'all in pasture, and capable of Grazing upwards of one Thousand Cheviot Sheep'. [191] By the Census of 1861 Balinatunie was deserted. [192]

When the Langlands family moved to Dalabhraddan, old and new neighbours contributed a day's ploughing on the farm, 'to testify their respect'. No fewer than forty ploughs turned out in April 1851, and a reporter to the *Campbeltown Journal* was moved to comment: 'In the face of cheap markets, and the general uproar as to rack-rents and sterile soil, it was gratifying to notice that the display of horse and harness would scarcely be equalled in any of the far-famed high-farming districts – Ayr, Renfrew, and Lanark.'[193]

60: Kintyre Agricultural Society

John Smith in 1798 referred to an agricultural society 'lately instituted in Kintyre, and favoured by the President of the Board of Agriculture with a parcel of agricultural reports, which are read with avidity, and may be the means of diffusing knowledge of useful facts, and exciting attention and a spirit of enquiry'. [194]

60. Looking north across Balinatunie ruins, with Auchenhoan in distance. Photograph by A. Martin, 1984.

61: Herring-fishing

Campbeltown's elevation to national importance as a fishing centre began about 1760 when it became an annual assembly port for a fleet of drift-netting 'busses' fitted out to capitalise on government subsidies. Investors in the buss fishery, known as 'adventurers', were generally local merchants, though some ship-masters also held shares; but the crews – from six to eighteen men on each vessel – were hired on agreed wages and had no share of profits. [195] In 1792, John Smith's analysis of the state of the buss fishery was uniformly pessimistic. His statistics for the previous seven years show, on average, 50 vessels employing 674 men and curing 7, 412 barrels of herring. [196]

In 1797, when the Duke requested a report on the 'General success of the Herring Fishing', the buss fishery was already in decline, and, with the phasing out, in 1800, of the bounty paid on busses' tonnage, the adventurers began withdrawing their capital. Fishing effort thereafter reverted to smaller, open boats until around 1840, when the scale again increased and smacks came into use. [197] But the industry would remain in the control of local capitalists, who were the fishermen's employers, until the final quarter of the nineteenth century, when ring-net fishing began displacing drift-netting, and lower investment costs in the new method allowed the fishermen themselves to invest in boats and gear, usually in partnerships which practised profit-sharing. [198]

The 5th Duke's interest in fishing was certainly not a casual one. He was, as his correspondence clearly shows, concerned with all enterprises which promised revenue for his estates and gainful employment for his tenantry, and the fishing industry was not the least of these concerns. He was Governor of the British Society for Extending the Fisheries, established in 1786, and was actively involved in the founding of Tobermory on Mull in 1789, though the village was never to become the thriving fishing station its planners hoped to create. [199]

62: Peat-cutting and draining of the mosses

Most of the listed properties are hill farms, but Aross, Darlochan, Durry, Clochkill, and Drumlemble are all in the low-lying Laggan, between Campbeltown and Machrihanish, and Kirkmichael and Achinleck (Auchaleek) are on the northern edge of the Laggan. At

61. 'The Herring Busse Sails into Harbour', a late eighteenth century Dutch engraving (De Jong, Amsterdam), from *The Herring* by Arthur Michael Samuel (London 1918).

62. Drift-net fishing in Loch Fyne, c. 1835. From W. Beattie's *Scotland Illustrated* (1835-38), drawn by artist-architect Thomas Allom (1804-1872) and engraved by Robert Wallis (1794-1878). Print in possession of A. Martin.

63. Neil Kelly, Lochside, with cartload of Moss peats for a Campbeltown distillery, c. 1925. Courtesy of Mrs Catherine Brodie, Campbeltown.

that time, 'moss', or wet peaty ground, had no agricultural value and required to be drained, sweetened by generous liming, and then sown with grass or clover. That 'wetlands' might have an ecological value transcending commercial interests – haphazard peat extraction aside – was a concept which belonged in the future.

The Laggan, before intensive draining turned the greater part of it into prime farmland, was largely a morass with lochs in it. The largest of these was Loch Sanish, drained towards the end of the eighteenth century by Col. Charles Campbell (p. 102). In Blaeu's *Atlas Novus*, published in 1654, the loch is represented as being immense; in 1857, Peter MacIntosh described it as having been 'about a mile in diameter'. [200] When James Watt visited Kintyre in 1773 to survey a line for the coal canal, he described 'a lake called Lough Sanish now drained and turned into meadow land'. [201]

In 1797, Alexander McWilliam in West Kilkeddan was obliged to 'turn into good land six acres of black heath below the houses by draining ploughing and liming', [202] and in 1799 Peter Clark in Baligregan had to 'lay out the sum of £200 sterling in improving the Moss of the said lands'. [203] In 1827, the leases of the Laggan farms of Durry and North and South Backs contained a reclamation incentive. For every acre of moss brought into cultivation with the prior agreement of the Chamberlain, and after a 'white and green crop' had been taken off it, the tenant would receive 'a premium of £4, he paying interest thereon in addition to his rent'. [204]

An anonymous contributor to the *Campbeltown Journal* in 1851 remarked on the improvements to the Laggan, which had brought 'hundreds of acres of inhospitable moss . . . into such a state of culture that, all sorts of crops, usually raised in these parts, are to be seen at the proper season of the year in heart-cheering luxuriance, where, but a short time ago, no crop or root could be seen but peats . . .'[205]

In a peninsula in which woodlands were scarce, and moreover largely out of bounds, peat was for centuries the main fuel. Most farms had peat deposits of their own, or access to nearby deposits, and the townsfolk of Campbeltown cut peats in 'mossrooms', those small portions of land leased from the Duke on the eastern edge of the Laggan, close to town (p. 138). With the growth of the whisky industry in Campbeltown, large quantities of peats were needed in the distilling process. In 1835, a lease was granted to Lieut.

64. The late Robert McInnes digging with his narrow-winged Hill peat-spade at the peat bank at Lochorodale. Photograph by A. Martin, June 1983.

65. The late John Harvey with his father George's broad-winged Moss peat-spade. George Harvey cut peats for Campbeltown distilleries as well as for his own use, and probably inherited the tool from his father. Photograph taken at Limecraigs by A. Martin, 29/9/1995.

Robert MacGregor, Campbeltown, Donald MacKay, and Kenneth Matheson, for the right to cut peat on specified mosses for sale to distillers, maltsters, and other inhabitants of Campbeltown. [206]

Laggan peat was supplied to distilleries well into the twentieth century, and an account of the cutting, drying, and carting of peats is contained in the present writer's *Kintyre Country Life*. John MacKay, the last of the commercial peat-cutters, would dig about 200 tons, or 400 cartloads, in a season. Payment would be collected from the distilleries by the Duke's agent, and the cutters would receive their money only after the Duke's share had been deducted. 'The Duke had the best o' it, ' John MacKay reasoned. 'He had nothing tae do. We had tae do the toilin. ' [207]

63: Rents and Removals

Tenants certainly were removed, as was the case before the 5th Duke's time, and after it, and as notes in the Estate leases show.

In 1747, the tenant in Darlochan was bankrupt and, according to the 3rd Duke's instructions, was to be 'removed and jailed'. [208]

James Brown and his sons, John and James, were put out of Homestone in 1820 owing to arrears of rent, which at £100 a year was at the higher end of the scale. [209]

In 1819, Lachlan McIsaac, tenant in Corrophin, renounced his lease of the neighbouring Learside farm Glenmurrell in favour of Donald McNaughton, Lephenstraw, but McNaughton's stock was sequestered in 1823, and the remainder of the lease was taken over by Malcom McKerral, tenant in Balnabraid, another neighbouring farm. [210]

The stock of Thomas Greenlees, Putichantuy, was sequestered in 1867, in which year he assigned the remainder of his lease to Angus McKeich, Campbeltown, who gave him a house and a cow's grass until expiry of the lease. [211]

At the end of his 19-year lease of Dunglas, Southend, taken in 1838, John Reid had to pay £33 additional rent because he had ploughed and sowed with corn and beans a field of 11 acres which should have been grass. [212]

Cottars, who were sub-tenants, were also prone to eviction, not by the landowner, but by his tenants, their superiors. In 1847, Archibald McKeich, farmer in Sunadale, took legal action to remove a cottar of his, John MacLellan, in a dispute over heritable property. [213]

By comparison with his immediate predecessors, the 5th Duke's conduct in these matters was not immoderate. Comments of Eric R. Cregeen's on the 3rd Duke's instructions to his Kintyre Chamberlain in 1758 are instructive: 'Almost the whole of this very long set of instructions concerns the collection of arrears of rent and the pursuance of tenants and tacksmen in arrears with legal action for the recovery of them. They exhibit the Duke's draconic and detailed control of the estate. There is little accent on improvement except in regard to the prevention of scourging the land [exhausting its fertility] before tenants remove, and on the other hand a decided tendency to take legal action against any tenant in debt to the estate and to recover what is owed by poinding his goods and by distress. '

The 3rd Duke, Archibald Campbell, died in 1761, and, having no legitimate heir, was succeeded by his cousin John, a son of John Campbell of Mamore, who was a brother of the 1st Duke. The 4th Duke's first set of Kintyre instructions, issued in the year of his succession, 1761, is also preoccupied with arrears. Tenants more than a year in arrears of rent at Candlemas were to be evicted and 'diligence used' in the collection of the debts; and rents were to be paid 'more timeously and punctually than in the late Duke's time', with July the deadline. [214]

As the present writer remarked in *Kintyre Country Life*: 'The system of farm-leasing itself encouraged failure. Farms were generally let for nineteen years; but a year or two before expiry of the lease, the farm would be advertised to let, regardless of whether the sitting tenant wished to remain. Effectively, the farm was being put up for private auction, and in most cases the highest bidder got the lease, providing he had sufficient capital or security to stock the farm. Rents were doubled or tripled at the stroke of a pen, though the bidders knew well that the farm was already heavily enough rented. Frequently these same men would be forced, a few years later, to beg a rent reduction or release from their rash commitment, or would seek to augment the holding by adding another to it, no matter at whose expense or inconvenience. In short, the leasing system encouraged the greedy and ambitious, who frequently had neither the capital nor the skill to succeed. John Smith, in 1798, put the landlords' case: "They say with some degree of justice, that the tenants only are to blame if they hurt themselves when allowed to make their own rents. " But he added: "They take too much for granted if they think the persons who offer are always better judges than themselves. "'[215]

Some Lowland farmers, of whom greater astuteness might have been expected, came into Kintyre in the early to mid-nineteenth century and brought distress or ruin upon themselves by offering rents which, they soon discovered, they could not meet out of the produce of their farms. A. I. B. Stewart, in 1990, examined the cases of some twelve of these 'Low Country tenants who came to Kintyre ... and who do not seem to have succeeded, apparently justifying the complaints of the native tenants that the rents were too high'.[216]

64: 'Clearances'

There is no evidence, which the present writer has been able to discover or authenticate, of wholesale 'clearances' on the Argyll estate in Kintyre. Clearance traditions exist associated with Ballochroy Glen and Skipness – in the time of the deeply unpopular William Fraser, who purchased Skipness Estate in 1843 – but if forcible removal of entire communities occurred, then proof is lacking.

Peter MacIntosh, in his description of depopulated Ballochroy Glen (p. 26), asked: 'Can the bleating of the sheep, the dogs' bark, and the chatter of the moorhen, delight the ear of the philanthrophist more than the joyful sound of the children amusing themselves with their innocent play in this glen?' This gentle, poetical question perhaps encapsulates the muted response in Kintyre to the encroachments of sheep-farming.

Since, as on the Mull of Kintyre and Learside (pp. 166-172), upland farmers were generally removed from their holdings not by force but by the Argyll's Estate's expedient of accepting higher bids from graziers, these 'clearances' proceeded with minimal fuss. The effect agriculturally was the same as if the tenantry had been forcibly evicted, but if anger and anguish were generated among the dispossessed, little trace of it has come down in literature or oral tradition. Elsewhere in the Highlands and Islands, the response was emphatically otherwise – see Sorley Maclean's essay 'The Poetry of the Clearances'[217] – but several reasons may be adduced for the indifference which apparently prevailed in Kintyre.

The Gaelic culture there, particularly in the south, was fragmenting and weak. Agrarian change had been implemented in Kintyre in the eighteenth century and with it went both the tacksman and the institution of the communal township with its rooted, inter-related population. Crofting, as an agricultural system, was insignificant in Kintyre, and the late nineteenth century agitations of the Land League had little relevance. The arrival, in the nineteenth century, of Lowland shepherds – reviled in many Gaelic communities elsewhere in the west – represented no great cultural shock, since Lowlanders had come in greater numbers to Kintyre in the seventeenth century, and kept coming, and a mutual accommodation had grown between the two communities, cemented ultimately by intermarriage. And when economic pressures dictated migration and emigration, the two groups went together.

65: Craigmore and Auchnabreck

Craigmore and Auchnabreck (Auchinbreck) were both Argyll Estate farms in the Carradale district. In 1729, when Craigmore – a 1-merkland holding – was let to Mary Campbell, widow of Patrick Campbell, minister of Killean, it was in the parish of Kilchenzie. Auchinbreck, in Saddell Parish, was a 3-merkland farm. In 1752, it was let to Archibald Campbell, then the 3rd Duke's Chamberlain, at a rent of £9 0s 9 1/3d, with, in addition, services to the Estate (36 carriages or horse-loads annually, 'if required', these being of peats or manure) and specific quantities of produce, which included – very specifically – '3 firlots Multure Meal of Kintyre measure at the rate of 20 Pecks to the Boll of the Old & Linlithgow Measure'. [218]

In the eighteenth century, according to John Smith, the only parishes in Kintyre containing significant plantations of woods were Saddell and Skipness and Kilcalmonell. In Saddell and Skipness, there was 'some planting' and a 'considerable quantity of natural wood; some of it not so well cared for as it ought'. [219] The planting of woodland and the protection of young – and existing – plantations from the destructive incursions of tenantry and livestock were recurring concerns of the 5th Duke.

The woodlands at Craigmore, which the Duke's own 'woodman', or forester, at Inveraray inspected and reported on, were clearly mature and valuable. This is apparent also from the 1791 lease of Craigmore granted to Dugald Stewart, into which was inserted an intimidating clause entitling the Duke to apply at any time to the Sheriff Depute of Argyll to send 'three persons of skill' to inspect the woods at Craigmore, 'and if these persons or the majority of them shall upon oath say that the woods have been hurt by cattle to the extent of five pounds sterling within the six months immediately preceding that then this present tack is to cease and be at an end and the said Duke to have it in his power at the following term of Whity [Whitsunday, 15 May, one of the term days] to remove the said Tacksman and his foresaids …'[220]

The Chamberlain, in his answer (No. 2), argued that without a 'regular Wood Ranger' – i. e. a resident guardian – it was difficult to effect legal detections, since depredations were 'uniformly committed under the cloud of night generally by handsaws to prevent noise'. The Duke, in his turn, responding in October 1801, dismissed this argument and placed responsibility entirely upon the tenant: 'The Law obliges every Tenant to preserve what are upon his possession and to make good the damage unless he can shew that it was done by another person and the law must be enforced. ' By 'handsaws' the Chamberlain presumably meant saws operated by one hand and therefore by one man, as opposed to two-man crosscut saws. This would suggest that only branches, or small trees, were being targeted.

66: Limestone

Crosshill farm lies to the south of Campbeltown, above the large Crosshill/Meadows housing estate, commenced in 1946, and the later (1979) Kintyre Gardens development. Crosshill steading was built on a limestone ridge, and Mr John C. Currie, who formerly farmed Crosshill, recalled that the fields to the north of the farm did not require drains, owing to the porous nature of the limestone; and the water from the spring on Barley Bannocks hill is noticeably calcareous. The main quarry was on the south-facing slope of the 'knowes' (the knolls of the ridge), overlooking Crosshill reservoir and south-east of the steading. A road was cut from the bottom of the quarry and ran east, rising at a shallow gradient along the south side of the knowes to a point just west of 'Flag-pole Hill' (NR 715 194). There was also a quarry in the stack-yard at Crosshill and another to the east, outside the stack-yard, both filled in. The limestone, Mr Currie presumes, was carted along the top of the knowes to a kiln, which was built into the bank at the western extremity of the knowes, south-west of the farm. [221] The hill, however, is now much overgrown with bushes, which conceal many of these man-made features.

66. Kilwhipnach lime-kiln and quarry, South Kintyre. Photograph by Judy Martin, 2011.

There is little trace of the large-scale commercial quarrying which the Duke appears to have been recommending, and which was carried on at, for example, Fort Argyll, on the opposite side of Campbeltown Loch, where a massive double-kiln remains (p. 113). Since the quarrier who was proposing to take the limestone quarry at Crosshill was 'killed in the Town quarry', and no other offer had been received, as the Chamberlain noted in his response, it may well be that the project lapsed.

In the eighteenth century, lime was used both as fertiliser and as mortar, though outwith the grander structures, such as churches and mansions, clay and mud were the standard mortars, as fillings for drystone walls, until the early nineteenth century. [222] The earliest lime-kilns were temporary turf structures built in the fields where lime was to be spread, but, by the end of the century, small, stone kilns had begun to be considered indispensable by the more progressive farmers. Larger kilns, as at Killellan and Kilwhipnach, both visible from the main Southend road, were built adjacent to quarries. [223]

The reference to ballast alludes to the practice of ships' which had discharged a cargo, and having no cargo to leave with, taking on stone to effect stability. One of the theories which attempt to explain the lumps of chalk and flint washed ashore on the northern Learside, links them with vessels sailing unladen to Campbeltown from County Antrim, in the north of Ireland, with beach-gathered ballast, which was dumped as the port of call neared.

67: Crosshill Farm

The Curries moved into Crosshill in 1944, replacing the Wilson family – still represented in South Kintyre – which had been the Duke's tenants for almost a century. Alexander Wilson, tenant in Knockbay, secured the standard 19-year lease in 1845 at a rent of £120 for the first three years and £130 for the remaining years. [224]

When the Curries moved in, domestic and sanitary conditions were basic. John Currie was told that there was a chain and hook suspended inside the chimney, on which a cast iron pot would be hung over the fire. There were four box-beds in the kitchen – two for the male servants and two for the female – and two of these beds were padlocked at night. There was a dry toilet at the bottom of the garden. Mr Currie understood that it 'worked all right except when there was east wind – then it could be challenging'. There is

67. Strath steading, with foal, c. 1960. Photograph by Mrs Betty Cockburn, Campbeltown.

a deep, stone-lined circular well at Crosshill, but, to Mr Currie's recollection, it was unused. Water was drawn from a hand pump at the well at Narrowfield and transported to Crosshill farmhouse in a horse-drawn whisky barrel on wheels. The annual charge for use of the water was 2 shillings. These living conditions were all modernised before John Currie's time. John's mother, Mrs Annie Campbell Currie (nee Craig), was descended from the Campbells of Glensaddell (p. 96) through her mother, Annie MacLeod Campbell. [225]

68: Little Straw

'Little Straw' – also Strabeg (Gaelic *beag*: little) or Stra Ichtrach – is now known as Bleachfield. 'Stramore' (Gaelic *mor*: big) – also Stra Uachtrach and Mickellstra (Scots 'mickle', large) – is now known as Strath, which represents Gaelic *srath*: valley. [226] 'Ichtrach' represents Gaelic *iochdrach*, 'lower', 'nether', and 'Uachtrach' represents Gaelic *uachdarach*, 'upper', 'higher', a common naming device with farms, in Scots and English too.

69: Willows

'Willow' covers many forms, which may be roughly categorised as sallows, or sallies, osiers, and the less definable group comprising crack-willow, white-willow and bay-willow. All, however, can be grown from cuttings, and coppice well, their wands being valuable in basket-weaving and interlaced as wattles to make domestic partitions and fences. The Duke's reference to 'the vicinity of Greenock' to his estate at Rosneath implies a market for his willow products in that town.

John Smith, in 1798, referred to a fast-growing 'Huntingdon willow', cited trees in Argyll with a diameter of from two to three feet, and mentioned a 'hoop willow', which he suggested should be raised in great quantities for the fishing industry, presumably for the manufacture of barrels for herring-curing. 'It is astonishing that in the neighbourhood of such a fishing town as Campbelton, which needs such quantities of hoops, which at present are both dear and distant, more attention is not paid to this article.' [227] Since willows thrive on ground too wet for any other crop, the economic advantage in their cultivation was obvious.

In his answer (No. 8), the Chamberlain countered with the observation that Limecraigs meadows, having been 'long drained and improved', were alternately under potatoes and oats and provided 'a very good return'. He reported that Campbell of Kildalloig had planted an area of marshy ground with willows, but, owing to 'the licentious depradations (*sic*) of the rabble in Campbeltown', who rooted up the young trees, he drained the ground that year and had 'a famous Crop on it'.

70: Ploughing

The above John Campbell, Bogside, in 1799 erected in Kirkwynd graveyard, Maybole, a memorial to his father Thomas, who died in that year at the age of 72. [228] In his instructions of the following year (No. 6), the Duke rejected the proposal, stating that he would rather have his own tenants instructed in ploughing with oxen 'than bring a stranger from Airshire'.

There is no description of the premium which had encouraged two Kintyre farmers to invest in plough-oxen, but on the island of Tiree in 1804 the Duke was offering £5 to the 'small tenant' who would plough at least five acres with two oxen, with or without a driver. A 'small tenant' he himself defined as one whose rent did not exceed £20. [229] Since his Kintyre tenants' rents at that period generally far exceeded that sum – £100 in exceptional cases – it may be assumed that premiums were proportionately higher. In any case, oxen never replaced horses in Kintyre and the experiment may be considered a failure. In Alexander Fenton's judgement, Scotland could be 'divided into lowland areas, where oxen were the main plough animals, and the higher or highland areas, where horses predominated'. [230]

One practice which the Duke offered premiums to eradicate, and which was eradicated, with or without those incentives, involved the horses' being led by a 'driver' at the head, walking backwards. As the nineteenth century progressed, the ploughman himself, by use of the reins, directed the entire ploughing operation from the stilts. As John Smith predicted in 1798: 'The ploughman who will not do without a driver, must soon be considered as unfit to be employed.' [231]

By the end of the eighteenth century, the old model of plough, which was heavy and required a team of four horses, had begun to be replaced by light ploughs on the model of James Small's patent of 1767, which required only two horses. Ploughing matches, which remain an annual feature in the Kintyre farmers' calendar, appear

68. A champion ploughman with champion horses. Archibald Ronald, Culinlongart, Southend, with Daisy (left) and Jean at annual ploughing match, East Backs, January 1939. This was the occasion of his winning his third Kintyre Agricultural Society medal with these horses, which had already won three medals with Archibald's brother Andrew in Dalmore, a remarkable record. Courtesy of Archibald Ronald, Campbeltown.

to have been introduced during the first quarter of the nineteenth century, through the influence of the Highland Society (now the Royal Highland and Agricultural Society). [232] Though most of the competitive ploughing is now understandably done with tractors, a horse section is still included and attracts a few entrants.

71: Illicit whisky-distillers

The tenants convicted of having been caught with an illicit whisky-still were: Thomas Brown, Machrimore; David Reid, Kildavie; Robert Colville, Glenmanuill; Peter MacBride, Largybeg; Colin McEachran, Glenahervie; Donald Campbell, Killeonan; Peter Galbreath, Laggan; James and John Harvie, Skeroblinraid, and Duncan McLean, Kylipoll (Calliburn). The following had quantities of 'wash' – fermented malt – ranging from 6 to 126 gallons: Donald MacLean, Corrylach; Hugh MacIliver, Remuil; Malcolm McMath, Auchinslisaig; John MacPhaill, Darlochan, and James McMillan, Cuilanlongart. Malting was being carried on by Donald McConnachy, Baligroggan; Lachlan Bowie, Largymore; John MacNaught, Druimnarianach; Hugh McMillan, Gartvain; Alexander Campbell, Strone, and Archibald Campbell Jnr. , Dailbhraddan. Alexander Campbell, Carrine, was caught with five gallons of illicit whisky. David Reid in Kildavie later satisfied the Duke, on oath, that he had no knowledge of the distilling, which had been 'carried on by his herd, and others not resident upon his Grace's property'. [233]

Ducal concerns about illicit whisky-distilling were nothing new. The 5th Duke's father complained in 1761 to his Kintyre Chamberlain, David Campbell, that tenants were breaking the law and damaging their farms by distilling 'whisky or aquavitae'. They were to be warned that they would be removed if they persisted, and the Chamberlain was to identify the culprits to the Duke. [234]

All such huffings and puffings, however, were to no avail. The economic reality was that small-scale distilling, usually organised in remote parts of the countryside to avoid detection, became a necessity to tenant farmers and their cottars, not least in the payment of rents to the Duke himself. For a study of illicit whisky in Kintyre, see the present writer's chapter on the subject in *Kintyre Country Life*. The activities of 'smugglers' persisted long enough to lodge in the annals of local journalism. The following report was published in the *Campbeltown Journal* of 4 March 1852:

69. This deservedly well-known photograph shows illicit whisky-distillers at work at an unidentified location; but the operators have been identified with reasonable certainty as Archibald McAllister – 'Baldy Ruadh' – at right, and his sons James – 'Big Jamie' – and Archibald Jnr., kneeling. The family, believed to have belonged to County Antrim, was connected with Kintyre through Helen McAllister, who married William Wilson and latterly lived in Southend. The original of the photograph was given to the parish priest in Campbeltown, Father James Webb, by a descendant of the distillers, Archibald Wilson, who died in 1957.

'A few days ago, we understand that Mr Murdoch, the officer of Inland Revenue, who surveys part of the Largy-side of Kintyre, accompanied by a Cuttersman, found a small quantity of malt on the Kiln attached to the corn mill of Tangy. The quantity found was enough to indicate that the kiln had been used for the illegal purpose of drying illicit malt, and that more of that commodity must be in existence not far away.

'On Friday last, the same party succeeded in locating the bothy in which they suppose the malt to have been made, choke full of good grain, in the process and some ready ground for mashing. This was at least six miles farther off than the mill. About a mile and a half away into a remote moor, they came upon a party of men busily employed preparing a house, partly built and partly sunk in the moss, for the purpose of bringing to the perfection of pure 'peat reek' whiskey, what had been begun in the establishment previously discovered. These unexpected visitors, of course, put their hand to the work and put a speedy termination to the hopeful labours of the lawless mountaineers.

'On Tuesday the 2nd inst. , again, the same party destroyed another distillery in a moor somewhere into the middle of the country between the head of Barr glen and the east coast of Kintyre. The owners thereof had just finished their distilling period and left the most of their utensils and a quantity of spirits in the bothy, no doubt concluding that no official would ever find out so perfect a hiding place. Again destruction was made to mark their progress. These places are, we understand, from sixteen to twenty miles from Campbeltown, where the detectors reside ...'

72. McAllister of Cour

The McAllister referred to on pages 59, 61, 62, 63, 65 and 66 of the Instructions appears to have been John, laird of Cour. He married Anna, a daughter of the Rev. Archibald MacNeill of Clachan. They had no family and he died in 1824. The main MacAlister family, that of Loup, was one of the most significant in Kintyre history. It descended from Alasdair Mor, younger son of Donald of Islay, Lord of the Isles, from whom the great Clan Donald took its name. Offshoots of the family included the MacAlisters of Tarbert, hereditary constables of the castle there, and the present MacAlisters of Glenbarr. [235]

Appendix: A Kintyre Boundaries Dispute

After the lay-out of this book had been completed, a copy of a fascinating legal document, dated 31/1/1736, was received: 'Depositions of the Witnesses adduced for John MacDonald of Largie against the Duke of Argyll'. It contains precisely the level of detail referred to on page 151, but space does not permit more than a few samples of the riches it contains.

In describing the boundaries of 'Bellochgerran' and 'Kilmory', the first witness, 56-year-old John MacIlchattan in Bellochgerran, names some thirty features, the vast majority of them small and long since forgotten, such as a stone called 'Clachvraigleinchraignacuineg' and an old dyke called 'Burngarvieguy'. From that document alone it may be deduced that the entire landscape of Kintyre, up until the nineteenth century and the coming of sheep, was packed with descriptive place-names, most of which have since vanished. In general, only the major geographical features – hills, streams, glens and suchlike – have survived in the interior of the peninsula.

MacIlchattan's father 'shewed him the said Marches when he was young, and particularly when there arose a Dispute betwixt Bellochgerran and Kilmory about a Piece of ploughed Ground near the Sea, which was then agreed by John Dow Campbel, who was then Tacksman of Kilmory, to belong to Largie'. Many social and agricultural customs are described, particularly in relation to the summer pastures or shielings, e. g. 'Archibald Oig Campbel' got permission from Macdonald of Largie to build 'Sheal-Houses' at Lecknacrouine 'for some weak Cows, that could not travel far, until they should be stronger'; but upon Archibald's death, Largie's grandson, assisted by 'some of the People of Rounahorin', pulled down the disputed huts.

Sources and Notes: Introductions

N. B. 'Kintyre Leases' were extracted by Duncan Colville from originals loaned to him by the 11th Duke of Argyll in 1958, and the compilation has been widely copied and circulated, while 'Kintyre Farm Leases' comprise bound volumes which are held in Argyll & Bute Council Archive, Lochgilphead. 'Argyll Papers' are in the archive at Inveraray Castle; catalogue only consulted.

1. The Duke was Colonel of the 54th Regiment of Foot and of the Argyllshire Fencibles. He was Commander-in-Chief of the army in Scotland in 1762 and 1767-78, and was created a Field Marshal in 1796. When he died, he was the senior field officer in the British Army, excepting only the Duke of York. *Scots Peerage*, I, pp. 386-87.
2. H. Paton (ed.): *The Clan Campbell*, vol. IV (Edinburgh, 1916), p. xx; A. McKerral, *The Clan Campbell* (1953), pp. 23-25; *Scots Peerage*, ut supra.
3. J. Smith, *General View of the Agriculture of the County of Argyll*, 1805, p. 14.
4. S. Johnson, *A Journey to the Western Islands of Scotland*, Glasgow 1825, pp. 117-18.
5. Knockbuy papers at Kilberry Castle; Trust Disposition dated April 20th, 1787, Scottish Record Office, Reg. of Deeds (Dalrymple), vol. 251, fo. 57.
6. A. McKerral, *Kintyre in the Seventeenth Century*, 1948, p. 86.
7. This is the total gross revenue from the Argyll lands, excluding other properties outside the county.
8. This means the lands under the management of the Chamberlain of Argyll, but the figure includes the feu-duties which he collected from the whole estate except Kintyre, and so exaggerates the relative importance of the older family lands in terms of the revenue which they yielded.
9. MS, letter of J. Campbell, Craignure, to Lord John Campbell, the future 7th Duke, June 28th, 1824, Inveraray Castle.
10. The 8th Duke of Argyll in Fyfe: *Scottish Diaries and Memoirs*, vol. II, p. 566.
11. No. 68, pp. 18-19.
12. E. R. Cregeen, 'A West Highland Census of 1779: Social and Economic Trends on the Argyll Estate', 1963, p. 12, unpublished.
13. A. Martin, *Kintyre: The Hidden Past*, Edinburgh 1984, pp. 6-12, & A. Martin, *Kintyre Families*, Campbeltown 2010, pp. 49, 50, & 55.
14. *Ibid.*, p. 2 & p. 40, & Rev. John R. H. Cormack, 'Three Kintyre

Books', *Kintyre Magazine* No. 21, pp. 4-5. He gives year of first edition as 1861.
15. A. Martin, *Kintyre Families, op. cit.* , p. 23. For an account of the Rev. Kelly and his eccentricities, see Col. C. Mactaggart, *The Lowland Church of Campbeltown*, Campbeltown 1924, pp. 15-17.
16. Dr Donald William Stewart, letter, 20/1/2011.
17. *Kintyre Magazine* No. 70, p. 5.
18. A. Martin, *Kintyre: The Hidden Past, op. cit.* , pp. 13-14.
19. *Antiquities of Killean and Kilchenzie*, 1934, p. 3, & A. Martin, *Kintyre: The Hidden Past, op. cit.* , pp. 76-77.
20. Donald William Stewart, *op. cit.*
21. 'Southend', *Campbeltown Journal*, 1/9/1852.
22. Adam McPhail, recorded by A. Martin, 3/7/1977.
23. D. J. Macdonald, *Antiquities of Killean and Kilchenzie, op. cit.* , p. 5.
24. 'Cuthbert Bede', *Glencreggan*, London 1861, Vol. 2, p. 30.
25. A. Martin, *Kintyre Magazine* No. 30, pp. 17-18.
26. A. Martin, *Ibid*. No. 63, pp. 20-21.
27. A. Martin, *Kintyre: The Hidden Past, op. cit.*, p. 3.
28. J. Smith, 'Allt Beithe – The Desertion of a Settlement', *Kist* 36, pp. 23 & 21.
29. Donald McCallum, 31/3/1977, & Calum Bannatyne, 12/6/1977, recorded by A. Martin.
30. William McGougan, 7/3/1977, recorded by A. Martin.
31. 'C', *Campbeltown Courier*, 22/8/1885.
32. *History of Kintyre*, 1857, pp. 68-69.
33. *Ibid.* , p. 39.
34. G. F. Black, *The Surnames of Scotland*, Edinburgh 1993, p. 66.
35. *The Oxford Names Companion*, Oxford 2002, p. 940.
36. A. Martin, *Kintyre Families, op. cit.* , p. 3. In 1836, John Beith fought a duel in Campbeltown, 'possibly the last regular duel fought in Scotland', according to Colonel Charles Mactaggart in 1924. Beith, an elder in the Lowland Church, was, as a consequence, suspended from that office for about two years. See Col. C. Mactaggart, *The Lowland Church of Campbeltown, op. cit. ,* p. 10.
37. Duncan C. MacTavish, *Commons of Argyll*, Lochgilphead 1935, p. 48.
38. Kintyre Leases, pp. 157, 162 & 163.
39. A few examples of those who prospered will suffice: David Colville (1813-98), iron and steel master – ancestor of the present Lord Clydesmuir – and John Colville (1844-1924) of the Glasgow Cotton Spinning Co. Ltd; Sir Nathaniel Dunlop (b 1830), chairman both of the Allan Line Steamship Company and of the Clyde Navigation Trust; the fabulously wealthy Alexander Fleming (1824-1909), ironmaster in Glasgow; brothers James (b 1848) and Samuel Greenlees (1850-

1939), pioneers in whisky-blending and in popularising Scotch whisky worldwide; and James Templeton (1802-85), who founded the carpet-making business which by 1881 employed more than 1100 workers. A. Martin, *Kintyre Families, op. cit.* , pp. 9, 13, 14, 19 & 72.
40. 'Gilbert Burns and his Family', *Campbeltown Courier*, 12/2/1921.
41. Kintyre Leases, p. 58A.
42. A. I. B. Stewart, 'Highland Mary: Saint or Sinner?', *Kintyre Magazine* No. 31, pp. 4-12, & Dr Gerard Carruthers, 'Fresh Light on Robert Burns's Note on Highland Mary', *ibid.* No. 68, pp. 16-18.
43. A. Martin, *Kintyre: The Hidden Past, op. cit.* , pp. 41-44 & Appendix 2, 'Surname Changes in Kintyre'; see also A. Martin, *Kintyre Families, op. cit.*
44. A. Martin, *Kintyre Magazine* No. 57, p. 18. For 'The Scots Dialect of South Kintyre', see A. Martin, *Kintyre: The Hidden Past, op. cit.* , pp. 15-21, & A. Martin, 'Dialect in South Kintyre', *Kintyre Magazine* No. 37, pp. 13-21.
45. *History of Kintyre, op. cit.* , p. 40.
46. A. Martin, *Kintyre Country Life*, Edinburgh 1987, p. 2.
47. E. R. Cregeen, 'A West Highland Census of 1779 . . . ', *op. cit.* , pp. 6-7.
48. *Ibid.* , pp. 22-23.
49. E. R. Cregeen, *Inhabitants of the Argyll Estate, 1779*, Edinburgh 1963, p. 3.
50. *Ibid*, pp. 115-119.
51. *Campbeltown Journal*, 29/4/1852.
52. *Campbeltown Courier*, 15/2/1903.
53. Donald McCallum, recorded by A. Martin, 6/8/1977.
54. A. Martin, *Sixteen Walks in South Kintyre*, Campbeltown 1994, p. 36.
55. D. J. Macdonald, *Annals of Killean*, Campbeltown 1934, p. 8; also in 'Traditions of Kintyre', *Argyllshire Herald*, 26/9/1874.
56. E. R. Cregeen, *Inhabitants of the Argyll Estate, op. cit.* , p. 3.
57. 'The Potato Trade As It Was And As It Is', *Campbeltown Journal*, 14/12/1853.
58. A. Martin, *Kintyre Country Life, op. cit.* , p. 43.
59. 'The Potato Trade . . . ', *op. cit.*
60. *Campbeltown Courier*, 14/7 & 21/7/1955.

70/71. The drystone wall of the nineteenth century sheep-fank at Innean Mor intersects, from left to right (west to east), an earlier turf dyke. Photographs by Judy Martin, 24/4/2011.

Sources and Notes: Commentaries

1. A. Martin, *Kintyre Country Life*, Edinburgh 1987, pp. 48 & 125-127.
2. Argyll Papers Bundle 1938, 30/11/1775.
3. E. R. Cregeen, *Argyll Estate Instructions: Mull, Morvern, Tiree, 1771-1805*, p. xviii.
4. Kintyre Farm Leases, p. 64.
5. J. Smith, *General View of the Agriculture of the County of Argyll*, Edinburgh 1798, pp. 40-41.
6. D. Colville & A. Martin, *The Place-Names of the Parish of Campbeltown*, Campbeltown 2009, p. 9.
7. *Ibid.*, pp. 36 & 54, & *Campbeltown Courier*, 6/9/1941.
8. *First Statistical Account*, Vol. 10, p. 550.
9. Kintyre Farm Leases, p. 181.
10. *Ibid.*, pp. 47, 86 & 177.
11. A. I. B. Stewart, 'Lachlan McNeill Buidhe', *Kintyre Magazine* No. 19, p. 18.
12. Rev. James Webb, 'Campbeltown in the 1715 & 1745 Stewart Rebellions', *Kintyre Magazine* No. 14, p. 5, & Colonel C. Mactaggart, 'Provosts of Campbeltown in 18th Century', *Campbeltown Courier*, 6/3/1924.
13. A. Martin, *Kintyre Country Life*, *op. cit.*, p. 124, & A. I. B. Stewart, 'A Melder wi' the Miller', *Kintyre Magazine* No. 23, p. 23.
14. Letter to author, 12/3/1996.
15. Col. H. Macneal, 'The History of the Brotche of Ugadale', *Kintyre Magazine* No. 3, pp. 5-6.
16. From notes made by A. Martin, 13/3/1996.
17. A. Martin, *An Historical and Genealogical Tour of Kilkerran Graveyard*, Campbeltown 2006, pp. 43-44; J. Macmaster Campbell, *The Island and House of Sanda*, Campbeltown 1924, pp. 28-37; A. I. B. Stewart, 'The Evolution of Gaelic Surnames in Kintyre', *Kintyre Magazine* No. 24, p. 26.
18. J. R. Maxwell-Macdonald, 'Largie', *Kintyre Magazine* No. 1, p. 8.
19. 'Cuthbert Bede', *Glencreggan*, London 1861, Vol. 2, p. 229, & M. C. Davis, *The Lost Mansions of Argyll*, Ardrishaig N. D., pp. 27-28.
20. F. F. Mackay, *MacNeill of Carskey: His Estate Journal, 1703-1743*, Edinburgh 1955, pp. 17-18, & A. McKerral, *Kintyre in the Seventeenth Century*, Edinburgh 1948, p. 168.
21. Notebook, Kintyre Antiquarian & Natural History Society archive, No. 331.
22. F. F. Mackay, *op. cit.*, pp. 21-22, & Una M. Robertson, *Carskey*, 1990,

pp. 1-2.
23. A. McKerral, *op. cit.*, pp. 11 & 169; Hew Shannon Stevenson, 'The Shannons of Lephenstrath', & K. Sanger, 'The McShannons of Kintyre: Harpers to Tacksmen', *Kintyre Magazine* No. 11, pp. 3-6, & No. 28, pp. 9-15.
24. Earle Lockerby, 'A Famous Author with Kintyre Roots', *Kintyre Magazine* No. 67, pp. 2-7.
25. A. Martin, *An Historical and Genealogical Tour of Kilkerran Graveyard*, *op. cit.*, p. 42.
26. A. McKerral, *op. cit.*, p. 83.
27. *Burke's Peerage & Baronetage*.
28. M. MacDonald, 'The Royal Charter and its Implications', *The Campbeltown Book*, Campbeltown 2003, p. 92.
29. *Campbeltown Courier*, 10/8/1907 & 28/2/1925, & Mr Joe Turner, 2/4/2011.
30. D. Colville, 'A Survey of the Place Names of the Burgh of Campbeltown', *Campbeltown Courier*, 1/5/1937.
31. Col. C. Mactaggart, 'Provosts of Campbeltown in 18th Century', *op. cit.*, 6/3/1924, & *Campbeltown Courier*, 18/4/1936.
32. A. McKerral, *op. cit.*, p. 81, & *Campbeltown Courier*, 25/1/1902.
33. Col. C. Mactaggart, *op. cit.*, & A McKerral, *op. cit.*, p. 59.
34. D. Mitchell, *Tarbert in Picture and Story*, Falkirk 1908, pp. 63-66.
35. D. Colville & A. Martin, *op. cit.*, p. 18.
36. R. L. Hills, 'James Watt at Campbeltown', *Kintyre Magazine* No. 42, p. 7.
37. N. Macmillan, 'Coal Mining in Kintyre', *The Campbeltown Book*, *op. cit.*, pp. 162-163, & *Inhabitants of the Argyll Estate, 1779*, ed. E. R. Cregeen, Edinburgh 1963, p. 115 & supplementary list, containing names of lessees, compiled by E. R. Cregeen post-publication.
38. R. L. Hills, *op. cit.*, p. 8; Dorothy Grant, undated typescript on the villages of Campbeltown Parish; *Machrihanish S. W. R. I. Village History Book*, 1996, p. 13; D. Colville & A. Martin, *op. cit.*, pp. 18 & 23.
39. Col. C. Mactaggart, 'Provosts of Campbeltown in 18th Century', *op. cit.*
40. *Inhabitants of the Argyll Estate, 1779*, ed. E. R. Cregeen, *op. cit.*
41. *Kintyre Magazine* No. 14, p. 18.
42. *History of Kintyre*, pp. 56-57.
43. Argyll Papers, Bundle 1960.
44. *Campbeltown Courier*, 20/3/1952.
45. D. Colville & A. Martin, *op. cit.*, p. 22.
46. *Argyll, An Inventory of the Ancient Monuments, Volume 1, Kintyre*, HMSO 1971, p. 202, & R. W. Munro, *Scottish Lighthouses*, Stornoway

1979, pp. 53 & 56.
47. Argyll Papers, Bundle 1937, 2/3/1790.
48. *Argyllshire Herald*, 6/4/1867.
49. R. W. Smith, *Kintyre Magazine* No. 66, p. 20.
50. Kintyre Farm Leases, p. 63.
51. N. M. K. Robertson, 'Account of Burial Places in Kintyre', *Campbeltown Courier*, 12/9/1885.
52. A. Martin, *Kintyre Country Life, op. cit.*, p. 143, & Scottish Record Office AD 14/16/62.
53. Col. C. Mactaggart, 'The Wreck of the "Charlemagne"', *Kintyre Magazine* No. 4, pp. 14-15.
54. C. Buchanan & D. Fairgray, *Kintyre and Gigha Dive Guide*, Campbeltown 1994, p. 16.
55. F. Bigwood, ed., *The Vice-Admiral Court of Argyll, Processes, etc. (1685-1825)*, North Berwick 2001, p. 7.
56. *Pigot & Co.'s New Commercial Directory of Scotland*, 1825-26, p. 208.
57. *Argyllshire Herald*, 29/2/1856.
58. *Ibid.*, 15/2/1856.
59. *Ibid.*, 7/3/1856 & 28/3/1856.
60. N. M. K. Robertson, *op. cit.*
61. *Fasti Ecclesiae Scoticanae*, Vol. IV., Edinburgh 1923, p. 52, & Col. C. Mactaggart, *The Lowland Church of Campbeltown*, Campbeltown 1924, pp. 11-12 & 14-15.
62. A. J. MacVicar, *The Rev. Dr. John Smith of Campbeltown*, Campbeltown 1934, p. 5.
63. D. Colville, 'A Survey of the Place Names of the Burgh of Campbeltown', *Campbeltown Courier*, 1/5/1937.
64. *First Statistical Account of Campbeltown*, Vol. X, p. 546.
65. A. McKerral, *op. cit.*, pp. 17 & 38-39.
66. Kintyre Farm Leases, p. 23, & D. Colville & A. Martin, *op. cit.*, p. 15, 'Castlemoil'.
67. Col. C. Mactaggart, 'The Limecraigs Duchess,' *Kintyre Magazine* No. 15, pp. 13-16.
68. *Second Statistical Account* of Campbeltown, p. 458.
69. A. Martin, 'Military Echoes', *Kintyre Magazine* No. 37, p. 32.
70. A. Martin, *Kintyre Families, op. cit.*, p. 40.
71. I. G. Lindsay and M. Cosh, *Inveraray and the Dukes of Argyll*, Edinburgh 1973, p. 393, n. 7.
72. I. M. Scott, 'John Smith D. D.', *Kintyre Magazine* No. 2, pp. 8-9.
73. A. J. MacVicar, *The Rev. Dr. John Smith of Campbeltown, op. cit.*
74. 'Traditions of Kintyre', *Argyllshire Herald*, 14/3/1874.
75. Argyll Papers, Bundle 1943, 16/8/1792.

76. Kintyre Estate Leases, Vol. 3, p. 381.
77. 'Traditions of Kintyre', *op. cit.*
78. *Chambers Biographical Dictionary*, ed. M. Magnusson, Edinburgh 1995, p. 511, I. G. Lindsay and M. Cosh, *op. cit.*, p. 377, n. 28, & E. R. Cregeen, *Argyll Estate Instructions, op. cit.*, p. 16, fn. 3 (quotation).
79. *Kintyre in the Seventeenth Century, op. cit.*, p. 181.
80. Stephanie Niederberger, Langlands family history, 2005 (unpublished).
81. *Campbeltown Courier*, 3/6/1933.
82. Old Parish Registers, Campbeltown & Southend.
83. *Campbeltown Journal*, 5/9/1851.
84. Kintyre Farm Leases, p. 39.
85. 'Cuthbert Bede', *Glencreggan*, Vol. 2, London 1861, p. 96.
86. A. Martin, *Kintyre Country Life, op. cit.*, pp. 6-7.
87. *Argyllshire Herald*, 30/8/1861.
88. D. Colville, *Third Statistical Account* (Argyll), 1961, p. 281.
89. A. Martin, 'Travelling People in Kintyre', an unpublished study.
90. Letter, 2/7/2010.
91. A. Martin, *Kintyre Country Life, op. cit.*, pp. 143-145.
92. A. Martin, *Ibid.*, pp. 144-45.
93. E. R. Cregeen, *Argyll Estate Instructions, op. cit.*, p. 17. These Morvern woods were a temptation to others without entitlement to their trees. John McCall and John Carmichael, crofters on the island of Lismore, were jailed for 40 days in 1852 for the theft of five cartloads of birch taken from 'the farm of Garrelos, Morven'. Two others, Duncan Carmichael and James Campbell, denied the charge and were dismissed. *Campbeltown Journal*, 8/1/1852.
94. Unpublished MS, transcribed by E. R. Cregeen, in possession of Mrs L. Cregeen.
95. A. Martin, *Kintyre Country Life, op. cit.*, pp. 9-11.
96. *Second Statistical Account*, p. 387.
97. L. Errington, *William McTaggart: 1835-1910*, Edinburgh 1989, pp. 15 & 21, & A. Martin, *Kintyre Country Life*, 2nd edition 2005, p. viii.
98. D. Colville & A. Martin, *op. cit.*, p. 48.
99. A. McKerral, *op. cit.*, p. 128.
100. *Pigot & Co.'s New Commercial Directory of Scotland*, 1825-26, p. 208.
101. *Kintyre Magazine* No. 14, p. 16.
102. Quoted by D. Colville in 'A Survey of the Place Names of the Burgh of Campbeltown', *Campbeltown Courier*, 8/5/1937.
103. A. Martin, *Kintyre Country Life, op. cit.*, pp. 131-135, & 'A Visit to Sanda', *Campbeltown Courier*, 5/9/1925.
104. A. Martin, *Kintyre Country Life, op. cit.*, p. 133.
105. Kintyre Farm Leases, p. 189.

106. E. R. Cregeen, *Argyll Estate Instructions, op. cit.*, pp. 185-187.
107. 'Cuthbert Bede', *Glencreggan, op. cit.*, Vol. 2, pp. 159-160.
108. *Ibid.*, pp. 157-158.
109. I. A. Fraser, letter, 15/7/2010.
110. D. Colville & A. Martin, *op. cit.*, p. 36.
111. Letter, 15/7/2010; transcript of Watt's notebooks, which are held in Birmingham Central Library, from D. E. Spilsbury, 15/7/2010.
112. *Argyll, An Inventory of the Ancient Monuments, Volume 1, op. cit.*, p. 201; N. Macmillan, 'Coal Mining in Kintyre', *The Campbeltown Book, op. cit.*, pp. 162-63; R. L. Hills, 'James Watt at Campbeltown', in *Kintyre Magazine* Nos. 41, 42 & 43; Col. C. Mactaggart, *Life in Campbeltown in the 18th Century*, Campbeltown 1923, p. 34.
113. *Campbeltown Journal*, 23/5/1851.
114. 'Bubly Jock', *Kintyre Magazine* No. 27, p. 4.
115. *Kintyre Magazine* No. 8, p. 21.
116. Letter, 20/8/2010.
117. 'Colonel John Lorne Stewart of Coll', *The Celtic Monthly*, No. 2, Vol. III, Nov 1894; Obituary, John Lorne Stewart, *Argyllshire Herald*, 6/7/1878; letter to E. R. Cregeen from Duncan Colville, 19/10/1954.
118. *Campbeltown Courier*, 5/3/1927.
119. Bundle 1927.
120. D. Colville & A. Martin, *op. cit.*, p. 45.
121. Bundle 1927.
122. Bundle 1928.
123. Southend Parish Register.
124. *Second Statistical Account*, Southend, p. 434.
125. Argyll Papers, Bundle 1922.
126. W. Crossan, 'Three Hundred Years of Education in Campbeltown', *The Campbeltown* Book, *op. cit.*, p. 173.
127. Argyll Papers, Bundle 1977.
128. *First Statistical Account*, Vol. 10, p. 555.
129. Quoted by E. R. Cregeen in *Argyll Estate Instructions, op. cit.*, p. 148, n. Other sources: Col. C. Mactaggart, 'Provosts of Campbeltown in 18th Century', *op. cit.*, & letter to E. R. Cregeen from Duncan Colville, 19/10/1954.
130. 'Kintyre Farm Leases', p. 34, & A. Martin, *Kintyre Country Life, op. cit.*, p. 17.
131. *The Concise Scots Dictionary*, Aberdeen 1985, p. 185.
132. On p. 12.
133. Kintyre Farm Leases, p. 34.
134. Argyll Papers, Bundle 1933, memorial of 6/9/1783.
135. Letter, 21/7/2010.
136. Argyll Papers, Bundle 1940, 31/10/1805.

137. A. Martin, *Kintyre Country Life, op. cit.*, p. 130.
138. Kintyre Estate Leases, Vol. 3, p. 77.
139. *Ibid.*, Vol. 2, p. 541.
140. I. MacDonald and A. I. B. Stewart, 'Sheriff Court, Tarbert, 1683', *Kintyre Magazine* No. 26, pp. 5-8.
141. A. Martin, *The Ring-Net Fishermen*, Edinburgh 1981, pp. 128-29.
142. Argyll Papers, Bundle 1933.
143. Kintyre Estate Leases, Vol. 3, p. 65.
144. MSS., transcribed by E. R. Cregeen, in possession of Mrs L. Cregeen.
145. Bundle 1970.
146. *Campbeltown Journal*, 5/9/1851.
147. *Ibid.*, 11/12/1851.
148. *Argyllshire Herald*, 30/8/1861.
149. Kintyre Estate Leases, Vol. 2, p. 43.
150. *Ibid.*, p. 52.
151. *Ibid.*, p. 93.
152. *Ibid.*, p. 98.
153. *Ibid.*, Vol. 3, p. 485, West Kildavie.
154. Kintyre Farm Leases, p. 144.
155. A. Martin, *Fishing and Whaling*, Edinburgh 1995, p. 41.
156. I. MacDonald and A. I. B. Stewart, *Kintyre Magazine* No. 26, pp. 3-12.
157. Duke of Argyll's Instructions for Kintyre, October 1759, from the papers of E. R. Cregeen.
158. Kintyre Leases, p. 146.
159. *Campbeltown Journal*, 14/7/1853.
160. Letter, 27/7/2010.
161. 9/9/1852.
162. Vol. XII, p. 481.
163. Argyll Papers, Bundle 1936.
164. R. W. Smith, letter 27/7/2010.
165. *Inventory of the Ancient Monuments, Volume 1, op. cit.*, p. 105; J. Cormack, 'The Churches of Campbeltown', in *The Campbeltown Book, op. cit.*, p. 114.
166. *Burke's Peerage & Baronetage*; A. J. MacVicar, *The Book of Blaan*, 1965, p. 24; Kintyre Farm Leases, pp. 123 & 152.
167. A. Martin, *An Historical and Genealogical Tour of Kilkerran Graveyard, op. cit.*, p. 17.
168. Col. C. Mactaggart, *Life in Campbeltown in the 18th Century, op. cit.*, p. 65.
169. Information transcribed from family bible in 1853 by Daniel Mactaggart.
170. Kintyre Farm Leases, pp. 97 & 142.

171. A. I. B. Stewart, 'The Duel', *Kintyre Magazine* No. 18, pp. 20-26.
172. Kintyre Farm Leases, p. 117.
173. Argyll Papers, Bundle 1943, 11/10/1771.
174. *Ibid*, Bundle 2020.
175. *Ibid*, Bundle 1931.
176. *List of Inhabitants upon the Duke of Argyle's Property in Kintyre in 1792*, Edinburgh 1991, p. 11.
177. Quoted in A. Martin, *Kintyre Country Life, op. cit.*, p. 9.
178. *Campbeltown Journal*, 29/7/1852.
179. Kintyre Farm Leases, p. 104.
180. A. Martin, *Kintyre Magazine* No. 40, pp. 26-29.
181. *List of Inhabitants upon the Duke of Argyle's Property in Kintyre in 1792, op. cit.*, Index of Places, p. 298.
182. A. Martin, *Kintyre Country Life, op. cit.*, p. 49.
183. J. Smith, *General View of the Agriculture of the County of Argyll, op. cit.*, p. 120.
184. Argyll Papers, Bundle 1927.
185. A. J. MacVicar, *The Book of Blaan, op. cit.*, p. 33.
186. A. Martin, *Kintyre: The Hidden Past, op. cit.*, p 26 & p. 44, fn. 3.
187. A. J. MacVicar, *op. cit.*, p. 25.
188. Kintyre Leases, p. 29. Balinatunie was clearly being sub-let earlier in the Langlands lease; a Loynachan (later Lang) family was associated with the holding. In October 1811, eight-year-old Catherine Loynachan, daughter of Lachlan Loynachan, Balinatunie, claimed to have seen a mermaid, as did John McIsaac in nearby Corphin. See A. Martin, *Kintyre: The Hidden Past, op. cit.*, pp. 191-92.
189. National Archives of Scotland, AD 4/30/102 & JC26/1830/212.
190. S. Niederberger, *op. cit.*
191. Kintyre Farm Leases, p. 76, & *Campbeltown Journal*, 11/4/1854.
192. A. Martin, *Kintyre Country Life, op. cit.*, p. 11.
193. 12/4/1851.
194. J. Smith, *General View of the Agriculture of the County of Argyll, op. cit.*, p. 300.
195. A. Martin, *The Ring-Net Fishermen, op. cit.*, pp. 4-5.
196. *First Statistical Account*, Vol. X, p. 553.
197. A. Martin, *The Ring-Net Fishermen, op. cit.*, p. 5.
198. A. Martin, 'The Campbeltown Fishing Industry', in *The Campbeltown Book, op. cit.*, p. 52.
199. E. R. Cregeen, *Argyll Estate Instructions, op. cit.*, pp. x, xxx &155.
200. D. Colville & A. Martin, *op. cit.*, p. 33.
201. R. L. Hills, 'James Watt at Campbeltown', in *Kintyre Magazine* No. 42, p. 7.
202. Kintyre Estate Leases, Vol. 3, p. 122.

203. *Ibid.*
204. *Ibid.*, Vol. 6, pp. 304, 522 & 529.
205. 29/3/1851.
206. Argyll Papers, Bundle 2015.
207. A. Martin, *Kintyre Country Life, op. cit.*, p. 94.
208. 'Instructions to Stonefield, Oct. 6th. 1747', in E. R. Cregeen's unpublished papers.
209. Kintyre Farm Leases, p. 110.
210. *Ibid.*, p. 105.
211. *Ibid.*, p. 166A.
212. *Ibid.*, p. 112.
213. Scottish Record Office, SC50/5/1847/6.
214. Unpublished MSS., transcribed by E. R. Cregeen, in possession of Mrs L. Cregeen.
215. *Op. cit.*, pp. 7-8.
216. *Kintyre Magazine* No. 27, pp. 6-7.
217. *Ris a' Bhruthaich*, Stornoway 1985, pp. 48-74.
218. Kintyre Farm Leases, pp. 68 & 11.
219. J. Smith, *General View of the Agriculture of the County of Argyll, op. cit.*, pp. 308-10.
220. Kintyre Estate Leases, Vol. 2., p. 30.
221. Letter, 17/8/2010.
222. A. Martin, *Kintyre Country Life, op. cit.*, pp. 140-142.
223. *Ibid*, p. 27.
224. Kintyre Farm Leases, p. 70.
225. J. C. Currie, letter, 17/8/2010, & *Campbeltown Courier*, 1/6/1950 (Glensaddell connection).
226. D. Colville & A. Martin, *op. cit.*, p. 43.
227. J. Smith, *General View of the Agriculture of the County of Argyll, op. cit.*, p. 166.
228. Monumental Inscriptions, Kirkwynd Cemetery, Maybole, compiled by D. & G. Killicoat, accessed via internet.
229. E. R. Cregeen, *Argyll Estate Instructions, op. cit.*, p. 87.
230. *Scottish Country Life*, Edinburgh 1976, p. 38.
231. *General View of the Agriculture of the County of Argyll, op. cit.*, p. 67.
232. A. Martin, *Kintyre Country Life, op. cit.*, pp. 18-19.
233. *Ibid.*, Appendix 1, p. 193, from Argyll Papers, Bundle 1921.
234. Unpublished MSS., transcribed by E. R. Cregeen, in possession of Mrs L. Cregeen.
235. A. Martin, *Kintyre Families, op. cit.*, p. 26

Index

Place-names have mostly been standardised in this index, for better comprehension, but variant spellings will be found in text. Divisions of farms by and large are not acknowledged – e. g. , 'Knockriochmore' is indexed under Knockrioch.

Acharua, 90
Achnaslishaig, 56
Alexander, James, Askomil, 113
Allt Beithe, 18 & illus. 7
Allt Leannan Sithe, 18
Anderson, John, Lintmill, 122
Anderson, Rebecca, 122
Andrew, David, Ballybrennan, 146
Ardnacross, 15, 65, 66, 153, 154, 155
Argyll Campbell family
  8th Earl and Marquess, 1, 89, 94
  9th Earl, 3
  10th Earl, 1, 94
  1st Duke, 92, 114
  2nd Duke, 1, 3, 4, 27, 114
  3rd Duke, 1, 2, 3, 4, 114, 127, 151, 154, 184, 185
  4th Duke, 1, 4, 110, 114, 185, 195
  5th Duke, 1-8, 11, 13, 23, 26, 33, 34, 38-79 (his instructions), 81, 82, 85, 89, 96, 100, 104, 106, 108, 113, 114, 119, 120, 121, 124, 126, 132, 134, 136, 140, 144, 146, 147, 148, 150, 151, 152, 153, 154, 156, 157, 159, 166, 172, 174, 176, 178, 184, 185, 187, 188, 190, 192, 193, 195, 199 fn. 1
  6th Duke, 6
  10th Duke, 34
Argyllshire Road Act, 1800, 31

Arinascavach, 56, 152
Armour family, Rosehill, 13 & illus. 4
Arnicle, 61, 86, 151
Aros, 71, 130, 181
ash trees, 59, 62
Askomil, 44, 113
Auchaleek/Achinleck, 34, 71, 181
Auchalochy, 113
Auchenhoan, 154, 172, 174, 176
Auchinbreck/Auchnabreck, 72, 75, 187
Auchinsavil (Southend), 60
'Ault more Killipol', 57
Ayrshire, 22, 23, 50, 76, 156, 176, 193

Backs (farm), 71, 181
Backs Water, 38, 81 & illus. 11
baile, 26
Balegreggan, 90
Balinatunie, 28, 172, 174, 176 & fn. 188 & illus. 60
ballast, 75
Ballimacvicar, 28
Ballimeanach (Kilchousland), 57
Ballivain, 106
Ballochgair, 57, 72
Ballochroy Glen, 26, 186
Ballybrennan, 54, 60, 146
Ballygroggan, 71, 168
Balnabraid, 127, 172, 184 & illus. 41

Balnamoil, 28, 168
Baltic, 50, 51, 124
Bannatyne, Calum, shepherd, 108
barley, 38, 40, 65, 76, 77, 81, 104, 122, 156, 197 (malted)
Barmollach, 62
Barr Glen, 16, 151, 197
Beachmore, 72
Beallachgoichan, 28
Bealochnahully, 152
beans, 78, 122, 184
bear – see barley
Bede, Cuthbert – see Bradley, Rev. Edward
Beith family, 22
Beith, Provost John, 22 & 200 fn. 36.
Bellenden, Mary, 1
Bellochgerran, 198
Ben Gullion, 16 & illus. 5
Bickett, James, 23
Blarferne, 81
Blary, 102, 152
Blasthill, 9, 90
Bleachfield (farm), 121
bleachfields, 48, 49, 53, 85, 121
Board of Trustees for Manufactures and Improvements in Scotland, 81
Borgadilbeg, 28, 168
Borgadilmore, 28, 168
boundaries, 39, 42, 47, 48, 53, 54, 59, 60, 61, 62, 63, 66, 151-52, 198
Bowie, Lachlan, Largymore, 195
Boyd, James, Carskey, 92
Brackenridge, Isobel, 176
Bradley, Rev. Edward, 90, 121, 136
Breakenridge, Jean, 23
Brecklate, 56, 60
British Society for Extending the Fisheries, 2, 178
Brolochan, Peter, 166

Brown, James and sons, Homestone, 184
Brown, Thomas, Machrimore, 174, 195
Bruce, King Robert I, 86
Bruce, Marrion, 104
'Bubly Jock', 141 & illus. 46
Buchanan, Robert, Achnasavil, 154
Buchanan, William, merchant, Tarbert, 148
Burns, Gilbert, 23
Burns, Robert, 23-24
buss fishery, 178 & illus. 61

Campbell:
of Airds, 7
of Asknish, 7
of Askomil, 44, 45, 113
of Blythswood, 99, 148
of Glencarradale/Carradale, 42, 65, 66, 78, 96, 157
of Glensaddell/Saddell, 60, 62, 96
of Kildalloig, 39, 77, 159, 193
of Skipness, 86, 96, 99
of Sonachan, 7, 114
of Stonefield, 7, 76, 96, 99, 100, 148
Alexander, Carrine, 195
Alexander, Strone, 195
Angus, Baillie, 159
Anne, Campbeltown, 176
Annie MacLeod, 192
Archibald of Askomil, 113
Archibald Jnr., Dalabhraddan, 195
Archibald of Knockbuy, 3
Archibald, Limecraigs, Chamberlain of Kintyre, 61, 161, 187
Archibald Oig, 198
Archibald of Succoth, 7
Archibald, father of 'Highland Mary', 23
Arthur, shoemaker,

Campbeltown, 176
Charles, Colonel, also 'Campbell of Barbreck', 38, 40, 41, 47, 53, 55, 75, 76, 77, 85, 102, 121, 181
Christian Hamilton, 166 & illus. 54A
D., of Combie, 55, 63
David, Baillie Depute, 168
David, Kintyre Chamberlain, 195
David, merchant, Campbeltown, 168
David, Rev., of Southend, 159, 161
Donald, merchant in Campbeltown, 147
Donald, lessee of Inneans, 70, 168
Donald, Killeonan, 195
Donald, Rev., of Southend, 159, 173-74
Dugald, Achnaba, 168
Dugald of Glencarradale, 155
Dugald of Inverawe, 90
Dugald, Rev., of Southend, 159
Duncan, Sir, of Auchinbreck, 113
Duncan, Sheriff Substitute, 63, 65, 66, 119
Elizabeth of Drumtroon, 144
Frederick, Captain, 141, 166
Gilles, 161
Grizel, 159
John, farmer in Bogside, Ayrshire, 76, 193
John Jnr., Campbeltown, 66, 67, 157
John Dow, 198
John MacLeod, of Glensaddell, 96, 125 (caption) & illus. 24
John, of Kildalloig, 159
John, of Mamore -see Argyll Campbells, 4th Duke
John, Major, 'hero of Mangalore', 90-100
John MacLeod, Dr, of Row, 99
John, tacksman of Scalpay, 174
Katherine Mary Edith, Kildalloig, 94-96 & illus. 21
Mary, Ardmore, 141
'Highland Mary', 23-24
Mathew, Major, Skipness, 99
Patrick, Rev., Killean, 187
Peter, window tax surveyor, 173
Robert, Baillie, Rosneath, 2, 7, 8
Scipio Duroure, Captain, 69, 161
Campbeltown, 15, 20, 26, 27, 31, 33, 34, 47, 49, 50, 51, 53, 54, 58, 59, 60, 63, 68, 76, 94, 96, 124, 132, 143, 147, 178, 181, 190, 192 & illus. 44
Campbeltown Town Council (also 'Town of Campbeltown'), 38, 46, 47, 53, 59, 61, 82, 94, 96
canal, 38, 43, 50, 51, 54, 75, 138-40 & illus. 47
Cantaig, 152, 170, 172
Cara Broonie, 18
Carradale, 30, 31, 148, 154-55, 187-88
'carriages', 81, 146, 187
Carskey, 92, 110, 155
Carskey mansion-houses, 92 & illus. 20
Castle Moil (or Askomil House), 113
Cattadalemore, 23
cattle, 3, 46, 59, 62, 119, 122, 130, 168, 186, 198
censuses, 27-28, 51, 121, 122, 138, 170, 176, 188
Charlemagne, wreck of, 108
Christlach, 54, 71, 126
churches, 15, 31, 44, 45, 65, 68, 173-74 & illus. 52, 58 & 59
Civil War, 11, 90, 113
Clachaig Glen, 26
Clachan, 30, 90

Clach-fhionn, 33
Clark, Daniel, 66, 67, 157
Clark, Peter, Ballygreggan, 181
clay, industrial, 53, 55, 147
'clearances', 186-87
Clifford, H. E. , architect, 122
Clochkeil, 72, 106, 127
Clyde, shipwrecked schooner, 109
Cnocan nam Ban, 16, 20
Cnoc Sithe, 20
coal and -mining, 40, 41, 43, 50, 58, 100, 124, 126, 140, 141
Coalwork Company of Campbeltown, 106
Coll, Island of, 4, 5, 141
Colville, David, ironmaster, 200 fn. 39
Colville, David, solicitor, 141
Colville, Duncan, xv, 199
Colville, John, Glasgow Cotton Spinning Co. Ltd, 200 fn. 39
Colville, Robert, Glemanuill, 195
Corphin, 81, 172, 184
Corrylach, Southend, 56
cottars, 5, 127, 130, 185
cotton, 49, 121
Craigaig, 9-11, illus. 2 & 3
Craigmore, 61, 62, 72, 75, 187-88
Craigs, 81, 139
Cregan, Loup, 146
Cregeen, Eric R. , xiii, 11, 27, 28, 33, 34, 185
Cregeen, Lily, xiv
crofting, 68, 70, 136, 187
Crossaig, 30
Crosshill, 60, 70, 75, 151, 173, 188, 190, 192
Crossibeg, 44, 47, 112
Cuilundune, 39, 42, 61, 85
Culinlongart, 142
Culloden, Battle of, 1, 116, 140
'Culmhor', 139
Cunison, Rev. John, 33

Currie, Annie, Crosshill, 192
Currie, John C. , Crosshill, 188, 190, 192
Curry, John, Askomil, 113

'Dailchoran', 57
'Dailquhasan', 100
Dalabhraddan, 176
Dalintober, 24, 96 & illus. 22
Dalivaddy, 77
Dalkeith, 136
Darlochan, 60, 72, 108, 181, 184
Davis, Michael C. , 92
Dempster, George, architect, 159
ditches, 54, 58, 61, 151, 152
Drumchrottan, 112
Drumgarve, 57
Drumlemble, 53, 54, 72, 85, 100, 108, 121, 124, 140, 147, 181
Drumore, Campbeltown, 30, 42, 54, 96, 138, 147
Drumorenabodach, 90
Dudgeon, Edward, Kildalloig, 96
Dunaverty, 154
Dunaverty, Massacre of, 89, 90, 92, 99
Dunbar, Robert, schoolmaster, 142
Dunlop, Sir Nathaniel, 200 fn. 39
Durry, 60, 72, 181
dykes, 61, 62, 63, 85, 119, 150, 151, 152, 153, 198 & illus. 70 & 71

Earadale, 9
Earl of Argyll's Rebellion, 1685, 132
Eden, 90
Eleric, 152
English farmers in Kintyre, 82, 156, 161
Episcopal Church, 140, 141
Erradil, 170, 172 & illus. 57
evictions, 8, 122, 141, 184-86
Experiment, wherry, 66, 157

fairies, 18, 20
farms and farming, 26, 27, 33, 38, 39, 40, 41, 42, 58, 59, 60, 62, 63, 65, 68, 69, 70, 73, 75, 76, 77, 78, 79, 168
farm plans, 59, 62, 150-51
Fenton, Alexander, 193
Feochaig, 56, 108
Ferrier, James, W. S., 2, 5, 6, 7, 52, 54, 55, 61, 68, 74, 82, 119, 134, 147
Ferrier, Susan Edmonstone, 119
fertilisers, 69, 75, 76, 134, 136, 153-54, 190
feu-duties, 4, 51, 55, 56
fishing – see herring and salmon
flax, 38, 81, 121
Fleming, Alexander, ironmaster in Glasgow, 200 fn. 39
flintlock pistol, Limecraigs, 114
'Flory Loynachan', dialect poem, 23
Flush, 130
folklore, 16-22
Forbes Mackay, Lieut. -Col. A., 92
Fort Argyll, 113, 190
'Forty-five Rebellion, 85, 86, 90, 99
Fraser, Ian A., 138
Fraser, William, Skipness, 186

Gaelic language in Kintyre, 11, 13-16, 24, 26, 130, 138, 159, 172, 174, 187
Galbreath, Peter, Laggan, 153, 195
gardens, 59, 60, 69, 102, 104, 130, 148, 172-73
Gartgreillan, 44, 57
Gartloisken, 71
Gartnacopaig, 90
Gartnacorach/Gartnagerach, 161, 171, 172
Gigha, 33
Gille Cochull nan Craiceann, 16
Glasgow, 121, 136, 155, 156, 166

glebes, 44, 47, 48, 112, 113, 116, 119
Glemanuill, 31
Glenahanty, 85
Glenahervie, 141, 152, 161, 170, 172
Glenbarr, 96, 102, 120, 152
Glencreggan, 136
Gleneadardacrock, 18 & illus. 6
Glenmurril, 56, 127, 150, 172, 184 & illus. 40
Glenramskill, 56
Gortan and variant names, 138
Gowdie, Mr, Lephenstrath, 110
Graham, Humphrey, 114
Greenlees, James, Peninver, 134
Greenlees, James, whisky-blender, 200 fn. 39
Greenlees, John, Balinatunie, 174
Greenlees, John, Lintmill, 122
Greenlees, Samuel, whisky-blender, 200 fn. 39
Greenlees, Thomas, Putechantuy, 184
Greenock, 24, 192

Harvey, James and John, Skeroblinraid, 195
Harvey, John, illus. 65
Harvey, William and Mathew, lightkeepers, 104
hedges, 52, 54, 58, 104, 152 & illus. 26 & 27
Hendry, Donald, Cantaig, 172
herring-fishing, 69, 70, 73, 74, 148 (tanning nets), 157, 178, 192 & illus. 62
herring, red, 65, 66, 67, 78, 157, 159
Highland Parish Church, 68, 69, 73, 75, 76, 116, 144, 159 & illus. 52
History of Kintyre (1857), 15, 20, 102

Holmer, Nils M., 16
Holmes, Mary, 130
horses, 31, 49, 113, 136, 140, 146, 187, 193, 195
houses and house-building, 31, 33, 51, 52, 54, 126-130, 190
Huie, William, Benton, 173

Innean Beag, 31, 69, 70, 166
Innean Dunain, 28, 105 & illus. 30
Innean Mor, 31, 69, 70, 166 & illus. 56
Inneans, 9, 166 & illus. 10
Inveraray, 2, 4, 5, 44, 50, 51, 54, 58, 62, 63, 124, 126, 141, 144, 150, 161, 176
Inverlochy (battle, 1645), 11, 113
iris, wild (*Iris pseudacorus*), 26 & illus. 8

James IV, King, 86, 90
J. G. Hall, shipwrecked brig, 110
Johnson, Dr Samuel, 3
Jones, John Paul, 161

kail-yards – see gardens
Kell, John, Ballybrennan, 54, 146
Kelly, Rev. Daniel or Donald, 13, 31, 142
Kelly, John and sons, Darlochan, 108
Kelly, Neil Munro – see Robertson, Neil Munro Kelly
Kelly, Neil, Lochside, 180 (illus.)
kelp industry, 6, 8, 50, 51, 52, 53, 67, 132, 134-38 & illus. 45 & 46
Keprigan, 56
Keramenach, 42
Kerr, James, Lintmill, 122
Kilchenzie, 141
Kilchousland, 116, 119 & illus. 34 & 35
Kilchrist, 85

Kildalloig, 94-96, 172
Kildavie, 56
Kilkerran (farm), 44, 55, 151
Kilkivan, 132
Killean, 46, 108, 142
Killeonan, 39, 42, 48, 71, 102
Killervan, 56
Killipole Loch, 100
Killocraw, 28
Kilmaluag, 102
Kilmashenachan, 90
Kilmichael/Kirkmichael, 44, 46, 47, 48, 71, 112, 116, 119, 181
Kilmory, 198
Kilwhipnach quarry, 190 & illus. 66
Kintyre Agricultural Society, 69, 70, 75, 176
Kintyre House and Drain Tile Work, 147
Kitchen, Sarah, 120
Knockhanty, 85
knockin stane, 104 & illus. 29 & 30
Knockmorran, 90
Knocknagrain, 65, 151
Knocknaha, 85, 86
Knockrioch, 71, 141
Knock Scalbert, 153

Laggan, The, 81, 130, 181
Laggan (farm, Glenlussa), 48, 57, 63, 153
Laggs, 28, 69, 70, 161, 166
Lagnacraig, 56
Laing, Rev. Alexander, Southend, 174
land measurements, 120, 121
Lands of Saint Ninian, 90
Langlands map (1801), 30-31, 100, 120, 157
Langlands, Agnes, 176
Langlands, Arthur, 120
Langlands, George, 26, 60, 62, 68, 70, 120, 121, 146, 150, 152, 174, 176

Langlands, Major George, 120
Langlands, Humphrey, 122
Langlands, John, Balnagleck, 120
Langlands, Matthew, 120, 176
Langlands, Ralph, 121, 122
Langlands, Richard, Balnagleck, 120
Langlands, Captain Roger, 120
Langlands, William, 4, 8, 50, 51, 58, 60, 62, 68, 70, 72, 74, 120, 146
Largiebaan, 85, 106, 108, 168
Largie castles, 90, 92 & illus. 19
Largieside, 15, 18, 33, 141, 197
Lean, John, Bristol, 55
Learside, 142, 161, 170-72, 176, 186 & illus. 9 (road)
Lecknacreive, 56
Lecknalarach, 102
Lephenstrath, 92
Lephincorrach, 61
Leslie, General David, 89
lime and limestone, 75, 77, 113, 188, 190 & illus. 66
Limecraigs and House, 44, 59, 63, 70, 76, 114, 151, 161, 173, 193 & illus. 33
Lintmill, 122-24, 140 & illus. 37
Littleson, Margaret Black, Dalkeith, 136
Livingston, Mary, 142
Loch an Eich, 16
Loch an t-Soluis, 100
Lochorodale, 106, 161
Lochsanish, 102, 130, 181
Lochsunart, 126 & fn. 93
Longrow Church, 112, 132
Lossit, 85, 100, 152
Lossit mansion-houses, 86, 89 & illus. 17
Lowland Church, 114, 158
Lowlanders in Kintyre, 13, 22-24, 27, 94, 144, 172, 174, 186, 187
Loynachan, Catherine and mermaid, 209 fn. 188

McAlester, John, Barmollach, 148
MacAlister landed families in Kintyre, 197
McAllister of Cour, 59, 61, 62, 63, 65, 66, 197
McAllister family, illicit whisky-distillers, illus 69
McArthur, Archibald, Auchinreoch, 31
McArthur, John, Tiree, 126
McArthur, Lachlan, Laggan, 153
McArthur, Neil, Auchinreoch, 154
MacBride, Peter, Largiebeg, 195
McCallien, W. J, geologist, 134
McCallum, Dugald, Campbeltown, 81
McCallum, Duncan, Auchinreoch, 154
McCallum, Neil, Auchinbreck, 154
MacCambridge, Flora, 90
McCaog, Mary, Corphin, 109 (caption)
MacColla, Alasdair – see MacDonald, Major-General Sir Alexander
McConnachy, Donald, Ballygroggan, 195
MacDonalds of Largie, 46, 47, 90, 198
MacDonalds of Sanda, 39, 89-90, 159
MacDonald, Major-General Sir Alexander, 11, 89
MacDonald, Ann, 159
MacDonald, Rev. Donald, 18, 130
Macdonald, Rev. D. J., 15, 16
MacDonald, Iain Lom, 11
MacDonald, Sir James, 18, 113
Macdonald, James, author, 144
MacDonald, Jimmy, Campbeltown, 9
MacDonald, Sir John Cathanach, 90

MacDonald, Murdo, 9 & illus. 56
MacDonald, Dr William, laird of Pennyland, 110
MacDougall, Helen, 116
McDougall, John, Brackley, 154
McDowall, Sheriff Charles, 40, 41, 70, 102, 104, 173
McDuff, Archibald, gardener, 40, 41, 70, 102, 104, 173
McEachran, Archibald, Southend historian, 92
McEachran, Colin, Glenahervie, 152, 195
McEwin, Ewin, 'the Craig', 154
MacFarlane sorcerer, Tarbert, 18
McFarlane, Charles, Lintmill, 122
McFarlan, Patrick, Tarbert, 148
McGill, Archibald, Arnicle, 61, 151
McGougan, William, Largie, 18
MacGregor, Lieut. Robert, 184
MacIlchattan, John, Bellochgerran, 198
Mcilgoune, Dougald, Barmollach, 148
MacIlliver – see McLiver
McIlmichael, Donald, Glenmurril, 150
McIlreavie, John, Ballybrennan, 146
McInnes, John, 'Dunaverty', 170
McInnes, Robert, illus. 64
MacIntosh, Peter, 15, 20, 22, 26, 102, 181, 186
Macintyre, Dugald Snr. and Jnr. , 114
McIsaac, John, Corphin, and mermaid, 209 fn. 188
McIsaac, John and Lauchlan Jnr. , Corphin, 81
McIssac, Lachlan, Corphin, 184
Mackays of Ugadale, 86
McKay, Captain Charles, 141
MacKay, Donald, Campbeltown, 184
MacKay, Donald, Erradil, 170
MacKay, Donald, Ugadale, 86
McKay, Effy, 122
Mackay, Farquhar, 86
MacKay, Flora, Erradil, 142
McKay, Hugh, 'Clerk to the Farming Society', 70, 76
MacKay, John, Auchadaduie, 173
MacKay, John, peat-cutter, 184
MacKay, Neil, Erradil, 170
MacKay, Peter, Erradil, 170
McKay, Peter, Knockstapple, 170
McKeich, Angus, Campbeltown, 184
McKeich, Archibald, Sunadale, 185
Mackenzie, Laurence, Collector of Excise, 69, 112
McKerral, Andrew, xv, 13, 120
MacKerral, Hugh, Brunerican, 173
McKerral, Malcolm, Balnabraid, 184
McKerral, William, Bleachfield, 124
McKillop, Janet, 168
McKinlay, Walter, Lossit, 152
Maclagan, Robert Craig, 15, 16
McLean, Donald, Corrylach, 195
McLean, Duncan, Calliburn, 195
MacLean, Sir Lachlan of Duart, 18
McLean, Malcolm, Glenbarr, 152
McLean, Marion, from Campbeltown, 99
McLean, Robert, thatcher Drumlemble, 152
Maclean, Sorley, 186
MacLeish, Rev. George, 157
McLellan, John, cottar, Sunadale, 185
Macleod, Colonel J. N. of Glensaddell, 96
Macleod, Dr Norman, Jnr. and Snr. , 96, 144 & 145 (caption)
McLiver, Hugh, Remuil, 148, 195
MacMarquis family, 11
McMaster, Ewan, schoolmaster, 142
McMath, Malcolm, Achnaslisaig, 195

McMillan, Archibald, Askomil, 113
McMillan, Archibald, Kilmichael (Carradale), 154
McMillan, Daniel, Kilmichael, 119
McMillan, Donald, Ronadale, 154
McMillan, Duncan, Carradale, 154
McMillan, Gilbert, Aird, 154
McMillan, Hugh, Gartvain, 195
McMillan, James, Culinlongart, 195
McMillan, Rev. William, Campbeltown, 161
MacMurchy family, 11, 16
McMurchy, smith in Kildavie, 173
McMurriche, John, Barmollach, 148
McNab, John, laird of Moy, 119
McNair, Robert, Smerby, 148
MacNaught, John, Druimnarianach, 195
McNaughton, Donald, Lephenstrath, 184
MacNeills of Carskey, 39, 60, 63, 92, 152
Macneals of Ugadale and Lossit, etc., 38, 42, 48, 53, 54, 59, 61, 63, 85, 86, 89, 94, 132
MacNeill, Anna, 197
MacNeill, Rev. Archibald, Clachan, 197
MacNeill, Elizabeth, aunt of 'Highland Mary', 23
MacNeill, Jessie, 144
MacNeill, Lachlan of Drimdrissaig, 144
McNeil, Major, 155
MacNeill, Margaret Farooza, 142
McNish, Donald, Lintmill, 122
MacPhail, John, Darlochan, 195
McPhail, Robert, Laggan, 153, 155
McQueen/McQuin, John, 176
MacShannon family, Lephenstrath, 11, 39, 92
McSporran, Donald, Askomil, 113
McStalker, John, Askomil, 113

Mactaggart, Colonel Charles, xv, 140
Mactaggart, Dr Charles Rowatt, 132
Mactaggart, Daniel, lawyer, 136, 166 & illus. 54B
McTaggart, Dugald, cottar, 130
McTaggart, William, artist, 130
MacVicar, Rev. A. J., 112, 116, 174
McWilliam, Alexander, Kilkeddan, 181
McWilliam, 'evicted farmer', 106

Macedonia, wreck of barque, 108
Macharioch, 90
Machribeg, 34
Machrihanish, 9, 18, 55, 85
maerl, 154
Mangalore House, 100
marches – see boundaries
marle, 63, 65, 66, 153-54
Martin, Judy, 9 & Ill. 10
Mary Pans – see Salt Pans
Matheson, Kenneth, 184
Mauchline, Duncan, Lintmill, 122
Maxwell, James, Chamberlain of Mull, 39, 53, 54, 59, 61, 104, 144, 146
Maxwell, Robert, 144
Mill Dam, 82 & illus. 13
mills and milling, 40, 41, 59, 61, 82, 86, 156-57 & illus. 12 (Campbeltown) & 15 (Knocknaha)
Mitchell, Samuel, Strath, 122
moles in folklore, 16
'Moninaclive', 51, 138
Montgomery, John, schoolmaster, 140
Montgomery, Lucy Maud, novelist, 94
Moreson, Donald, Tarbert, 148
Morgan, Charles, 109
Morvern, 5, 81, 126 & fn. 93, 144
moss & 'moss rooms' – see peat

Moy, 42, 138
Muasdale, 16, 22, 34, 122
Mucklach, 42, 60
Muir, John, Balinatunie, 174
Mull, 5, 136, 144, 151, 178
Mull of Kintyre, 18, 126, 168, 186 & illus. 28
Mull of Kintyre Lighthouse, 31, 40, 41, 104, 108 & illus. 28
Murdoch, Mr, officer of Inland Revenue, 197

Narachan, 61
Northumberland, 120, 146
Nugent, Gerry and Pat, 114

oats (meal), 76, 77, 81, 184, 187, 193
O'Loynachan, Donald, Glenahervie, 152
oxen (plough), 76, 193

Park (farm), 72
Parkfergus, 130
Paterson, Annie Sillars, 23
peat and peat-cutting, 20, 43, 50, 58, 69, 70, 71-72, 73, 82, 138, 181-84 & illus. 63
peelygrass, 42, 104
Peninver, 33, 54, 57, 134, 136, 142
Penlaughton, 90
Pennysearach, 90
Pickan, Alexander, Kildavie, 173
ploughing, 176, 193-95 & illus. 68
pollarding, 62
Polliwilline, 28, 106, 173
Port Crannaig, 157
postal service, 31
potatoes, 33-34, 52, 77, 122, 130, 193

Ramsay, Duncan, Lintmill, 122
Ranachan, 152
red herring – see herring
Reid, David, Kildavie, 173, 195

Reid, John, Dunglas, 184
Remuil, 56, 148
rents and arrears of, 4, 6, 38, 40, 43, 44, 45, 46, 48, 53, 73, 74, 81, 113, 130, 146, 181, 184-86, 190, 193, 197
Revie, Archibald, miller, 82
Revie, John, Lintmill, 122
roads and tracks, 30-31 & illus. 9 & 10
Robertson, Rev. George, 44, 45, 48, 110, 111
Robertson, Neil Munro Kelly, 13, 110, 112
Robinson, Dr Gary, 9, 153
Ronachan, 62
Ronald, Archibald and Andrew, 194 (caption)
Rosehill, 31 & 14 (caption)
Rosneath, 2, 3, 4, 5, 6, 44, 63, 76, 192
rowans, 148
Rowatt, Alexander, factor, 132
Rowatt, Alex, surveyor, 151
Rowatt, Dr Charles, 50, 51, 54, 58, 60, 86, 132, 138

Sabbath desecration, 22
Sac Ban, 16
Saddell Castle, 99 & illus. 23
salmon-fishing, 65, 66, 154-55
Saltcoats, brigantine, 106
Salt Pans, 100, 110, 155 & illus. 25
Sanda, 134 & illus. 18
schools and schoolmasters, 44, 52, 54, 59, 60, 61, 68, 70, 81, 110, 142, 144, 161 & illus. 49
Scots language in Kintyre, 13
Scott, Sir Walter, 23, 119
Scottish Society for the Propogation of Christian Knowledge, 59, 142, 144

Semple, Dugald, 'Apostle of the Simple Life', 125 (caption)
serpents, mythical, 16
Sharp, Thomas, Corphin, 109 (caption)
Sheanachie, 172
sheep, 26, 63, 120, 142, 166-71, 176
shepherds, 28, 31, 168, 187 & illus. 55
shipping, 50, 51, 58, 60, 96, 124-25, 155, 157 & illus. 51 (wherry)
shipwrecks and plundering from, 43, 106, 108, 110
Sinclair, Duncan, shepherd, 108
Sitheach, 18
Skeroblingorry, 71
Skeroblinraid, 152
Skipness, 155, 186 (see also Campbells of Skipness)
Small, James, 193
Smerby, 22, 28, 112, 148
Smith, Archibald, Ballybrennan, 146
Smith, Rev. Dr John, 44, 46, 48, 81, 82, 112, 116, 119, 144, 149, 153, 154, 156, 176, 178, 187, 192, 193 & illus. 36
Smith, Robert, Askomil, 113
Smith, Robert W. , Linlithgow, 124, 141, 147
Socach, 170, 172
soum, 62
Southend, 33, 159-60, 173-74
starch (farina) factories, 34
Stewart, Anthony, traveller, 124
Stewart, Archibald, Skeroblinraid, 152
Stewart, A. I. B. , 85, 86, 138, 140, 142, 186
Stewart, Charles, Rev. , Campbeltown, 112

Stewart, Christeane, 89
Stewart, Dugald, Craigmore, 188
Stewart, Duncan of Ardsheal, 141
Stewart, Duncan of Glenbuckie, Chamberlain of Kintyre, 140-41, 155, 159, 173
Stewart, Duncan, Peninver, 136
Stewart, John Glas of Benmore, 140
Stewart, John Lorne of Coll, 141, 166
Stewart, John, schoolmaster, 142
Stewart, Lorn MacNeill of Knockrioch, 142
Stewart, Margaret, 141
Stewart, Mary, 112
Stewarton, 82, 141
stipends, 60, 65, 75, 78, 81, 112
Strath, 72, 75, 121, 122, 192 & illus. 67
Straw – see Strath
Strone, 42
Success, shipwrecked schooner, 110

tacksmen, 4, 5, 27, 187
Tangy, 22, 102, 197
Tarbert, 18, 148
Tayinloan, 16, 30, 31
Taylor, John, schoolmaster, 142
Taylor, Lauchlan, Auchinchoirk, 120
Taylor, Mary, 120
teinds, 4, 38, 40, 41, 65, 66, 81, 176
Templeton, James, carpet-manufacturer, 200 fn. 39
Thompson, Richard, Northumberland and Ballybrennan, 146
Thomson, Neil, Cregan, 148
timber, 3, 50, 51, 52, 53, 54, 58, 60, 75, 76, 106, 110, 124, 126, 147

221

Tiree, 4, 5, 126, 193
Tirfergus, 85, 152 & illus. 14
Tollemache, Elizabeth, Duchess of Argyll, 114, 168
Tomaig, 141, 142
Tonrioch, 82, 85
Torrisdale, 28, 61, 155, 157
Townley, Lieut. Thomas, 161
Townsley families, 124
Traigh Ghruineart, Battle of (1598), 18
Train, Thomas, 168
Travellers, 124 & illus. 38
trees – see woods
Trench Point, 113
Turner, John, Tonrioch, 38, 40, 41, 47, 82, 85, 156

Ugadale, 85
Ugadale Brooch, 86 & illus. 16

water, 18, 192
Watson, James, Askomil, 113
Watson, John, Campbeltown, 40, 41
Watson, William, Claongart, 31
Watson, William Jnr., insurance agent, 108
Watt, James, engineer, 139, 140, 181
Watt, Robert, 159
Webb, Fr. James, 104
wheat, 40, 41-42, 59, 63, 65, 146, 156-57, 176
Whinhill, 147
whisky, 65, 78, 156, 157, 184, 195-97 & illus. 69
Whitehill, 102
willows, 53, 76, 77, 151, 192
Wilson, Alexander, Knockbay and Crosshill, 190
Wilson, James, flax-dresser, 81
witches, 20, 148

wood and woodlands, 48, 55, 56-57, 59, 65, 70, 73, 76, 114, 147-48, 172, 187-88 & illus. 50
wood-cutting, illegal, 44, 45, 148, 157, 188, 193
wool manufacture, 122

www.ingramcontent.com/pod-product-compliance
Lightning Source LLC
Chambersburg PA
CBHW051121160426
43195CB00014B/2291